MacDIA
THE TERRIBLE
CRYSTAL

By the same author

Poetry
SOCIETY INEBRIOUS
THE VOYAGE
TO FIND THE NEW
A PERPETUAL MOTION MACHINE
PENGUIN MODERN POETS 15 (with Morgan and Brathwaite)
THE STATE OF THE NATION
THE AULD SYMIE
HE WILL BE GREATLY MISSED
A CENTURY OF PEOPLE
A PINT OF BITTER
SCOTLAND, YES
THIS FINE DAY
IN THIS CORNER: SELECTED POEMS 1963–83

Stories
HAMMER AND THISTLE (with Morrison)

Criticism
THOM GUNN & TED HUGHES
GEORGE MACKAY BROWN
THE BALLAD
(ed) SMOLLETT: AUTHOR OF THE FIRST DISTINCTION
(ed) THE SEXUAL DIMENSION IN LITERATURE
THE SENSUAL SCOT
MODERN SCOTTISH LITERATURE

Anthologies
THE PENGUIN BOOK OF SOCIALIST VERSE
THE MARTIAL MUSE: SEVEN CENTURIES OF WAR POETRY
THE CAMBRIDGE BOOK OF ENGLISH VERSE 1939–75
MAKING LOVE: THE PICADOR BOOK OF EROTIC VERSE
THE BAWDY BEAUTIFUL: THE SPHERE BOOK OF IMPROPER
    VERSE
MOUNTS OF VENUS: THE PICADOR BOOK OF EROTIC PROSE
DRINK TO ME ONLY: THE PROSE (AND CONS) OF DRINKING
A SCOTTISH POETRY BOOK

MacDIARMID
THE TERRIBLE
CRYSTAL

Alan Bold

The poetry I seek must therefore have the power
Of fusing the discordant qualities of experience,
Of mixing moods, and holding together opposites,
And well I know that the various facets
Of sensibility, sensuous, mental, and emotional,
And its alternating moods
Cannot be fully reconciled
Save in an imaginative integrity
That includes, but transcends, sensibility as such.
      Hugh MacDiarmid, 'The Terrible Crystal'

And the likeness of the firmament upon the heads
of the living creature *was* as the colour of the
terrible crystal, stretched forth over their heads above.
                              Ezekiel 1:22

Routledge & Kegan Paul
London, Boston, Melbourne and Henley

First published in 1983
by Routledge & Kegan Paul plc
39 Store Street, London WC1E 7DD,
9 Park Street, Boston, Mass. 02108, USA,
296 Beaconsfield Parade, Middle Park,
Melbourne, 3206, Australia, and
Broadway House, Newtown Road,
Henley-on-Thames, Oxon RG9 1EN

Set in Linotron Baskerville by
Input Typesetting Ltd, London
and printed in Great Britain by
Redwood Burn Ltd,
Trowbridge, Wiltshire

Library of Congress Cataloging in Publication Data

Bold, Alan Norman, 1943–
MacDiarmid: the terrible crystal.
Includes bibliographical references and indexes.
1. MacDiarmid, Hugh, 1892–1978
—Criticism and interpretation.   I. Title.
PR6013.R735Z585 1983   821'.912   83–3075

ISBN 0–7100–9493–0 (U.S.)

TO RONALD STEVENSON

Our wonderment will have no end, and yet
From the very beginning we feel at home.

'Plaited Like the Generations of Men'

CONTENTS

Acknowledgments   viii
Bibliographical Note   ix
Chronology   xi

1 The Mind Alone   1
2 Names for Nameless things   45
3 To prove my Saul is Scots   84
4 Frae Battles, Mair than Ballads   122
5 This Stone World   157
6 Alone with the Alone   197

Notes   239
Glossary   244
Index of Poems   247
General Index   249

ACKNOWLEDGMENTS

In the course of writing this book I discussed various points at various times with various colleagues and correspondents and found that the spirit of MacDiarmid moves in a harmonious way. Among my fellow enthusiasts are individuals as diverse as David Daiches, Ian Hamilton Finlay, W. R. Aitken, Dougald McMillan, G. E. Davie, Michael Grieve, Tom Scott, Duncan Glen, J. K. Annand, Maurice Lindsay, John Bett and Ronald Stevenson. None of these is in any way responsible for the opinions expressed in the following pages but I thank each of them for an encouraging interest in my research.

I would like to thank Mrs Valda Grieve and Michael Grieve for permission to quote from the poetry and prose of Hugh MacDiarmid; and W. R. Aitken and Michael Grieve for permission to make all page references to *Complete Poems 1920–1976* as edited by them and published in two volumes in 1978 by Martin Brian & O'Keeffe to whom grateful acknowledgment is also made.

I am indebted to Gordon Wright for allowing me to adapt and expand the Chronology from his *MacDiarmid: An Illustrated Biography*, Edinburgh, Gordon Wright 1977.

After I had chosen the title for this book I discovered that Routledge had, in 1940, published *The Terrible Crystal* by M. Chaning-Pearce. Appropriately that book discusses the thought of Kierkegaard, a man much admired by MacDiarmid, and evokes a vision 'of a terrible and intense candour of spirit wrought to a diamond-like induration and brilliance.'

BIBLIOGRAPHICAL NOTE

The appearance in 1978 of the two-volume *Complete Poems 1920–1976*, edited by Michael Grieve and W. R. Aitken, and published by Martin Brian & O'Keeffe of London, made a full and reliable text of MacDiarmid's poetry available for the first time. In the present study all poetic quotations are followed by numbers in parentheses which refer to appropriate pages in *Complete Poems*; four dots represent the poet's punctuation, three dots denote omissions. The books I found most useful in my research are listed in the notes at the end of the book; those who require a complete MacDiarmid bibliography (up to 1980) should consult the relevant section in W. R. Aitken's *Scottish Literature in English and Scots: A Guide to Information Sources*, Detroit, Gale Research Company 1982. In the following pages specific sources are identified by the abbreviations listed below.

Annals = *Annals of the Five Senses*, by C. M. Grieve, Montrose, C. M. Grieve, 1923.

Cencrastus = *To Circumjack Cencrastus, or The Curly Snake*, by Hugh M'Diarmid, Edinburgh, Blackwood, 1930.

Collected = *Collected Poems*, by Hugh MacDiarmid, Edinburgh, Oliver and Boyd 1962.

Company = *The Company I've Kept*, by Hugh MacDiarmid, London, Hutchinson, 1966.

Conversation = *The MacDiarmids: A Conversation*, by Hugh MacDiarmid and Duncan Glen, Preston, Akros, 1970.

[ix]

Festschrift = *Hugh MacDiarmid: A Festschrift*, edited by K. D. Duval and Sydney Goodsir Smith, Edinburgh, K. D. Duval, 1962.

Joyce = *In Memoriam James Joyce: from A Vision of World Language*, by Hugh MacDiarmid, Glasgow, Maclellan, 1955.

Kist = *A Kist of Whistles*, by Hugh MacDiarmid, Glasgow, Maclellan, 1947.

Lap = *A Lap of Honour*, by Hugh MacDiarmid, London, MacGibbon & Kee, 1967.

LP = *Lucky Poet*, by Hugh MacDiarmid, London, Jonathan Cape, 1972.

Metaphysics = *Metaphysics and Poetry*, by Hugh MacDiarmid in conversation with Walter Perrie, Hamilton, Lothlorien, 1975.

NLS = MacDiarmid archive in the National Library of Scotland.

SE = *Selected Essays of Hugh MacDiarmid*, edited by Duncan Glen, London, Jonathan Cape, 1969.

Studies = *Contemporary Scottish Studies*, by Hugh MacDiarmid, Edinburgh, Scottish Educational Journal, 1976.

Thistle = *A Drunk Man Looks at the Thistle*, by Hugh MacDiarmid, Edinburgh, Castle Wynd Printers, 1956.

Uncanny = *The Uncanny Scot* by Hugh MacDiarmid, edited by Kenneth Buthlay, London, MacGibbon & Kee, 1968.

CHRONOLOGY

My life has been an adventure, or series of adventures, in the exploration of the mystery of Scotland's self-suppression.

LP, 381

1892 *11 August: born at Arkinholm Terrace, Langholm.* I am of the opinion that 'my native place' – the muckle toon of Langholm, in Dumfriesshire – is the bonniest place I know, by virtue, not of the little burgh in itself . . . but of wonderful variety and quality of the scenery in which it is set. (SE, 53)

1894 It was some fourteen months later that I was caught in the act of trying to commit my first murder – attempting, in short, to smash in the head of my newly-born brother [Andrew] with a poker, and, when I was disarmed, continuing to insist that, despite that horrible red-faced object, I 'was still Mummy's boy, too.' (LP, 218–19)

1899 *Enrolled in primary department, Langholm Academy. Moved to house in Library Buildings.* It was that library, however, that was the great determining factor. My father was a rural postman, his beat running up the Ewes Road to Fiddleton Toll, and we lived in the post office buildings. The library, the nucleus of which had been left by Thomas Telford, the famous engineer, was upstairs. I had constant access to it, and used to fill a big washing-basket with books and bring it downstairs as often as I wanted to. . . There were upwards of twelve thousand books in the library (though it was strangely deficient in Scottish books), and a fair number of new books, chiefly novels, was constantly bought. Before I left home (when I was fourteen) I could go up into that library in the dark and find any book I wanted. . . I certainly read almost every one of them. . . (LP, 8–9)

1904 *Transferred to secondary department, Langholm Academy.* But even as a boy . . . I drew an assurance that I felt and understood the spirit of Scotland and the Scottish country folk in no common measure, and that that made it at any rate possible that I would in due course become a great national poet of Scotland. (LP, 3)

1905 *Taught in Langholm South United Free Church Sunday School.* My parents were very devout believers and very Churchy people. . . (LP, 40) Another poet – Thomas Scott Cairncross, who was, when I was a boy, minister of the church my parents attended, introduced me to the work of many poets . . . but . . . subsequently ceased to be friendly with me. . . (LP, 222) *Taught English by William Burt and Francis George Scott* who were teachers at Langholm Academy when I was a boy . . . and, in my opinion, [rank] among the strictly limited number of the best brains in Scotland. . . (LP, 228–9)

1908 *Admitted as pupil teacher to Broughton Higher Grade School and Junior Student Centre, Edinburgh.* [George Ogilvie] my English master at the Junior Student Centre in Edinburgh was a man in ten thousand, who meant a very great deal to me. . . (LP, 228–9) *Joined the Edinburgh Central Branch of the Independent Labour Party of Great Britain and the Edinburgh University branch of the Fabian Society.*

1909 Edited **The Broughton Magazine**.

1911 *Death of father, James Grieve.* A lean, hardy, weather-beaten man, he died at forty-seven after a few days' illness of pneumonia. He had never been ill in his life before. (LP, 18) *Left Scotland to work in South Wales on the* **Monmouthshire Labour News**. My father died suddenly before I was finished at the Junior Student Centre. I took immediate advantage of the fact to abandon my plans for becoming a teacher. That is one thing which I have never, for one moment, regretted. . . If I had gone on and qualified and become a teacher, my sojourn in the profession would have been of short duration in any event, and I would have been dismissed as Thomas Davidson and John Maclean and my friend, A. S. Neill, were dismissed. (LP, 228–9)

1912 *Returned to Langholm.* The old Radicalism was still strong all over the Borders, though already a great deal of it had been dissipated away into the channels of religious sectarianism and such moralitarian crusades as the Temperance Movement, the Anti-Gambling agitation, and so forth. . . But what I personally owed to the Langholm of that time was an out-and-out Radicalism and Republicanism, combined with an extreme anti-English feeling. (LP, 225) *Moved to Clydebank to work on* the **Clydebank and Renfrew Press**. *Rejoined Independent Labour Party. Moved to Cupar, met Peggy Skinner.*

1913 *Moved to Forfar to work on* **The Forfar Review**.

1915 *Enlisted.* I served in the Royal Army Medical Corps in the First World War, rising to the rank of Quarter-Master-Sergeant. From 1916 to 1918 I was in Salonika with the 42nd General Hospital, which, located on the outskirts of the city towards Kalamaria, was established in the marble-floored premises of L'Orphenilat Grec. I was invalided home with malaria in 1918, but, after a period in a malaria concentration centre near Rhyl, was pronounced A1 again and fit for another spell of service overseas. After a brief stay near Dieppe, I was posted to the Sections Lahore Indian General Hospital stationed at the Château Mirabeau at Estaque near Marseilles. This hospital had been established to deal with Indian and other Asiatic soldiers who had been broken down psychologically on the Western Front. We had always several hundred insane there and the death-rate was very high, culminating in the great Influenza Epidemic in 1918 when our patients had little or no power of resistance and died in great numbers. The officers of the hospital were all Indians, mostly Edinburgh-trained, and there were only, in addition to myself, four white N.C.O.s. I returned to Britain and was demobilised in 1920. (Company, 184)

1918 *Married Peggy Skinner.* [I] came back with an *idée fixe* – never again must men be made to suffer as in these years of war. (Annals, 89)

1919 *Found job with* **The Montrose Review** *and moved to Montrose.*

1920 *Moved to Kildermorie, E. Ross and Cromarty. Edited* **Northern Numbers**. Looking back, and recollecting my own conviction even as a mere boy that I was going to be a famous poet, it is surprising that I wrote little or nothing until after I was demobilized in 1919. (LP, 65)

1921 *Returned to Montrose to work for* **The Montrose Review**. *Edited* **Northern Numbers: Second Series.**

1922 *Edited* **Northern Numbers: Third Series**. *Founded and edited* **The Scottish Chapbook**. I became editor-reporter of *The Montrose Review*, and held that position until 1929. I threw myself whole-heartedly into the life of that community and became a Town Councillor, Parish Councillor, member of the School Management Committee and Justice of the Peace for the county. (Company, 184)
Began to use pseudonymn Hugh MacDiarmid. It was an immediate realization of [the] ultimate reach of the implications of my experiment which made me adopt, when I began writing Scots poetry, the Gaelic pseudonym of Hugh MacDiarmid (Hugh has a traditional association and essential rightness in conjunction with MacDiarmid). . . (LP, 6)

1923 *Edited* **The Scottish Chapbook**, *edited* **The Scottish Nation**, *published* **Annals of the Five Senses**, *contributed to* **The New Age**. When Orage gave up *The New Age* [in 1922] and went to America to promulgate the doctrines of Ouspensky and Gurdjieff I took over the literary editorship of *The New Age* and was a prolific contributor to it over my own name and various pseudonyms for

tish Admiralty and engaged in servicing vessels of the British and American Navies in the waters of the Clyde Estuary. (Company, 187) **Lucky Poet**.

1945 *Registered as unemployed in Glasgow. Revived **The Voice of Scotland***.

1948 *Left the Scottish National Party.*

1950 *Visited Russia with members of the Scottish-USSR Friendship Society. Moved to Dungavel House, Strathaven.* At a meeting of the Saltire Society the Earl of Selkirk praised my work for Scotland and the quality of my lyrics, and a little later at his instance his brother, the Duke of Hamilton, offered me a commodious house adjacent to his Lanarkshire mansion of Dungavel, near Strathaven. Standing in a fine wood, it is an ideal dwelling, but unfortunately we had barely moved in and got ourselves settled when the National Coal Board bought over the whole estate, to establish a School for Miners in the mansion and in the adjoining lodges like ours houses for the school staff. So we had to get out. (Company, 188) *Received a Civil List Pension.* I received a letter from the Prime Minister's office asking if I would accept a Civil List pension. This was a Godsend and put me on my feet at last. (Company, 189)

1951 *Moved into Brownsbank Cottage, near Biggar, Lanarkshire.* It was in a derelict condition, not having been occupied for several years, but it had the supreme advantage of being rent-free, and my wife speedily made it not only habitable but comfortable. We had no 'mod cons', and were getting too old to put up with really primitive conditions. In a year or two, however, some of the Edinburgh University students, members of the Young Communist League, and other friends came to the rescue and did all the necessary digging, draining, etc., and we soon found ourselves equipped with a kitchenette, bathroom, hot and cold water, flush lavatory, and electric light and other gadgets. The long spell of hardship and near destitution was over and after about twenty years' tough struggle we were very comfortably

several years – until, in fact, Orage returned to England. (Company, 271)

1924 *Peggy gave birth to Christine. Edited **The Northern Review***

1925 **Sangschaw**.

1926 **Penny Wheep**. I was in the thick of the General Strike too. I was the only Socialist Town Councillor in Montrose and a Justice of the Peace for the county, and we had the whole area sewn up. One of my most poignant memories is of how, when the news of the great betrayal came through, I was in the act of addressing a packed meeting mainly of railwaymen. When I told them the terrible news most of them burst into tears – and I am not ashamed to say I did too. (Company, 158) **A Drunk Man Looks at the Thistle. Contemporary Scottish Studies**.

1927 *Founded the Scottish Centre of PEN.* **Albyn. The Lucky Bag. The Present Position of Scottish Music**.

1928 *Founder member of the National Party of Scotland.*

1929 *Peggy gave birth to Walter. Moved to London to edit **Vox**.* In 1929 I left Montrose and went to London to become London editor of *Vox*, a radio critical journal which had been promoted by Compton (afterwards Sir Compton) Mackenzie. . . Alas, *Vox* was under-capitalised and premature – radio was not sufficiently far developed to yield an adequate readership concerned with critical assessments of home and foreign programme material of all kinds; and very shortly the venture collapsed. (Company, 186) [In December 1929] I had fallen from the top of a London double-decker motor-bus going at speed, and landed on my head on the pavement, sustaining severe concussion. I did not fracture, but it was a miracle I did not break my neck. (LP, 38)

1930 *Separated from Peggy.* **To Circumjack Cencrastus**. I realized, with terrible distress, that, against my will, the ties between my wife and two children, Christine and Walter, were about to be broken no less completely than I had allowed the ties between myself and my relatives in Langholm and elsewhere to break. (LP, 19)

Moved to Liverpool to work as public relations officer. After
. . . one most unfortunate interlude in London, and a
subsequent year in Liverpool (equally unfortunate, but
for other and far more painful reasons, and owing perhaps to a considerable extent to my own blame), I have
been desperately anxious not to leave Scotland again. . .
(LP, 41)

1931 *Divorced from Peggy. Met Valda Trevlyn in London.* My
domestic affairs were in a bad way and I was divorced
in 1931. Shortly afterwards I married again. I had,
however, no money or income. . . (Company, 186) **First
Hymn to Lenin and Other Poems.**

1932 *Moved to Thakeham in Surrey. Valda gave birth to Michael.*
My friends included, too, such extraordinary characters
as Count Geoffrey Potocki de Montalk, editor of the
Right Review (who went . . . about London wearing a
long red cloak – as did his brother, Count Cedric – and
whose cottage at Thakeham in Sussex I 'took on' while
he was in gaol for publishing obscene literature). . .
(LP, 48) **Second Hymn to Lenin. Scots Unbound and
Other Poems.**

1933 *Moved to the Shetland island of Whalsay.* I came to Whalsay,
this little north Isle of the Shetland group, in 1933. I
was absolutely down-and-out at the time – with no
money behind me at all, broken down in health, unable
to secure remunerative employment of any kind, and
wholly concentrated on projects in poetry and other
literary fields which could bring me no monetary return
whatever . . . I could not have lived anywhere else . . .
without recourse to the poorhouse. We were not only
penniless when we arrived in Whalsay – I was in ex-
ceedingly bad state, psychologically and physically.
(LP, 41, 45) *Expelled from the National Party of Scotland.*

1934 *Joined the Communist Party of Great Britain.* My coming to
Communist membership was not the resolution of a
conflict, but the completion, as it were, of a career. . .
From the beginning I took as my motto – and I have
adhered to it all through my literary work – Thomas

Hardy's declaration: 'Literature is the written expression of revolt against accepted things.' (LP, 232) **Stony
Limits and Other Poems.** *Death of mother, Elizabeth.* My
mother . . . and I were always great friends and had a
profound understanding of the ultimate worth of each
other's beliefs. . . (LP, 224)

1935 *Nervous breakdown.* I have been Scotland's Public Enemy
No. 1 for over a decade now, and I have certain
accounts to settle while (a recent very grave illness
prompts the phrase) there is yet time. (LP, 34) **Second
Hymn to Lenin and Other Poems.**

1938 *Edited* **The Voice of Scotland.** *Expelled from the Communist
Party for Nationalist deviation.*

1941 *Conscripted for National Service.*

1942 *Left Shetland.* In February [1942] I had to abandon
my Shetland retreat, and since then I have been doing
hard manual labour in big Clydeside engineering shops.
Going from one extreme to the other like this is, of
course, in keeping with my (and Gurdjieff's) philosophy
of life, and, happily, at fifty, my constitution has been
able to stand the long hours, foul conditions, and totally
unaccustomed, heavy and filthy work perfectly well
. . . my Leontiev-like detestation of all the bourgeoisie,
and, especially, teachers, ministers, lawyers, bankers,
and journalists, and my preference for the barbarous
and illiterate lower classes of workers, has been completely confirmed by my Clydeside experiences. (LP,
xxxiii) *Rejoined the Scottish National Party. Member of SNP
National Council.*

1943 *Transferred to the Merchant Service.* I had made a good
recovery from a serious general break-down I had had
in 1935, but the very rough conditions at Mechans
[engineering firm] and the fact that I suffered serious
injuries when a stack of copper-cuttings fell on me and
cut both my legs very severely led me to seek a transf
to the Merchant Service. This was granted and I
came first a deck hand – and then first engineer – o
Norwegian vessel, M.F.V. *Gurli*, chartered by the

ensconced in a house of our own with every likeli-
hood that it would prove a permanency. (Company,
188–9)

1955 ***In Memoriam James Joyce***. *Again revived **The Voice of
Scotland**.*

1956 *Rejoined the Communist Party.* I rejoined [the Communist
Party] at the time of what I would call the suppression
of the threatened counter-revolution in Hungary. Those
who came out then, I think, did so for reasons I would
call purely sentimental. They had probably never been
convinced Communists and the party was well shot of
most of them. (Uncanny, 170) *Visited China with the
British-Chinese Friendship Society.*

1957 *Awarded Honorary LL.D. by Edinburgh University.*

1959 *Visited Czechoslovakia, Rumania, Bulgaria and Hungary as
part of the Burns bi-centenary celebrations.*

1961 ***The Kind of Poetry I Want***.

1962 ***Collected Poems***. It was in 1962, however, that the real
break-through came. The occasion of my seventieth
birthday was celebrated all over the world. There were
scores of articles about my poetry in newspapers and
periodicals in every so-called civilised country. I had
hundreds of greetings telegrams and letters from many
countries – so many that for several days round about
11th August . . . Biggar Post Office had to run what
was virtually a shuttle-service several times a day to
deliver the masses of mail. (Company, 189)

1963 *Presented with the William Foyle Poetry Prize for 1962.*

1964 *Visited Canada. Communist candidate for Kinross and West
Perthshire in General Election.* It was essential to oppose
the Prime Minister [Sir Alec Douglas-Home], as a
Communist and as a Scotsman. (Company, 203)

1966 ***The Company I've Kept***.

1967 *Visited the USA.*

1971 *Visited Italy.*

1973 *Visited Ireland.*

1976 *Visited Canada.*

1978 *Awarded Honorary Litt.D. by Dublin University. 9 September: Died in hospital in Edinburgh. 13 September: Buried in Langholm Cemetery.* **Complete Poems**.

Chapter One
THE MIND ALONE

The supreme reality is visible to the mind alone.
'Lament for the Great Music' (475)

The supreme reality is visible to the mind *alone*.
In Memoriam James Joyce (888)

Although he gleefully introduced an element of intellectual
ostentation into his poetry, Hugh MacDiarmid was not a
wilfully obscure poet. When a MacDiarmid poem is difficult
or inaccessible it is generally because the concept is complex,
elusive or unfamiliar. In 1932 the poet collected, in his volume
Scots Unbound and Other Poems, a discursive piece called 'Depth
and the Chthonian Image', which is composed with considerable care as is evident from both structure and texture. The
poem, in Aggrandised Scots, consists of ten 24-line stanzas
rhyming (ambitiously) *abcbddeffebbcbadgghihijj*. It is arranged
as an address to another introduced as early as the second
line:

> *Absolvitur ab instantia* is decreed
> In every case against you men array.
> Yours is the only nature stiflin' nocht,
> Meetin' a' the experiences there are to ha'e
> And never meetin' ane o' them raw-edged.
> Ripe, reconcilin' mind, sublimely gauged,
> Serene receptiveness, nae tongue can speak
> Your fair fey form felicitously enow,

Nae subtle mind seek your benmaist howe
And gar your deepest implications beek. (346–7)

It is not immediately apparent what or who the poet has in
mind. The poem is dedicated to John Macnair Reid, a fellow
Scottish writer, and the title suggests a reference to a deity
such as Demeter dwelling underground. More significantly
the poem is subtitled 'On looking at a ruined mill and thinking of the greatest' and the image of the mill is taken up by
the poet in the second verse-paragraph:

Forever ample baith in scouth and skill,
Watchin' your aws by nicht it seems to me
The stars adreigh mimic their drops and 'mang hands
There is nae nearer image gi'en to life
O' that conclusive power by which you rin
Even on, drawin' a' the universe in,
Than this loose simile o' the heavenly hosts
Vainly prefigurin' the unseen jaups
Roond your vast wheel – or mair waesome ghosts
O' that reality man's pairt o' and yet caps
Wi' Gods in his ain likeness drawn
            – Puir travesties o' your plan. (347–8)

In the third verse-paragraph MacDiarmid associates 'you'
with 'the invisible' (348) and reaches out into infinity for an
appropriate image of the eternal. He then comes to a mystical
conclusion and insists on the unity, the 'aneness', of the
mystery:

You're no' its meanin' but the world itsel'.
Yet let nae man think he can see you better
By concentratin' on your aneness either.
He pits his mind into a double fetter
Wha hauds this airt or that, no baith thegither.
You are at aince the road a' croods ha' gane
            And alane wi' the alane. (349)

[2]

At the time this poem materialised in print MacDiarmid was known, in Scotland, as a lyric poet intent on literary expansion along the lines of *A Drunk Man Looks at the Thistle* (1926) and *To Circumjack Cencrastus* (1930); in England, and elsewhere, he was more damagingly categorised as a hagiographer of Lenin who had perpetrated *First Hymn to Lenin and Other Poems* (1931) and *Second Hymn to Lenin* (1932). MacDiarmid, however, resisted classification and astute readers of his work would have noticed a spiritual quality running through his lines and implicit in the spaces between the lines. MacDiarmid was searching for a unity, for 'aneness', but displayed in himself such endless variety that his search had to be for the unity-in-diversity that Plotinus regarded as the fragmentary nature of the Mind as an image of the One, the mystical source of creation. Like Plotinus, MacDiarmid was a visionary and in his contemplation of a ruined mill there is an affinity with the way Plotinus himself 'turned aside from the spectacle of ruin and misery in the actual world, to contemplate an eternal world of goodness and beauty.'[1] A poetic pantheon that could accommodate both Plotinus and Lenin could only be associated with an unusually eclectic writer and MacDiarmid was a prolific literary activist who relished incongruity and delighted in provocation. Critics then, as now, were uncomfortable with his intellectual restlessness and his stunning range of reference.

Turning back to the poem there emerges an imaginative programme based on the neoplatonism of Plotinus; MacDiarmid assumes that the earthly can only be connected with its eternal Idea by means of an intellectual vision. Typically MacDiarmid approaches the central theme from different angles and his neoplatonic perception opens on to an autobiographical aside. MacDiarmid recalls that he is the force behind a movement (the Scottish Renaissance) so he extrapolates and considers the energy that moves the earthly mill and, beyond that, the universal source that motivates the One, the greatest, the eternally creative principle:

Ein Mann aus dem Volke – weel I ken
Nae man or movement's worth a damn unless
The movement 'ud gang on withoot him if
He dee'd the morn. Wherefore in you I bless
My sense o' the greatest man can typify
And universalise himsel' maist fully by. (351)

Here the movement of MacDiarmid's verse is by creative
conflation; a many-layered notion is set up, examined, and
then slowly stripped down to a quintessential core. In other
poems he is equally capable of reversing the motion and
endlessly expanding and illustrating a central insight. In
'Depth and the Chthonian Image' MacDiarmid is condensing
a mass of conceptual material into an important symbol.
Behind the ruined mill is the Ideal mill and (by analogy)
behind the physical limitation of the poet there is the intellectual vision of the One. MacDiarmid wants to dismiss the
everyday irrelevancies that come between man and the intellectual vision which he symbolises as 'the terrible crystal, the
ineffable glow.' (352) Appropriately enough this image is
buried towards the end of the poem like a treasure the poet
has been searching for. When he comes across 'the vital
vision' (353) and sees the 'radiant licht' (353) he has attained
a unity with the universe. He has found the terrible crystal
of creativity.

Throughout all his work MacDiarmid seeks the vital vision.
His poetry is a consistent search for the source of universal
creativity and he firmly believes that 'in ages like our own all
the ostensible themes and subjects of the poet will tend to be
in the first place simply allegories for the creative process
itself.' (LP, 337) In pursuit of 'the terrible crystal, the ineffable glow' MacDiarmid regards everything as grist to his
mill. He makes no attempt to be systematic but rejoices in
the multifarious nature of his search since he dislikes speci-
alisation and feels that 'watertight compartments are useful
only to a sinking ship.' (657) Whenever he was questioned
on the apparent inconsistency of his thought he was quick to
dismiss the charge as irrelevant:

[4]

The variety and the enormity of the world and the
infinite possibilities of the human mind are such that
contradictions are inevitable for anyone who has a certain
depth of intellectual perception. Only shallow minds
fancy that they are being consistent. And they can only
be consistent within a very narrow ambit. As soon as
they endeavour to take in the whole, they are lost,
completely lost, unless they have learned to juggle with
contradictions. (Metaphysics, [5])

On the other hand MacDiarmid loved to parade his intellectual credentials to such an extent that he claimed he had
been educated at Edinburgh University when he had been
nothing of the kind.[2] In a pseudonymous description of *To
Circumjack Cencrastus*, MacDiarmid promotes himself as an
intellectual virtuoso:

The author shows an astonishing knowledge of the whole
range of modern European philosophy and religious
speculation, and has obviously been profoundly
influenced by Nietzsche, Bergson, Soloviev, Husserl, and
others. This is a familiarity which is sufficiently unusual
in lay circles in Scotland to-day to constitute a merit in
itself. (Uncanny, 136)

I think MacDiarmid was an intuitive, not a systematic,
thinker who was attracted to insights rather than, say, epis-
temology. He enjoys dropping the names of philosophers
whose work confirms his own suppositions. The citation of a
great name, MacDiarmid feels, lends intellectual authority to
his work which is consequently riddled with references. Plato,
Hegel and (by extension) Marx are perfect examples of philosophers who were made to measure for MacDiarmid. The
concept of the dialectic (whether dialectical idealism as in
Plato, dialectical absolutism as in Hegel, or dialectical materialism as in Marx) supported the contradictory nature of
MacDiarmid's character. By assuming that great minds invariably think alike he was able to give his idiosyncratic
nature the status of an ideology.

[5]

Christopher Murray Grieve was born in Langholm on 11 August 1892 and his alter ego Hugh MacDiarmid was buried in Langholm on 13 September 1978. Between these dates a new poetic presence reared its inventive head in Scotland and increasingly impinged on the consciousness of the literary world at large. In becoming Hugh MacDiarmid, Christopher Murray Grieve acted in accordance with his own fundamental belief that 'to improve his own character is a man's surest means of improving the world.' (LP, 4) Grieve was born with few social advantages and, for the remainder of his life, endured various stages of poverty and hardship. Yet he never acknowledged defeat (since to do so would be to surrender to a negative national impulse), was always ready to fight for the various causes he believed in, and artistically his work represents a triumphal arch (with the apex achieved midway through life) through which future generations of Scots can pass. He did not accept the quietist role of a poet as a man who should confine himself to lyrical impulses. MacDiarmid wanted to reshape Scotland in his own assertive image. When he defined his role it was in activist terms. 'My function in Scotland', he said, 'has been that of the cat-fish that vitalizes the other torpid denizens of the aquarium' (LP, xxv); and, again, 'I have, in fact, thought it part of my job to keep up perpetually a sort of Berserker rage, or *riastral*, in the way of the old heroes.' (LP, 79)

The story of MacDiarmid's poetry begins in Langholm though it certainly does not end there. Langholm did not only feature in his poetry as a source of local colour or as a point of reference; it shaped the movement of his mind. Langholm is a Border burgh six miles from the English frontier; it is small but significant and earned, in the eighteenth century, the sobriquet the Muckle Toun because it was then much larger than the neighbouring burghs. It has a history of disputation as it dominated the Debatable Land, an area claimed for centuries by both Scotland and England until, in 1552, the issue was settled on paper, though not in the realm of folklore. In 1445, just outside Langholm, the battle of Arkinholm was fought between forces representing James, 9th earl of Douglas, and James I of Scotland. The result was the fall of the House of Black Douglas and an important victory for the Scottish crown eager to establish itself as a respected central authority. Christopher Murray Grieve was born in Arkinholm Terrace; his birthplace, therefore, bore the name of the burgh's most celebrated battle. MacDiarmid regarded himself as 'a fechter' (309) and was capable of coming out with rhetorical questions rich in regional pride: 'Fear? What's fear to a Border man?' (310) He came, he said, 'Frae battles, mair than ballads' (1150) and during his career he made sure that (to quote the title of one of his occasional sequences) *The Battle Continues.*

MacDiarmid's reputation has been, like his poetry, an argumentative issue. Until the posthumous publication, in 1978, of the two-volume *Complete Poems 1920–1976* MacDiarmid's work was relatively inaccessible and for years great critical claims for or against him had to be supported by references to poems in small editions or in little magazines or, after 1962, to the woefully incomplete *Collected Poems.* As a result there were, while the poet was alive, two critical groups operating a MacDiarmid assessment centre. The first group comprised those who worshipped uncritically at the shrine of a quintessentially Scottish institution while the second group largely ignored the poetry. Members of the first group were usually disciples who attempted to write in the grand style of the master and imagined that MacDiarmidist mannerisms would constitute the stuff of a rejuvenated Scottish Renaissance. Members of the second group were either ignorant of the work or too lethargic to acquire the texts on which they could come to an informed judgment about one of the century's most demanding poets.

This unstable critical situation disfigured books about literature, and (for example) the history of the 1930s will have to be rewritten in the light of MacDiarmid's achievement. MacDiarmid published, in 1931, his *First Hymn to Lenin and Other Poems* and C. Day Lewis recognised the pioneer nature of the book since he noted in 1934 that MacDiarmid's collection 'was followed by a rush of poetry sympathetic to Communism or influenced by it.' (LP, 158) In the 1930s Mac-Diarmid also published *Second Hymn to Lenin* (1932), *Scots Unbound and Other Poems* (1932), *Stony Limits and Other Poems* (1934), *Second Hymn to Lenin and Other Poems* (1935) as well as prose works and a miscellany co-written with Lewis Grassic Gibbon. Yet three representative books about the 1930s ignore or avoid MacDiarmid. Robin Skelton's anthology of *Poetry of the Thirties* (1964) has no reference to or contribution by MacDiarmid; A. T. Tolley's *The Poetry of the Thirties* (1975) drops his name once; Samuel Hynes's *The Auden Generation* (1976) has no mention of MacDiarmid though, as we have just seen, C. Day Lewis was aware of the influential nature of his work and an irascible Auden letter of 1931 refers to MacDiarmid as 'a fearful intellectual snob and prig.'[3]

Ignorance and uncritical adulation have also been responsible for the inability of observers to understand MacDiarmid's involvement in the experimental literature of the 1920s, though he made his intentions clear enough by stating, for instance in 1926,

> The peculiar relations now establishing themselves
> between literature and linguistics make it obvious that a
> speedy and successful use of synthetic Scots would give
> Scotland a short cut into the very forefront of
> contemporary creative experimentalism. (Studies, 117)

MacDiarmid's position becomes much clearer if we regard him as a contemporary of Joyce, Eliot and Pound rather than as a poet intent on renewing traditional Scottish verse. The Victorian world he was born into provided an evolutionary ideology that was subsequently expressed in an idiosyncratic manner for modernist artistic methods were impressed on his imagination through his reading of the great literary experimentalists. To MacDiarmid, dialect Scots was contaminated with the kailyard and he used Synthetic Scots, quite deliberately, as an indigenous equivalent of Joycean prose or the poetic idiom associated with Pound and Eliot. The fact that the pseudonym Hugh MacDiarmid was first used, and the first MacDiarmid lyric published, in 1922 is of crucial importance: MacDiarmid's appearance came in the creative interval between the publication of Joyce's *Ulysses* in February and Eliot's *The Waste Land* in October of that *annus mirabilis* of modernism. MacDiarmid constantly emphasised his experimental ambitions but his disciples thought that his use of Scots was purely emotional and his detractors adhered to the preconceived notion that the use of Scots must be, *ipso facto*, reactionary. MacDiarmid's poetry, which spanned more than half a century, is not to be defined by decades though he was experimental in the 1920s, political in the 1930s, philosophical in the 1940s. This book looks at the poetic achievement as an unusually unified text in a marvellously varied context.

MacDiarmid's poetry – exquisitely abbreviated or epic, Scots or English, lyrical or stridently didactic – is a search for the source of creativity conducted by a man who had availed himself of what he called (in *In Memoriam James Joyce*) 'the fifth dimension, individuality' (836). This emphasis on individuality, the belief that 'the individual is the only foundation/On which any social order may safely build,' (1120) is related to an evolutionary ideal since the poet is 'exclusively concerned with the highest forms of life.' (575) MacDiarmid believed that every human being had a duty to realise his or her immense spiritual potential and felt he could best demonstrate this by attaining an astonishing individuality himself. MacDiarmid did not regard individuality as an excuse for inhuman egotism or antisocial escapism but felt that the fully conscious individual could attain a spiritual unity with the universe. The idea is expressed as early as his first book:

> He believed recurrently that his own thought was part of the consciousness which sustained the world, and he expected to find a rational quality in its final outlines as well as in human history. He started anew from himself around an anthropomorphic universe, and went in search of a larger self which was the reflection and confirmation of his own. . . (Annals, 69)

Since the uniqueness of the philosophically selfconscious individual impressed MacDiarmid he felt it was his poetic duty to be as singular as possible. MacDiarmid admired eccentrics (Scottish or otherwise) and responded enthusiastically to writers who went their own way regardless of fame or fortune. His dislike of conventionality, his love of polemic, his penchant for provocation: these elements constitute the character at the centre of the poetry. MacDiarmid is a character created by Grieve; an idealisation of himself. Those unfamiliar with MacDiarmid's work as a whole suspect that he is a mass of irreconcilable contradictions, a confused and inconsistent author who could readily endorse Henry Jekyll's opinion that 'man is not truly one, but truly two'.[4] Not so. MacDiarmid, a dialectician by nature, wanted a visionary synthesis to heal the 'broken unity of the human spirit'. (753) Certainly a superficial glance at MacDiarmid's career would reveal apparent contradictions: the nationalist Anglophobe who sang a communist international, the voice of the people who despised the mob, the militant materialist who rejoiced that 'there are few of the great mystical experiences I have not had'. (LP, 268) MacDiarmid was, however, consistent in his contradictions, for he believed that Scottishness was a state of mind capable of creating lasting edifices from ideas explored in the to-and-fro of open argument. Long before he endorsed the Marxist theory of dialectical materialism MacDiarmid believed in thesis and antithesis; and in the poetic vision that makes a synthesis out of extremes. In a celebrated moment his immortal Drunk Man said:

> I'll ha'e nae hauf-way hoose, but aye be whaur
> Extremes meet – it's the only way I ken
> To dodge the curst conceit o' bein' richt
> That damns the vast majority o' men. (87)

That quatrain has the resonance of a credo.

MacDiarmid was proud of the consistency of his contradictions. In 1972, looking back over his life without any of the usual Grand Old Mannerisms, he referred pugnaciously to his paradoxical nature:

I am accustomed to being accused of all sorts of contradictions, to which I have often merely answered, like Walt Whitman, 'I contradict myself. Very well! I contradict myself.' But I am interested to note that many of those who have written about me and my work now tend to agree that under the apparent inconsistencies and contradictions there is a basic unity, and they refer their readers to my first book, *Annals of the Five Senses* [1923], in which I express the main ideas of all my subsequent work. (LP, xi)

Annals of the Five Senses opens with an inventive composition called, appropriately enough, 'Cerebral'. It describes the stream-of-consciousness flowing through the mind of a young journalist as he works, under the pressure of a deadline, on an article on the Scottish element in Ibsen. MacDiarmid, or Grieve as he was then, finds his material in the act of creation itself. He is exhilarated by the cerebral process as it searches for a creative outlet. Linguistic creativity is the subject and object of his writing:

He was athrill with the miracle of sentience, quivering in every filament of his perceptions with an amazing aliveness. All his thoughts were to him (although all the while away down in the unguessable depths of his being, where the egos of his actualities and his appearances debated without end in the forum of the absolute, doubts may have been expressed as to what was becoming in a man of his years), every one of them sweet, careless, fragrant interpretations of the gratitude of being alive – Elysian fields of cogitation where all happy words which had endeavoured in honesty and humility to express for him raptures beyond adumbration, after their patient services of signification, entered into their full felicity – brilliant, joyous, poignant pages of appreciation, as sensitive and magical as the mind of youth ever lent to the wonder of being.
   Continually the spirit of poetry broke blossoms about his head. (Annals, 7)

The ecstatic appreciation of the way words work on a poetic level is still providing MacDiarmid with his theme in a book published more than thirty years after *Annals* for in *In Memoriam James Joyce* (1955) he is still 'athrill with the miracle of sentience' and even expressing his excitement in a similar way:

> Easy – Quick – Sure – The exact word
> You want – when you want it.
> Elusive words easily captured and harnessed.
> New ideas spring to your mind.
> Your imagination is stirred by this simple
> But wonderful Idea and Word Chart.
> It puts words and ideas at your finger tips,
> It will enable you to open the flood-gates of the mind
> And let the torrent of drama and tragedy –
> Human strife, flaming love, raging passion,
> Fiendish onslaught, splendid heroism –
> Flow from your pen, leap into type
> And fly to your readers, to grip them and hold them
> Enthralled by the fascinating spell of your power. (805)

All his creative life MacDiarmid's primary concern was with the cerebral act of creation as experienced by himself as a representative of the evolutionary ideal he adhered to. Wallace Stevens, a poet MacDiarmid admired, opened part XXII of 'The Man With The Blue Guitar' by asserting 'Poetry is the subject of the poem'; so it was for MacDiarmid who felt, to recall a point worth repeating, that 'in ages like our own all the ostensible themes and subjects of the poet will tend to be in the first place simply allegories for the creative process itself.' (LP, 337) MacDiarmid did not see this as a limitation since he conceived poetry to be the creative monument humanity builds on its own behalf, a process that is never finished, is literally eternal. Poetry, for MacDiarmid, was 'The greatest poo'er amang men.' (326) In one of the programmatic parts of the unfinished *Impavidi Progrediamur* (in which he appears as 'The Man for whom Gaeldom is waiting') he says:

He has a craving for essentials.
The miracle of literature,
Of culture, in racial history
Is that it is at once the bow and the mark,
The inspiration and the aim.
'In the beginning was the Word,'
But the Word is also
'The last of life for which the first was made.' (1375)

MacDiarmid's pursuit of the word perceived as a multifaceted poetic symbol – the terrible crystal – led to his habit of 'adventuring in dictionaries' (823) and the lexical texture of his poetry has caused confusion over the nature of his art.

MacDiarmid's crucial childhood experience was exposure to a mass of books (see Chronology) and in 'Cerebral' he speaks of

the effect of his sense of personal insignificance, of physical inadequacy – of having paralysed his creative faculties by over-reading – of being merely a 'strong solution of books' as 'full of quotations as Shakespeare' – and so forth. . . (Annals, 20)

This is a source of anxiety in many creative artists who suspect that omnivorous reading may undermine the imagination. On 22 September 1846 Flaubert wrote to his mistress Louise Colet on the same subject, expressing similar fears 'about excessive reading killing the imagination, the individual element, the one thing, after all, that has some value'.[5] MacDiarmid had peculiar problems with his omnivorous reading for he occasionally failed so obviously in integrating secondary material into his work that he attracted charges of plagiarism. When the novelist Glyn Jones wrote to the *TLS* pointing out that (apart from the title and the first line) MacDiarmid's poem 'Perfect' comprised a linear arrangement of a passage in Jones's story 'Porth-y-rhyd', MacDiarmid replied:

I have always used quotations from many books in some

of my poems but have always been careful to attribute such quotations to their sources when I knew these. In this case . . . I either automatically memorized it and subsequently thought it my own, or wrote it into one of my notebooks with the same result.[6]

In the heated correspondence that followed MacDiarmid defended himself by referring to impeccable authorities:

As Mr T. S. Eliot said: 'Minor poets borrow, major poets steal' and my own practice in much of my later work has been like that of Mr Ezra Pound who, in one of his essays, says he takes his material from wherever he can find it and endeavours to transform the assemblage into an artistic unity, the test being that in the upshot the whole (i.e., what in sum he makes of these discrete materials) is more than the sum of the parts.[7]

For MacDiarmid, then, the main aesthetic issue is not inspirational originality or linguistic purity but an organisational ability to arrange words (from whatever source) into an impressive artistic whole.

Although his Mature Art project has long stretches of declamation about the kind of poetry he wants, MacDiarmid has made few statements on the nature of poetry in general or his poetry in particular. When he discusses his art it is generally in terms of its educative properties so that 'I dream of a literary equipment which may bring immense erudition to bear on the general unsanity of mankind, on the appalling mindlessness of almost everybody.' (LP, 407) Poetry, MacDiarmid believes, is a spiritual instrument for changing the world; or for enabling its spiritual qualities to be apprehended. As he believes that poetry is the supremely creative agency at large in the universe MacDiarmid takes its artistic importance for granted. He is not given to abstract aesthetic statements of his poetic intentions though it is obvious that his quest for a dictionary-derived language (first Synthetic Scots, then Aggrandised Scots, then Synthetic English) was based on his belief, acquired during his years in the army, that 'most of the important words were killed in the First

World War'. (1156) To use the language of everyday exchange was a betrayal of the potential of poetry and Grieve felt that prevailing styles in English and Scots were inadequate. A new linguistic idiom had to be created and Grieve watched admiringly the attempts of the 'men of 1914' – as Wyndham Lewis termed himself, Pound, Eliot and Joyce – to create it. Pound's artistic commandment to 'make it new' was taken very seriously by the Scottish poet.

In his isolated reflections on the nature of poetry MacDiarmid emphasises his interest in the texture rather than the structure of verse:

> Making poems . . . is very like diamond-polishing – the 'dop' in which the diamond or poem is held being the poet's cortical understanding, and the 'schyf' on which the 'dop' is held down to polish the diamond being reason in the fullest sense. (LP, 56)

The poem as diamond is linked, in MacDiarmid's mind, with his quest for the terrible crystal of creativity. In his poem 'Diamond Body' (apparently written on Linga) he watches 'the brilliant light', 'the pure white light/Of the divine body of truth' (1087) then, after considering appearance and reality in a cave (both real and Platonic), he ends by asserting: 'I have achieved the diamond body.' (1088) This note of resolution is rare in MacDiarmid's characteristically restless poetry; it also occurs at the end of another Shetland poem, 'Island Funeral', where he listens to 'this island note,/This clear old Gaelic sound' (581) and concludes triumphantly 'I have heard it and am content for ever.' (583) The cerebral act of creation therefore allows the poet to touch the terrible crystal and understand the universal importance of his individuality. MacDiarmid is convinced that the 'true poet never merely articulates a preconception of his tribe, but starts rather from an inner fact of his individual consciousness' (LP, 59) to which the poet might add:

Remember, I speak
Never of the representative individual man as man,

But always of the artist as the great exception
To the whole human order of things. (1172)

In his most considered statement on the nature of poetry
MacDiarmid stressed the philological genesis of his work:

Because of a profound interest in the actual structure of
language, like Mallarmé's, like Mallarmé I have always
believed in the possibility of 'une poésie qui fut comme
déduite de l'ensemble des propriétés et des caractères
du langage' – the act of poetry being the reverse of what
it is usually thought to be; not an idea gradually shaping
itself in words, but deriving entirely from words – and it
was in fact (as only my friend F. G. Scott divined) in this
way that I wrote all the best of my Scots poems. (LP,
xxiii)

MacDiarmid's celebration of the suggestive power of words
was not, of course, meant as an insult to the intellect

For if it's no' by thocht that Poetry's wrocht
It's no' by want o' thocht (232)

The notion of linguistic response is MacDiarmid's rationalisation of his poetic instinct and appetite for lexical adventure;
his poetry displays a concern with the transformational power
of words to develop 'The ineluctable individuation of personality' (1119). The art of MacDiarmid is in the nature of a
voyage across an ocean of words with the poet trawling for
the choicest specimens, aware that some catches will be better
than others. Appropriately enough MacDiarmid's favourite
imagery relates to angling and fishing and he speaks from
experience when he says (in a poem omitted from *Complete
Poems* but reproduced from the original manuscript in
Festschrift):

Fishers know it's at night
Their harvest is got.
Daylight's only of use
For disposing of the 'shot'.

The poet as fisher of words is linked to the parable of Christ the fisher of men and it is a hallmark of MacDiarmid's poetry that it encourages images to clash before they coalesce. Thus neoplatonist ideas intermingle with Christian symbolism and Old Testament archetypes coexist with the intellectual supermen who emerge from MacDiarmid's evolutionary idealism.

Immodesty is another aspect of MacDiarmid's poetry. In his lyrics he tends to romantic egotism and in his Shetland period to solipsism yet the poetic self is rooted in reality. In celebrating himself MacDiarmid is (like Whitman) rejoicing in himself as an especially heroic human being who has achieved, through articulation, a glimpse of universal unity, of 'aneness'. MacDiarmid is more likely to consider himself as an example of evolution in action than to dwell on autobiographical detail. During his poetic career MacDiarmid held tenaciously to his evolutionary ideal and it transcends, and actually explains, his party politics. The last sentence of Trotsky's *Literature and Revolution* (1924) proclaims that the average human type will rise to the heights of an Aristotle, a Goethe, a Marx and that, in the future, new peaks will rise. MacDiarmid takes this seriously in his poetry and the evolutionary ideal gives an optimistic tone to his verse. MacDiarmid tossed ideas in the air with the nonchalance of an expert juggler and some he jettisoned when his mood changed. The evolutionary ideal was crucial, though, as he indicated in his autobiography:

> the belief that the Future lies with ordinariness, the
> ordinary man . . . is the very nadir of contemptible
> demagoguery; on the contrary . . . scientific development
> and a better social order can tap genius in every human
> being and create a society in which men like the greatest
> philosophers, poets, and scientists in human history will
> no longer be, as they have always been hitherto, very rare
> exceptions, but the rule – most men will be of a stature
> like that of Plato or Homer or Shakespeare. And I believe
> that is coming, as the result of scientific discoveries, very
> speedily – the time when the earth will be occupied by 'a

race of people all of whom come up to the level of what
we now call "genius". . . .' If Communism did not mean
that – if it only meant doing away with a great deal of
hardship and preventible pain and disease and death – if
it only meant raising the economic level of everybody
until it was as high as that of the wealthiest man in the
world to-day, I would not move a little finger to assist the
process. (LP, 237)

MacDiarmid's contempt for the masses, for 'maist folk' (*passim*), is based on his conviction that the unconscious individual is a living insult to the evolutionary ideal. He is unwilling
to compromise, to come down to the level of the man in the
street, and he regards the struggle for economic freedom as
a marginal issue:

> Man does not cease to interest me
> When he ceases to be miserable.
> Quite the contrary!
> That it is important to aid him
> In the beginning goes without saying,
> Like a plant it is essential
> To water at first;
> But this is in order to get it to flower,
> And I *am concerned with the blossom*. (1060)

Since the evolutionary ideal is to produce intellectual supermen, MacDiarmid frequently appeals to the future (when
such mental mutations will be theoretically commonplace) or
addresses his intellectual equals (like Lenin or Doughty) or
settles for speaking to himself. Until the evolutionary ideal is
achieved, however, the poet must be a man able to take his
place among the poorest people aware that 'lack of money
does not spell poverty of spirit' (820) and that the poorest
folk (according to both Christian and Marxist thought) carry
the seeds of the future:

And until that day comes every true man's place
Is to reject all else and be with the lowest,
The poorest – in the bottom of that deepest of wells
In which alone is truth; in which
Is truly only – truth that should shine like the sun,
With a monopoly of movement, and a sound like
    talking to God. . . . (1043)

When he turns from the heights of evolutionary idealism to
the nature of everyday reality MacDiarmid stresses the
animal origins of man. He points to the biological past in
order to show the necessity of a creative evolution into the
future. In the process the poetic record of the past becomes
something powerful and vivid. In 'Gairmscoile' he insists that
'Deep i' the herts o' a' men lurk scaut-heid/Skrymmorie monsters' (72) and in 'Song of the New Economics' recalls 'our
rash progenitors' with their 'Prehensile tails and . . . primae-
val/Forest economy of nuts'. (397) 'Second Hymn to Lenin'
contains an evolutionary argument for overcoming 'breid-
and-butter problems':

> They s'ud be like the tails we tint
> On leavin' the monkey stage;
> A' maist folk fash aboot's alike
> Primaeval to oor age. (325)

and 'Ode to All Rebels' reminds the reader of his evolutionary
inheritance:

> Folk recognise – wi' regret it may be –
> Man's kinship wi' the maist laithsome brute
> Jogglin' his protudin' sternum there
> And lettin' his animal noises oot. (505)

As expressed in the poetry the ultimate aim of MacDiarmid's evolutionary ideal is the attainment of oneness – 'aneness' – with the universe. As he puts it in *In Memoriam James
Joyce*:

[19]

> The spiritual evolution from vile humanity
> To authentic manhood and onward
> To participation in self-universal
> Is an operation which bases itself
> On a full realization of the transiency
> Of spatial and temporal conditions (877)

All MacDiarmid's ideological prognostications derive from a basic faith in the upward movement of spiritual matter. As the individual is unique so is the individual nation (hence MacDiarmidian nationalism); and as the individual seeks universal expression so the individual nation tends towards interdependence (in MacDiarmidian communist theory anyway). MacDiarmid's ideology is no technical textbook affair but a bundle of insights derived from his impressionistic reading. His longing for oneness with the universe is an instinctive impulse that was complicated by references to other writers – like Plotinus or, nearer home, the Scottish poet John Davidson who thought 'that Man must rejoice in being, because, made up of the same ingredients as the Universe, he is, in fact, the Universe made conscious, and therefore inherently a creature of greatness.'[8] MacDiarmid's poem 'Of John Davidson' shows how deeply he was impressed by his predecessor's personality and what a profound impact Davidson's suicide had on him in 1909:

> something in me has always stood
> Since then looking down the sandslope
> On your small black shape by the edge of the sea,
> – A bullet-hole through a great scene's beauty,
> God through the wrong end of a telescope. (362)

Davidson was the kind of poet MacDiarmid always valued: a man differentiated from the mass (or 'the feck') by a unique talent. In drowning himself Davidson became, for MacDiarmid, the artist as self-sacrificial victim. As a young man MacDiarmid was a diligent student of the Bible and his work is saturated with biblical imagery and iconography. The truly admirable figure is always a man who comes with a message that is ignored by the majority, a man of integrity who carries an unbearable burden and is then sacrificed so that lesser men might take notice of the message. Davidson is such a figure in MacDiarmid's pantheon and is therefore worthy of MacDiarmid's complete approval. Though, as we shall see, MacDiarmid utilises the Christian symbolism of martyrdom he is also attracted to the Old Testament notions of the Prophet and the Outcast. 'I knew that the programme I embraced made me a sort of Ishmael' (LP, 234) MacDiarmid maintained, and Davidson had made Ishmaelitism a part of his own programme since his 'The Testament of a Man Forbid' opens with the statement 'Mankind has cast me out.'

MacDiarmid, too, had been cast out and his universal longings led back to the Langholm that had sustained him as a boy. He always regarded Langholm as an incomparably beautiful place and his descriptions of it reveal a romantic attitude not often permitted in his otherwise combative prose:

> Scotland is not generally regarded as a land flowing with
> milk and honey. . . Nevertheless, it can do so at times. . .
> It certainly did so in my boyhood – with a bountifulness
> so inexhaustible that it has supplied all my subsequent
> poetry with a tremendous wealth of sensuous satisfaction,
> a teeming gratitude of reminiscence, and that I have still
> an immense reservoir to draw upon. My earliest
> impressions are of an almost tropical luxuriance of
> Nature – of great forests, of honey-scented heather hills,
> and moorlands infinitely rich in little-appreciated beauties
> of flowering, of animal and insect life, of strange and
> subtle relationships of water and light . . . and of a
> multitude of rivers. . . (LP, 219)

There is a phrase, 'Out of the world and into Langholm', MacDiarmid is fond of quoting and indeed the poem 'The Dog Pool' uses it as an introduction to a rare expression of the limitations of booklore:

Oot o' the world and into the Langholm!
There's mony a troot in the auld Dog Pool
Livelier, praise be, than ocht you can write.
Lean owre as you used to ga'en to the school
And see the broon shadows and ivory beaks
    Bonnier than ony book bespeaks. (1252)

The earthly paradise is clear to MacDiarmid for it looks like Langholm. However the universal unity is something to be imagined and the man who wishes to reach it climbs up on a ladder made from the books he has read and when he is within touching distance of his goal abandons the props

Even as a man who rises high
Kicks away the ladder he has come up by. (757)

Like Wittgenstein, whose image that is, MacDiarmid uses words to reach silence; he attempts to express the ineffable.

As a youngster in Langholm MacDiarmid's source book was the Bible and he first came close to poetry through a theological connexion. As befitted the son of a church elder, Christopher Grieve taught in the Sunday School, won certificates for his religious knowledge and gravitated to the home of the local minister, Rev. Thomas Scott Cairncross, who ran Langholm South United Free Church from 1901 to 1907. When he first met Grieve, Cairncross was attracted by the intelligence of the youth though somewhat abashed by his energy (finding him at times, so Cairncross's son-in-law told me, an unsettling influence in Sunday School). While in Langholm, Cairncross published (locally) a collection of poems, *The Return of the Master* (1905), containing 'Langholm' and 'Crying the Fair' which alludes to the Common Riding with its display of 'the Thistle and the Bannock' and thus anticipates symbols MacDiarmid was to use in *A Drunk Man Looks at the Thistle*. After leaving Langholm, Cairncross published several books including a Kailyardish novel, *Blawearie* (1911), and a work of popular theology, *The Making of a Minister* (1914). He also continued to write poems and kept in touch with C. M. Grieve who corresponded with Cairncross during the First World War and included eight of the minister's poems in the First Series of his poetry annual *Northern Numbers* (1920). Grieve was undoubtedly impressed by Cairncross's prowess as a poet and stunned by the modernity of the minister's verse. The following lines are from Cairncross's description of Langholm:

> It lies by the heather slopes
> Where God spilt the wine of the moorland
> Brimming the beaker of hills. Lone it lies,
> A rude outpost: challenging stars and dawn,
> And down from remoteness
> And the Balladland of the Forest
> The Pictish Esk trails glory,
> Rippling the quiet eaves
> With the gold of the sun. (LP, 222)

MacDiarmid admitted he 'thought that was great stuff when I was a boy of twelve to fourteen' but later came to distrust 'such backward-looking resignationism and sentimental dreaming'. (LP, 223) Theoretically, yes: but these lines of Cairncross, with their paradisal Langholm and excessive alliteration, certainly had a permanent influence on Grieve. Even in a mature work such as 'A Golden Wine in the Gaidhealtachd' there are faint verbal echoes of Cairncross's manner:

> In Scotland in the Gaidhealtachd there's a golden
>   wine.
> Carelessly and irreligiously quaffed it might be taken
> For a very fine champagne. But it is not an effervescing
>   wine
> Although its delicate piquancy produces a somewhat
>   similar effect upon the palate. (721)

It is important to realise, when we are confronted by the apparent originality of MacDiarmid's poetry, that he was influenced at an early age by some obscure and unfamiliar models.

It is remarkable, in fact, how loyal MacDiarmid was to his earliest influences. He was weaned from the ways of the kirk by his reading and by need for new intellectual challenges. At Langholm Academy he was taught by two stimulating teachers, Francis George Scott and William Burt. Scott was an intensely opinionated man who believed in the possibility of an internationally important art emanating from Scotland. It is likely that he discussed these ideas with Burt and that something of the two teachers' excitement was communicated to their most perceptive pupil. MacDiarmid later recalled his early view of Scott:

As a matter of fact I was his blue-eyed boy, the star pupil. But one did not need to be a star pupil to know – indeed, I think all of us recognised at once – that Mr Scott was out of the ordinary run of teachers, and was, in fact, an eagle among sparrows; or rather, a lion in a den of Daniels, which in regard to the Scottish public he has remained ever since. I think that the basis that was laid then for our later friendship and collaboration was the fact that we were both imbued with the frontier spirit.[9]

In 1933, when MacDiarmid had established himself as Scotland's most inventive artistic mind, he still looked to Scott for advice and guidance as the bedfast poet William Soutar noted in his diary after a visit:

I enjoyed Scott immensely: his mentor-relationship with Grieve very interesting: a psychological touchstone: granting Scott's imaginative insight – why does Grieve depend so much upon his criticism: the reflex in Scott's case – as it seems to me – is to patronize Grieve: however, perhaps the relationship keeps Grieve more balanced: I don't think Scott is a big man – his penchant for song-setting rather suggests that – but he is a very interesting type.[10]

The 'mentor-relationship' was to have an important part in

the making of MacDiarmid's masterpiece *A Drunk Man Looks at the Thistle*.

In 1908 Grieve left Langholm to become a pupil teacher at Broughton Higher Grade School and Junior Student Centre in Edinburgh. It was the first step in a career that would, after all, reverse the Langholmian proverb as Grieve went out of Langholm into the world. And, just as he had been drawn to Cairncross and Scott in Langholm, so he found an inspirational figure at Broughton where the English teacher, George Ogilvie, became the man to whom his first serious literary efforts were addressed. Ogilvie was a lover of poetry, an enthusiast of Scottish literature, and a Socialist. Grieve also formalised his political commitment the year he first met Ogilvie, for in 1908 he joined the Independent Labour Party. It seems that Grieve's earliest work – including much of the material in *Annals of the Five Senses* – was written for Ogilvie's approval. In November 1920 the poet, then a married man, still turned to Ogilvie:

I have turned to you in every need with utter confidence. I have loved you above all men and women. Do you think I want money or position or reputation? No. Do you think that it matters to my wife, for instance? I may dedicate my poems to her but do you think she reads them? And if she did do you think she would understand them, or me? No! I need not write. I can dream my books and enjoy them in my head. But I try to write incessantly and cannot help doing so because your commendation of my work is my only desire. (NLS)

Ogilvie introduced Grieve to A. R. Orage's magazine *The New Age*. With contributors like Shaw, Wells, Havelock Ellis, T. E. Hulme, Ezra Pound (and eventually Edwin Muir and C. M. Grieve) the weekly represented a platform for modernism in the arts and socialism in society. Grieve believed that *The New Age* was 'the most brilliant journal that has ever been written in English, and small though its circulation was it reached all the liveliest minds in Great Britain and further afield.' (Company, 271)

To a considerable degree MacDiarmid modelled his artistic features on the intellectual image cultivated by *The New Age*. He liked its elitist tone, its polemical approach, its assumption that the artist was a shaper of society, its Nietzschean notion of the artist-as-redeemer. Through Orage, MacDiarmid was drawn to the Social Credit economics of Major C. H. Douglas who was certainly a prophet ignored in his native Scotland and therefore ready for deification by MacDiarmid who boasted 'I frequented "Douglasite" circles a good deal and associated with Major C. H. Douglas himself.' (LP, 48)

Another poet who advocated Social Credit, Ezra Pound, was enthusiastically admitted to MacDiarmid's pantheon. MacDiarmid agreed 'with almost everything Ezra Pound says in his *How to Read*' (LP, 137) and saw in Pound's jump from the formal concision of *Hugh Selwyn Mauberley* to the sprawling epic aspirations of the Cantos an irresistible precedent. Orage, Douglas and Pound were all outsiders, as was MacDiarmid's favourite contemporary writer – James Joyce. MacDiarmid's first book, *Annals of the Five Senses*, was written in 'English in a complicated style of prose' which MacDiarmid gladly acknowledged was 'very considerably affected' (Uncanny, 170) by the writing of Joyce. MacDiarmid's *A Drunk Man Looks at the Thistle* was conceived as a poetic equivalent of (or answer to) *Ulysses* and other MacDiarmid poems, from the ecstatically onomatapoeic 'Water Music' to the extended *In Memoriam James Joyce*, are addressed to the Irish master. It is no coincidence that most of MacDiarmid's cultural heroes experienced some form of martyrdom. Pound was persecuted by a country unable to appreciate his patriotism, a fate that justifies MacDiarmid's casting of the poet in contemporary society:

> The poet a Tarzan among apes all
> Suddenly murderously inimical. (609)

Joyce, too, attained cultural martyrdom of a sort, suffering

exile and poverty while bestowing incomparable artistic rich-
ness on the world that rejected him.

By nature and nurture MacDiarmid was attracted to individuals distinguished by (to adapt a favourite epithet of his)
myriad-minded (894) dedication. Most of his favourites have
an eccentric or outrageous quality. When he names names he
is liable to cite men of genius alongside figures guaranteed
épater les bourgeois:

> I have a fine array of the works of my favourite writers,
> Rainer Maria Rilke, Charles Doughty, Stefan George,
> Paul Valéry in poetry, Leo Chestov in philosophy,
> Pavlov's *Lectures on Conditioned Reflexes*, and Lenin, Stalin,
> Marx, Engels, Adoratsky, and other dialectical materialist
> writers. (LP, 46)

MacDiarmid translated Rilke magnificently, responded to
Valéry's interest in the connexion between science and poetry, appreciated Doughty's philological programme, and
admired the organisational ability of Lenin; but when he cites
Chestov as 'my favourite philosopher' (LP, 28) I suspect he
is teasing and testing the reader, though MacDiarmid did
pick up many insights into Russian philosophical idealism in
conversation with Prince D. S. Mirsky, the friend to whom
he dedicated his 'First Hymn to Lenin'. It should always be
remembered that there is a playful element in MacDiarmid's
pronouncements. He was a man with a wonderfully developed
sense of humour and a mischievous nature and when he drops
a name it does not follow that he is on intimate terms with
the whole body of work associated with that name. Mac-
Diarmid's poetry is never a systematic exploration of a philosophical or political doctrine. When he responds to a source
he enlarges on it with reference to his own poetic imagination:
'I am a poet; our fools ask me for logic not life.' (415)

Two examples illustrate MacDiarmid's attitude to sources.
He was much taken with the universalism of Vladimir Sergeyevich Solovyov. Just as he responded to Plotinus's sense
of being 'alone with the Alone', (786) and John Davidson's
faith in man as the consciousness of the universe, so he

admired Solovyov's image of the universe as an interplay between God and the object of God's thought – Sophia, the Wisdom of God. In 1923 MacDiarmid summarised Solovyov's metaphysic as follows:

> According to Solovyov there is no opposition between the universal and the individual. . . Sophia is not only the perfect unity of all that is *sub specie aeternitatis*, but also the unifying power in the divided and chaotic world, the living bond between the Creator and the creature. Sophia is for ever seeking to bring back to herself the existence that has split off from the original whole, and by becoming incarnate in the lower world, to attain complete and perfect realization of the ideal union between God and the universe. (SE, 40)

Now that notion obviously excited MacDiarmid who could see the poetic justice in an image that permitted the poet to attain universal unity by embracing a feminine ideal. It is an image he put to use in *A Drunk Man Looks at the Thistle* in invoking the figure of the mystical bride. On a less intense level there is 'Hymn to Sophia: The Wisdom of God' in which he stresses the healing power of Sophia as the feminine principle of unity and rebirth:

> Our broken cries of shame dispute
>   Death's pitiless and impious law
> As the whole Earth with straining hearts
>   Towards thee we draw. (455)

Another Russian, Dostoevsky (or Dostoevski as MacDiarmid usually spells it) provided MacDiarmid with an example he could adapt in his own way. Just as Dostoevsky had his Russian Idea – 'in which he pictured Russia as the sick man possessed of devils but who would yet "sit at the feet of Jesus" ' (SE, 67) – so MacDiarmid would reply with his Gaelic Idea. Dostoevsky is a crucial presence in *A Drunk Man* and the Gaelic Idea, aired throughout *To Circumjack Cencrastus*, is gradually built up into the cornerstone of MacDiarmid's

cultural programme. Dostoevsky and Solovyov are used se-
lectively by MacDiarmid the poet. They take their place in
the pantheon alongside heroes such as Sir Patrick Geddes,
Denis Saurat, Kaikhosru Shapurji Sorabji, John Maclean,
Lenin, Francis George Scott, Major Douglas, Ezra Pound,
James Joyce, Charles Doughty and others. These names
appear in MacDiarmid's prose and poetry as symbols of artistic integrity and political perspicacity. They are called on
to provide the human – or superhuman – element in his
poetry. Although MacDiarmid is a poet who celebrates individuality in principle he does not describe or discuss many
recognisable individuals in his work; he addresses other intellectual supermen (Lenin, Joyce, Doughty) but only occasionally encounters everyman. His long narrative piece on
'Tam o' the Wilds and the Many-Faced Mystery' begins by
claiming that 'Tam was a common workin' man' (368) then
rightly rejects that in view of Tam's extraordinary passion for
learning. The poet's father, James Grieve, is the subject of
'The Watergaw', 'Kinsfolk', 'At My Father's Grave', 'Fatherless in Boyhood' but the man is only evoked by his absence.
There is no verbal portrait of him. Apart from James Grieve
the only other actual figure who features regularly in the
poetry is the poet's second wife Valda to whom the Cornish
Heroic Song is addressed. MacDiarmid's poetry portrays
ideal and imaginary figures rather than actual individuals
and this, of course, is consistent with MacDiarmid's cerebral
approach.

What MacDiarmid does so successfully is to develop an
essentially poetic method of containing all his contradictions.
In this he asserts his Scottishness, for it is a quintessential
feature of Scottish thought to encourage the clash of ideas in
order to achieve what the poet's friend G. E. Davie called 'a
distinctive blend of the secular and the sacred.' (Company,
240) Byron (referring to Burns) described this distinctive
Scottish quality as The Antithetical Mind, Stevenson embod-
ied the schism in Dr Jekyll and Mr Hyde, G. Gregory Smith
referred to it as The Caledonian Antisyzygy and R. D. Laing
drew attention to The Divided Self. MacDiarmid's own per-

sonality exhibited a contrariness that confused him until he was able to elevate it into a literary principle that served him for a long creative lifetime. He always had an exaggerated respect for academic credentials and was delighted when, in 1919, he was provided with professorial authority for his own love of contradiction. In simultaneously holding paradoxical viewpoints, in exhibiting 'myriad-mindedness', (894) Grieve saw he was being fundamentally Scottish. Such, at any rate, was the contention of G. Gregory Smith's *Scottish Literature* which had a profound impact on Grieve since he subsequently used the book as the basic sermon on which to preach the Scottish Renaissance. What struck Grieve with the force of a major revelation was Smith's account of The Caledonian Antisyzygy:

> [Scottish] literature is remarkably varied [and] becomes, under the stress of foreign influence and native division and reaction, almost a zigzag of contradictions. The antithesis need not, however, disconcert us. Perhaps in the very combination of opposites – what either of the two Sir Thomases, of Norwich and Cromarty, might have been willing to call 'the Caledonian antisyzygy' – we have a reflection of the contrasts which the Scot shows at every turn, in his political and ecclesiastical history, in his polemical restlessness, in his adaptability, which is another way of saying that he has made allowance for new conditions, in his practical judgement, which is the admission that two sides of the matter have been considered. If therefore Scottish history and life are, as an old northern writer said of something else, 'varied with a clean contrair spirit,' we need not be surprised to find that in his literature the Scot presents two aspects which appear contradictory. Oxymoron was ever the bravest figure, and we must not forget that disorderly order is order after all.[11]

MacDiarmid appropriated the Caledonian Antisyzygy as the apotheosis of contradiction. It became his faith. When he later came to a serious consideration of Marx, the theory of

Dialectical Materialism must have seemed second nature to him as the making of a synthesis out of thesis and antithesis was his own strongest creative instinct. In launching his one-man Renaissance MacDiarmid had his pantheon as cover and the Caledonian Antisyzygy for platform. Naturally there had to be a counterpoint to the pantheon and we might call this his hitlist since he used up a lot of energy in attacking those he regarded as his cultural enemies. Perhaps chief among those open to literary assassination was Sir Harry Lauder whose commercialisation of the pathetic image of the comic Scot deeply offended MacDiarmid. Sir Harry was integrated into the rich texture of *A Drunk Man*, victimised in such occasional poems as 'Allelauder', and was generally remade in the image of a contemporary Judas:

> The workers have not too much fun in their lives
>   And gladly they paid you well.
> You took their cash; and double-crossed them then
>   And sold them into Hell. (1288)

Another apparently harmless figure was Mrs Marjory Kennedy-Fraser, the collector of Hebridean folksongs, who was angrily dismissed as an ally of sentimentality and Celtic Twilightry:

> Mrs Kennedy-Fraser's Hebridean songs – the whole
> Celtic Twilight business – I abhor. . .
> Give me Gaelic poets and composers again
> Who will stand first and foremost as Sibelius stands,
> Towering overwhelmingly over the Palmgrens and
>   Järnefelts. . .
> For harsh, positive masculinity,
> The creative treatment of actuality
> – And to blazes with all the sweetie-wives
> And colourful confectionery. (573–4)

Yet another was Lauchlan Maclean Watt, minister of Glasgow Cathedral and (in 1934) Moderator of the General As-

sembly of the Church of Scotland. In 1926 MacDiarmid
described Watt's efforts to write Scots poetry as 'atrocities'
(Studies, 118) and in 1930 Watt had the temerity to reply
with an attack on *To Circumjack Cencrastus*. For that act of
aggression he became the subject of MacDiarmid's satirical
poem 'An Apprentice Angel' and was thereafter cited as a
synonym for mediocrity:

> Now let Ramsay MacDonald and Lauchlan Maclean
>   Watt,
> Harry Lauder and Morton of the 'Rangers'
> And all the other 'great Scots' of to-day. . . . (1282)

More important figures on the hitlist are those former
friends MacDiarmid fell out with. He deplored F. G. Scott's
antisemitism, he parted company with Neil Gunn and decided
to champion Fionn Mac Colla as the truly representative
novelist of the Scottish Highlands, and he sustained a pro-
longed campaign against Edwin Muir who was MacDiarmid's only real rival for the poetic crown of twentieth-century
Scotland. During the 1920s Muir and MacDiarmid were
friends and colleagues. Muir greatly admired MacDiarmid's
Scots poetry; however his suggestion, in *Scott and Scotland*
(1936), that 'Scotland can only create a national literature by
writing in English'[12] outraged MacDiarmid. Muir granted
that MacDiarmid had written some remarkable poetry but
had changed nothing since it remained true that 'Scotsmen
feel in one language and think in another.'[13] MacDiarmid hit
back at this act of treachery by calling Muir 'a leader of the
white-mouse faction of the Anglo-Scottish *literati* and a pala-
din in mental fight with the presence of a Larry the Lamb'
(LP, 21) and by insisting that:

> . . . when I want to clinch the matter – when I rise to the
> height of my theme – I do not pass into English because
> Scots is inadequate, but I pass from dialect Scots little
> different from English into the real Mackay! – phrases of
> pure Scots a man cannot come by unless he is thinking in

Scots and has recovered for himself, and achieved a
mastery of, the full canon of that magnificent tongue.
These two instances alone completely demolish Mr
Muir's case, and I would certainly be unable to express
my profoundest ideas in English at all. (LP, 22)

The two examples are from, respectively, *A Drunk Man Looks
at the Thistle* and 'The Seamless Garment'. They are interesting as MacDiarmid has italicised what he considers to be
singularly successful effects only obtainable in Scots:

> We wha are poets and artists
> Move frae inklin' to inklin',
> And live for oor antrin lichtnin's
> In the haingles atweenwhiles,
>
> Laich as the feck o' mankind
> Whence we breenge in unkennable shapes
>   *– Crockats up, hair kaimed to the lift,*
>   *And no' to cree legs wi'!* . . . (100)

and

> Ailie Bally's tongue's keepin' time
>   To the vibration a' richt.
> Clear through the maze your een signal to Jean
>   What's for naebody else's sicht
> Shorts skirts, silk stockin's – *fegs, hoo the auld*
> *Emmle-deugs o' the past are curjute and devauld!* (313–14)

When MacDiarmid draws attention to his own poetic efforts it is almost always to exhibit a certain textural effect, as
above. Yet his repertoire is wider than such examples suggest
and his work has a rare conceptual quality. MacDiarmid's
approach to poetry is angular – as is the movement of his
verse. He regards his subject as a target and comes at it from
various angles. In *A Drunk Man* the method works perfectly
for there are so many ways of looking at the symbolic thistle.

In *To Circumjack Cencrastus* the method is less successful because the target is not so attractive to the poet. The angular method is omnipresent in the poetry and in MacDiarmid's general aesthetic. Discussing his radical work in Synthetic Scots he recalled his hostility to extant work in dialect Scots:

> What I said to myself, roughly, was: I wonder if it is just a question of angle of approach. If you approach the problem of Scots from a different angle you'd produce something quite different from this post-Burns sentimental Scots stuff. And I did that. And I produced 'The Watergaw' and then I went on from there. And, of course, they wouldn't believe it. (Conversation, [41–2])

As he contemplated longer poems he widened the angle until he reached *The Kind of Poetry I Want*:

> In photographic language, 'wide-angle' poems
> Taking in the whole which explains the part,
> Scientifically accurate, fully realized in all their details
>   (1020)

For all its unrolling of great names MacDiarmid's poetry is not obviously modelled on the actual poems of another poet. He was quite adamant about his originality:

> Basically, I don't think I've been influenced by anybody at all. I'm a great admirer of Valéry and others but I haven't been influenced by them. I'm not writing the kind of stuff they were writing at all. (Metaphysics, [17])

I have already suggested that MacDiarmid retained elements of the earliest poetry he was exposed to and though he is the opposite of a Shelleyan sensitive plant he certainly learned from Shelley and from classical English masters like Milton. From his own early reading of contemporary poetry he admired the Irish Revivalist poets; the Georgians (whose house-organ *Georgian Poetry* he emulated in his annual *Northern Numbers*); and he gained some notion of the possibilities of discursive poetry from Thomas Sturge Moore's poem 'Sent

from Egypt with a Fair Robe of Tissue to a Sicilian Vine-
dresser', as he acknowledged in 'Cornish Heroic Song for
Valda Trevlyn'. (704) His early ambitions as a romantic
sonneteer show the influence of Keats and Rupert Brooke,
whose pose as a poetic prophet appealed to Grieve (and to
thousands of other young men). His poetry in English is also
influenced by Doughty, Blake, Hopkins and Whitman. Mac-
Diarmid's Scots poetry is more influenced, in conception if
not in execution, by the linguistic experimentation of Joyce
than by the Burnsian tradition. He regarded the Burns Cult
as a barrier and knocked it down in *A Drunk Man*. He also
demonstrated that Burns was not the only Scottish poet and
enthused over the great Scottish Makars: Dunbar, Henryson
and Gavin Douglas. MacDiarmid was especially excited by
European poetry; at least by the idea of European poetry as
it came to him through the medium of translation. He
admired Valéry and borrowed from him the steady application of the *idée fixe* which came naturally enough to a man
who instinctively kept approaching a given subject obsessively. He also had an attachment to Symbolism and knew
(through translations) the work of Russian Symbolists such
as Blok and Hippius. The pursuit of the moon through *A
Drunk Man* reveals a Symbolist approach though it is typical
of MacDiarmid that he should juxtapose Symbolism with a
down-to-earth realism. Extremes, after all, meet.

From the Bible, I have suggested, MacDiarmid derives
much of his Symbolism: the artistic Prophet not honoured in
his own country, the poetic Saviour sacrificed on a cross of
ignorance, the David battling against Goliath, the sacred
significance of stones. The biblical notion of survival through
spiritual struggle was reinforced by the energetic aesthetic
MacDiarmid derived from the existential urgency of
Nietzsche and Dostoevsky. In a sonnet written on the occasion
of the centenary of Henri-Frédéric Amiel in 1921, MacDiarmid alludes to Amiel's aboulia and provides a powerful antidote to be administered by Nietzsche and 'his Russian peer'
Dostoevsky:

Ah! few there be who win to your plateau
Flat though you lie colossal peaks below,
And untraversable save to how few
The way to your horizon whence uprear
The forms of Nietzsche and his Russian peer
Whom scaling not none may the future view. (1219)

MacDiarmid's imagery, as opposed to his Symbolism, is often
based on his personal interests and activities. He put it like
this:

> Two of the great images that have always played a
> dominant part in my poetic life have been the horse and
> the ship, which is not surprising, since I come of a race of
> horse-lovers on the one hand and on the other have spent
> so much time at sea in all manner of craft. . . (LP, 418)

Although *The Kind of Poetry I Want* contains a description of
'two great galloping horses' (614) that remark is slightly misleading as neither of these images is predominant in Mac-
Diarmid's work. Perhaps the horse is cited as a gesture
towards his rural origins, for MacDiarmid never came to
terms with urban imagery. 'As I look at some of my recent
poems,' MacDiarmid said in 1941, 'I find that there has been
an enormous extension of the instrument of the knowledge of
natural history and allied subjects upon which my poetry is
played.' (LP, 267) Actually the knowledge of natural history
is there from the beginning; what changed was MacDiarmid's
referential range and willingness to exchange the lyrical instant for a patient variation on a theme.

Although MacDiarmid's great work of the 1920s was consciously modernist in tone his work differs from that of the
two most celebrated modernists in an important respect. In
Ulysses, Joyce brought Homer's contemporary counterpart to
the streets of Dublin; in *The Waste Land*, Eliot contrasted
classical culture with life in a sprawling metropolis. Modernism was, largely, an urban phenomenon, an imaginative answer to mechanisation. MacDiarmid's muse is ill-at-ease in
the city since he is an essentially rural man. He was brought

up in Langholm, created his masterpiece in the small town
of Montrose, developed his Synthetic English poems in Shetland, and settled down in a country cottage in Lanarkshire.
The unhappiest periods of his life were associated with cities:
with London where he found himself out of sorts and out of
work; with Liverpool where he despaired as his marriage
broke up; with Glasgow where he was unemployed after the
Second World War. 'I do not like Edinburgh (or any city
very much),' he said, 'for I have never been able to find one
that was not full of reminders of the fact that Cain, the
murderer, was also the first city-builder.' (LP, 105) His poems
on Glasgow and Edinburgh show a hatred of cities; 'Reflections in a Slum' dwells on the soul-destroying aspects of urban
squalor; and in 'Dìreadh II' he contrasts 'the real Scotland'
with 'Edinburgh and Glasgow, which are rubbish'. (1175)

We know that MacDiarmid's concept of the world was
shaped by his early life in Langholm and the contours of that
little town, surrounded on all sides by hills, implanted in the
poet an image of completion which he tries to return to by
way of his search for unity, for 'aneness'. MacDiarmid has
said that 'Langholm presents all the manifold and multiform
grandeur and delight of Scotland in miniature' (LP, 222): for
Scotland read the universe and there is the layout and landscape of MacDiarmid's poetry. In his best poems he surveys
the world from the top of one of Langholm's hills, looks down
with a knowing gaze. In his first book the poet refers to 'a
bird's-eye view, as Milton's Satan first saw Paradise.' (Annals, 99) His own view goes further than that in simulating
a God's eye-view of Paradise:

> I see the world as the Gods may,
> Like a grey boulder drowned beneath
> A shining pool of Space
> Whereon no shadow falls. (1223)

The Paradise looked down on has a Langholm look about it
as MacDiarmid goes, in a spiritual sense, out of the world
and into Langholm:

[37]

Sin' frae the Eden o' the world
Ilka man in turn is hurled,
And ilka gairden rins to waste
That was ever to his taste (137)

From his God's-eye viewpoint MacDiarmid makes value
judgments on the world and finds it in need of unity, of a
healing intellectual vision, of a mystical union with Sophia.
By keeping his visionary distance MacDiarmid avoids the
dreaded majority for

I have always been an outsider except to a chosen few; I
do not share any of the interests of the mass. Their
unexamined lives do not seem to me worth having.
(Company, 104)

From the vantage point he prefers MacDiarmid can sweep
aside the masses. In 'Gairmscoile' he says

Maist folk are thowless fules wha downa stir,
Crouse sumphs that hate nane 'bies wha'd wauken
them (74)

and in *A Drunk Man* he claims

The core o' ocht is only for the few,
Scorned by the mony, thrang wi'ts empty name. (86)

The poet must therefore make his observations from his
mountain top which can be Parnassus or Olympia or something more tragic:

Schiehallion and Calvary are one.
All men at last hang broken on the Cross,
Calling to One who gives a blackening sun.
There is one hill up which each soul is thrust
Ere all is levelled in eternal loss,
The peaks and plains are one. The end is dust. (1208)

Whether singing on Parnassus, looking down from the Olympian heights, ensconced on Schiehallion or crucified on Calvary the poet has had to soar to reach his lonely, if exalted, position. For this reason MacDiarmid's poems are packed with references to soaring. The three Dìreadh poems are based on the image of ascent and MacDiarmid lifts them higher with references to eagles and the upward movements of other animals. Naturally, then, mountains are peaks to be scaled. Schiehallion is a favourite, another is Liathach:

> The north face of Liathach
> Lives in the mind like a vision
> From the deeps of Coire na Caime
> Sheer cliffs go up
> To spurs and pinnacles and jagged teeth.
> Its grandeur draws back the heart.
> Scotland is full of such places.
> Few (few Scots even) know them. (1055)

When the poet has scaled the imaginative heights the mountain-top perspective is not enough for MacDiarmid has metaphysical matters to settle and moves out into deep space to regard the earth from afar. Many of the lyrics in *Sangschaw* utilise the cosmic viewpoint and in 'Dìreadh III' MacDiarmid draws attention to the fact that 'I see all things/In a cosmic or historical perspective too.' (1190) This 'cosmic consciousness' (481) is a mood that suits MacDiarmid and enriches his scientifically orientated later poetry. It gives him yet another angle on human (or superhuman) affairs. It also brings him closer to his creative source, to 'the terrible crystal, the ineffable glow' (352) since stars shine like crystals and as thought soars above the physical so it begins to express the inexpressible. MacDiarmid valued the idea of silence; he ended *A Drunk Man* with a coda to personified Silence and also enlarged on the matter in conversation:

> I regard silence as the great reservoir out of which
> articulation and expression come and as long as we are

conscious of that enormous resource then we are not inclined to attach too much importance to any particular thing we may say in a given thing. We can always refer it back to the source and the source can accommodate anything. (Conversation, [52])

Wittgenstein, who reached similar conclusions about the importance of silence, felt that there was an international language of gesture and MacDiarmid uses it in his work. Sometimes thought is revealed not by reported speech but by the wordless eloquence of particular gestures, particularly manual gestures. In 'The Hole in the Wall' he recalls a gesture in Langholm:

> Like when Uncle Dick wi' his pinkie crookt
>   Made yon gesture o' his,
> A raither slow line, half-blocked, half-reprovin',
>   And suddenly Liz
>   – Dirty Dick! Liz-Quiz! –
> In a slightly buoyant anapaestic tone
>   Threw the dog a bone,
> And a wealth o' new rhythms was syne let loose
> To mither's dismay, a' through the hoose. (309)

and, in 'The Glass of Pure Water', he urges the reader:

> Look at the ridge of skin between your thumb and
>   forefinger.
> Look at the delicate lines on it and how they change
> – How many different things they can express –
> As you move out or close in your forefinger and thumb.
> And look at the changing shapes – the countless
> Little gestures, little miracles of line –
> Of your forefinger and thumb as you move them.
> And remember how much a hand can express,
> How a single slight movement of it can say more
> Than millions of words – dropped hand, clenched fist,
> Snapping fingers, thumb up, thumb down,

Raised in blessing, clutched in passion, begging,
Welcome, dismissal, prayer, applause,
And a million other signs, too slight, too subtle,
Too packed with meaning for words to describe,
A universal language understood by all. (1042)

Remember that when he is acknowledging the importance of
this fundamental sign language, MacDiarmid is speaking as
an artist whose ideal is 'A universal language understood by
all.'

Though MacDiarmid describes himself as 'a singer after
the fashion/Of my people – a poet of passion' (482) his passion
is an intellectual rather than a physical affair. When Mac-
Diarmid stresses physicality it is generally to allude to its
limitations since it is (in neoplatonic terms) an imperfect
approximation of an eternal ideal. For example the orgasmic
intensity of sex is an earthly surrogate for a spiritual or mystical experience:

I have seen this abhyasa most clearly in the folk of
   these slums,
Even as I know how every one of the women there,
Irrespective of all questions of intelligence, good looks,
   fortune's favour,
Can give some buck-navvy or sneak-thief the joy
   beyond compare –
Naked, open as to destitution and death, to the
   unprudential
Guideless life-in-death of the ecstasy they share –
Eternity, as Boethius defined it, – though few lovers
   give it his terms –
'To hold and possess the whole fulness of life anywhere
In a moment; here and now, past, present and to
   come.' –
The bliss of God glorifying every squalid lair. (564)

The erotic passages in *A Drunk Man*, 'Harry Semen', 'Ode to All Rebels' are likewise intimations of mystical immortality.

When MacDiarmid turns from evolutionary idealism and metaphysics he is more inclined to contemplate natural beauty than to consider other people. There are many allusions that indicate his origins. Often there are references to birdwatching ranging from the laverock in 'The Watergaw', to the long 'The Nature of a Bird's World' section planned as part of *Impavidi Progrediamur*. In 'On a Raised Beach' MacDiarmid brings in an ornithological image at a crucial moment, and in 'Tam o' the Wilds and the Many-Faced Mystery' the poet displays his ornithological expertise:

> He heard the corn-buntin' cry 'Guid-night'
> And the lark 'Guid-mornin',' and kent by sight
> And call-note the Osprey and the Erne,
> The Blue-Hawk and the Merlin and the Kite,
> The Honey Buzzard and the Snowy Owl,
> The Ring Ouzel, the Black Cap, the Wood Wren,
> The Mealy Redpole, the Purple Heron, the Avocet,
> The Gadwell, the Shoveller, and the Raven. (375)

The countryman in MacDiarmid also loves angling and he is fond of using the salmon image as it occurs in 'The Diseased Salmon', 'The Salmon Leap' and is integrated into the symbolism of 'Lo! A Child is Born'. When the poet wants a Gothic touch he also turns to fishy images which appear in 'Deep-Sea Fishing'

> I suddenly saw I was wrang when I felt
> That the gapin' mooths and gogglin' een
> O' the fish were no' what we should expect
> Frae a sea sae infinite and serene. (438)

and reappear in 'Ode to All Rebels'

> But as the lourd earth is the same alow
> Tho' insubstantialised in the sunshine

I see the slack mooth and gogglin' een
Ahint this glory and ken them for mine (505)

'Above all,' MacDiarmid recalled, 'when I think of my
boyhood, my chief impression is of the amazing wealth of
colour.' (LP, 221) As we might expect from a natural dialectician colour, for MacDiarmid, is principally a matter of black
and white with the poet himself 'Preferring darkness rather
than light.' (LP, 105) In *A Drunk Man* he describes darkness
as 'oor natural element', (148) in 'Milk-Wort and Bog-Cotton'
he is aware of 'deep surroondin' darkness', (331) in 'Ode to
All Rebels' he feels 'Blindin' licht is waur than the dark',
(504) and in 'Kinsfolk' he says 'My clan is darkness'. (1149)
Darkness is human, so white becomes the colour of purity
and superhuman conception. In 'A Moment in Eternity' he
sees 'a white light deeper in God's heart', (7) in 'I Heard
Christ Sing' there is 'a white sword loupin' at the hert/O' a'
eternity', (21) in *A Drunk Man* the universal bride 'carries the
bunch/O' thistles blinterin' white' (102) and in 'Harry Semen' he refers to seed 'Passin' frae white to purer shades o'
white'. (485)

MacDiarmid's manner, like his matter, is illustrative. All
through his poetry he has pursued a Socratic method of argument by analogy so that the poetry progresses by an accumu-
lation of similes. In 'Ballad of the Five Senses' he describes
the world by piling up similes:

For the warl' is like a flourishing tree,
And God is like the sun,
But they or I to either lie
Like deid folk i' the grun'. (39)

The technique is basic to all his poetry, from the Scots verse
to the English epics. In 'Sea-Serpent' MacDiarmid packs four
similes into one eight-line stanza:

Round the cantles o' space Leviathan flickered
Like Borealis in flicht

Or eelied thro' the poorin' deeps o' the sea
Like a ca' o' whales and was tint to sicht,
But aye in its endless ups-and-doons
As it dwined to gleids or walloped in rings
God like a Jonah whirled in its kite
But blithe as a loon in the swings. (49)

In the Mature Art project the similes are usually appropriately epic but also liable to be frequent and vivid;

So this is what our lives have been given to find,
A language that can serve our purposes,
A marvellous lucidity, a quality of fiery aery light,
Flowing like clear water, flying like a bird,
Burning like a sunlit landscape. (822)

The other-worldly quality of MacDiarmid's work is the
result of a gift that he took seriously enough over a long life.
Technically he can be slipshod, using (in spite of Ezra
Pound's aesthetic principles) archaisms, inversions, abstractions and rhyming fillers such as 'I wis'. (327) His best work,
though, is unique; cerebral in conception and nurtured in an
emotional matrix. He once defined his mission as a determination 'To serve Scotland . . . and . . . to write . . . a poetry
of strange architecture.' (LP, 423) This strange architecture
will bear closer examination.

Chapter Two
NAMES FOR
NAMELESS THINGS

here's a language rings
Wi' datchie sesames, and names for nameless things.
  'Gairmscoile' (74)

It is appropriately ironical that the best-known bit of English verse associated with the name of Hugh MacDiarmid should be the montage, or found-poem, 'Perfect'. At a time when MacDiarmid's poetic work was hardly discussed at all in the literary journals erudite correspondents were quick to write to the *TLS* expressing an opinion on 'Perfect' when the Welsh writer Glyn Jones revealed that he, and not MacDiarmid, had actually composed the words that were subsequently arranged into poetic lines. It is additionally ironical that MacDiarmid should be almost exclusively associated with his poems in Scots since the majority of his work is in English – although he was careful to call the language of his earliest efforts a 'complicated' English (Uncanny, 170) and to apply the term Synthetic English (SE, 79) to his later work. Mac-Diarmid claimed that his 'earliest literary efforts were all in Scots' (LP, 17) yet he also noted that Burns 'was taboo in my father's house and quite unknown to me as a boy'. (LP, 191) Scots was, in a creative sense, an experiment that came between his conventional English beginnings and his unconventional English endings. Miraculously enough the experiment succeeded beyond his wildest expectations because the cerebral conception took place in an emotional matrix. Nevertheless the poetic career of Hugh MacDiarmid was built on the early English verse of Christopher Murray Grieve.

From an early age Grieve regarded poetry as the supreme method of imposing the individual personality on the environment. It was a way of taking solipsism seriously. He wrote verse as a student teacher and enclosed examples in his letters to George Ogilvie, his mentor at Broughton. These poems – such as 'Tryst in the Forest', 'She Whom I Love' and 'To Margaret' – are written in a conventional Georgian diction and express orthodox sentiments of romantic love. 'Tryst in the Forest' tries to convey an atmospheric morbidity by vague abstraction:

> With starry eyes she comes to me
> Between the dim trees there.
> Love is the rosebud at her breast
> And Time the ribbon in her hair. (1113)

In the second, and final, quatrain Love and Time have given way to Dust and Death. Ezra Pound, in the rules for writing he formulated in 1913, warned the apprentice poet: 'Don't use such an expression as "dim lands of *peace*". It dulls the image. . . Go in fear of abstractions. . . Use either no ornament or good ornament.'[1] The early Grieve was no modernist, but in the process of learning his poetic manners from his Georgian contemporaries. What a poem like 'Tryst in the Forest' does reveal is an antithetical approach since the two quatrains are connected by juxtaposition.

Like everything else poetry changed under the impact of the First World War. To the poets who lived long enough to tell of the barbed wire, shell-holes and rat-infested trenches on the Western Front the quiet Keatsian resignation of a Rupert Brooke was anathema. Grieve was spared the horrific conditions that produced the descriptively abrupt and psychologically brittle poems of Owen and Sassoon. His war was relatively pacific. He enlisted, in Sheffield, in 1915 and went to the Eastern Front. To begin with, Grieve's most powerful emotion was homesickness which explains the sentimentality

of his poem 'Beyond Exile'. Dated 'Salonika, 1916', it reads
like a hymn to the virtues of the kailyard:

> No stranger's roof-tree covers me,
>   Albeit I travel far and wide,
> And sundering leagues but closer bind
>   Me to my darling's side.
>
> And if I pass the utmost bourne
>   Why, then, I shall be home again –
> The quick step at the quiet door,
>   The gay eyes at the pane! (306)

Sometime after writing these nostalgic lines Grieve had his
first attack of cerebral malaria. He recovered sufficiently to
resume his duties in Salonika but the crisis, in conjunction
with the emotional extremism induced by the war, pressurised
him into a very different kind of poetry from 'Beyond Exile'.
'La Belle Terre Sans Merci' dispenses with the predictable
rhythms and rhymes of 'Beyond Exile' and uses the pathological imagery that characterises certain stages of the poet's
development. Salonika is apostrophised thus:

> O Siren of the wrecking shores,
> O Mirage of the desert lands,
> Mother of whores
> With leprous hands –
> 'Unclean! – Unclean!'
> O prostituted skies,
> Worthy of Paradise,
> O luring hills whose glory is a lie,
> The calm crystalline light that on Olympus lies
> The alabaster is of Death embalmed,
> A lantern for the damned
> To light their orgies by! (1199)

It is worth noting, first, the image of the 'luring hills' (which,
here, falsely mirror the greater glory of higher hills); and,

second, the 'calm crystalline light that on Olympus lies'. As early as 1916 or 1917 (when this poem was written) Grieve had a vision (albeit an unsteady one) of the creative source he was determined to track down, or up. The terrible crystal of creativity was clearly in his mind.

Grieve hoped to publish a collection of his war poems under the title *A Voice from Macedonia* or *A Voice from Salonika*. He sent the MS to George Ogilvie who placed it, provisionally, with Erskine MacDonald; impatient with that firm's procrastination over a decision Grieve then offered the book to John Buchan at Nelson's. Buchan liked the poems though he explained to the impatient Grieve that such a book could not realistically be projected for publication until after the war. In the event Grieve abandoned the project, though he thought well enough of 'Beyond Exile' to preserve it (after its first appearance in the *Broughton Magazine* of Summer 1919) in *Northern Numbers* in 1920 and, incongruously, in *First Hymn to Lenin and Other Poems* (1931). It is obvious that Grieve was composing copiously during the war years for his letters to Ogilvie are full of plans and forebodings. In 1916 he wrote to Ogilvie:

> One of the chief considerations in the psychological
> tangle from which I have never freed myself is
> undoubtedly the fact that I have never done anything
> worthwhile. Never a day but what I have said is,
> 'Tomorrow I will write the Fine Thing – then I will write
> to him again.' (NLS)

Grieve was determined to attain some kind of immortality. Among his early poetic plans was a grand scheme for a series of *Sonnets of the Highland Hills* and by 1922 he had decided on one hundred sonnets mainly because (he told Ogilvie) from such a sustained effort he would be able 'to write two or three sonnets which will live – which will rank with the great sonnets of British literature.' (NLS)

Although this project too was abandoned eleven of these *Sonnets of the Highland Hills* are preserved. They are workman-like and use the antithetical tension built into the sonnet form to provide an exposition in the octave and a paradoxical resolution in the sestet. As the collective title shows the poems use the climbing imagery that Grieve was to retain throughout his subsequent poems; they are also assertively emphatic, are frequently punctuated by exclamation marks. These sonnets usually build up to a climax and the upward movement of apsiration is an important and permanent feature of Mac-Diarmid's poetry. Much Georgian verse cultivated the dying fall with poets beginning bravely and then succumbing to defeat before the impossible challenge of real life. Grieve's spirits are lifted as he rises to a challenge. His direction is positive and the sonnets are defiant. Often the octave includes an observation that allows the poet to process the landscape through his consciousness; this coming together of observed object and perceived subject comprises the theme of the poem. In sonnet after sonnet Grieve goes through his stylistic routine which is seen to advantage in 'The Wind-bags', written in November 1920 at Gildermorie where the poet had taken a job teaching two children at a side school. After setting the stage with a bleak landscape, the poet makes his melodramatic entrance:

> And I, in wild and boundless consciousness,
> A brooding chaos, feel within me press
> The corpse of Time, aborted, cold, negroid.

This poet is looking for something elusive, something special, and is willing to thole the elements in search of a solution which turns out to be an option on the two possibilities open to him:

> Aimless lightnings play intermittently,
> Diffuse, vacant, dully, athwart the stones,
> Involuntary thunders slip from me
> And growl, inconsequently, hither, thither
> – And now converse, see-saws of sighs and groans,
> Oblivion and Eternity together! (1207)

Grieve, naturally, chose Eternity.

[49]

After the First World War Grieve went out of his way to make a reputation for himself as a poet. In 1920 he edited the First Series of *Northern Numbers* and the Third (and final) Series appeared in 1922. As he gladly acknowledged, Grieve used his editorship of this annual anthology to gain an entrance to the public domain by rubbing shoulders with those who passed as poetic celebrities in Scotland. As soon as he had made use of their names Grieve subsequently dumped his older colleagues so that he stood out as the up-and-coming poet. By the beginning of 1922 Grieve's first book, *Annals of the Five Senses*,[2] was about to materialise in print. In fact the Edinburgh publisher, T. N. Foulis, could not produce the book because of financial difficulties and Grieve himself published it, from his Montrose address at 16 Links Avenue, in June 1923. The six poems that appeared in *Annals* should properly be considered before the appearance of Grieve's experimental alter ego. One of the poems, 'A Moment in Eternity', was subsequently incorporated in *To Circumjack Cencrastus* and was included in MacDiarmid's *Collected Poems*. It is, in many ways, his showpiece of writing in English.

'A Moment in Eternity' is the first poem published by Grieve that demonstrates his quality and enunciates the poetic programme he had decided on. Like other poems from the same source the piece is an analogue of the creative process as experienced by an individual as he ponders on intimations of immortality, considers 'my eternal life' (3). Stylistically the poem uses several modes and merges them into an idiosyncratically individual vision: there is the ethereal quality of early Milton (the Milton of 'L'Allegro'), the informed lyricism of Shelley (the Shelley of 'Ode to the West Wind'), the Symbolist method of approaching a poetic metaphor (here the poet as Creative Tree of Life) from various angles, Grieve's own love of similes (so that poetic metamorphoses are constantly shifting in the interests of contrast and counterpoint), and an excessively obvious reliance on alliteration that may derive from Grieve's journalistic training (as the journalist habitually binds copy with the device of alliteration). The poet, in this poem, is the Tree of Life; as such he is acutely conscious of Keats's supposition (in a letter of 27 February 1818 to John Taylor) that 'If poetry comes not as naturally as the leaves to a tree it had better not come at all.' He is rooted in a local reality (which will be Scotland in all its facets in Grieve's later poems) but branches out sublimely. When God – as an inspirational creative spirit – visits him he springs into new life and puts out leaves or, to follow the simple logic of the central metaphor, poems. As leaves scatter throughout the world (as in Shelley's aforementioned ode), so the poet's poems can achieve wide distribution and, ideally, reach the highest height of all, the summit of evolutionary idealism. So Grieve sees his creations (his leaves, his poems)

> Lifted toward the unexplored
> Summits of Paradise. (5)

As the poem begins the Tree is shaken by the creative force. The poet is thus set into motion, is 'a multitude of leaves' (3) ready to put into 'the infinite air/The everlasting foliage of my soul'. (4) When one leaf-poem reaches 'the unexplored/Summits of Paradise' there is a transformation. This seminal leaf can give birth to a new tree and, with hindsight, it is tempting to identify the new tree with the new poet that Grieve was about to create in the name of Mac-Diarmid. The new tree-poet is different, more fantastic than Grieve and shining with an other-worldly light (which is the terrible crystal of creativity):

> I was a crystal trunk,
> Columnar in the glades of Paradise,
> Bearing the luminous boughs
> And foliaged with the flame
> Of infinite and gracious growth,
> – Meteors for roots,
> And my topmost spires
> Notes of enchanted light
> Blind in the Godhead!
> – White stars at noon! (5)

Grieve's intellectual vision sees the source of creativity shining in the new tree, the newly created poet. He salutes this poetic saviour emerging from the intellectual vision:

> I knew then that a new tree,
> A new tree and a strange,
> Stood beautifully in Heaven. (6)

The tree-poet equation holds and the source of growth is 'Crystal and burning-gold and scarlet'. (6) To this new tree-poet Grieve attributes a light, a brilliance that will impinge on the universe created by God:

> And when on pinnacles of praise
> All others whirled
> Like a white light deeper in God's heart
> This light would shine,
> Pondering the imponderable,
> Revealing ever clearlier
> Patterns of endless revels,
> Each gesture freed,
> Each shining shadow of difference,
> Each subtle phase evolved
> In the magnificent and numberless
> Revelations of ecstasy
> Succeeding and excelling inexhaustibly,
> – A white light like a silence
> Accentuating the great songs!
> – A shining silence wherein God
> Might see as in a mirror
> The miracles that He must next achieve! (7)

In Symbolist terms this predicts the coming and career of the poetic prophet who will illuminate the darkness with the white light (or terrible crystal of creativity) and will ascend on a hill (or mountain, depending on which metaphor is current) as he rises to a speech that is God-like in its ineffability. Such is the task Grieve will entrust to MacDiarmid.

Of course there is a realisation that the poem-bearing tree can also become a Christ-bearing cross, an image of suffering and self-sacrifice. At the end of the poem Grieve addresses himself to the creative principle, to the God-like power gifted individuals can discover in Sophia:

> *O Thou,*
> *Who art the wisdom of the God*
> *Whose ecstasies we are!* (8)

The other poems in *Annals* are interesting rather than achieved; they show the poet searching for a style that will express his sense of creative urgency and the images he is beginning to rely on. 'The Fool' is an anecdotal redaction of Nietzsche, 'The Following Day' a meditation on the crucifixion theme that is to become so important for the poet. 'Spanish Girl' reveals the poet's closely textural and loosely structural processes at the trial-and-error stage. The poem is, ostensibly, a celebration of a girl the poet has known in Salonika. Grieve does not approach the subject directly but opens on the image of a star which dissolves into a rose which, in turn, becomes a shell – 'Loosen the rose and put it to my ear!' (11) – which is given back to the girl as a rose. This to-ing and fro-ing, this ebb and flow of imagery, can produce complexity or it can result in prolixity. Here there is a bit of both. The rose is a familiar image of feminine fragility, of sexual vulnerability; Blake, one of Grieve's favourite poets, used it as such in 'The Sick Rose' in *Songs of Experience*. Grieve leans on this connotation and leads on to the secondary sexual image of roses as breasts:

> It is good to lie here
> In endless mornings pale and clear
> And see the roses trembling on the sill
> And your breasts quivering still! (13)

That pictorial scene, coming closely on a vivid portrayal of the Spanish girl standing by a lattice, is derived from Grieve's

familiarity with European poetry. It has the ring of someone
who has read Baudelaire and Rilke and Blok. However the
physical presence is not integrated into the theme which has
implications that, at the time of writing, escape Grieve:

> When will the tyrannous rose wither
> And let us lapse together
> Vacant in space? (12)

That rhetorical question will be answered in the work of
MacDiarmid; in the context of 'Spanish Girl' the epithet
'tyrannous' is misplaced. Stylistically the poem is an exercise
in fine writing, the principle of it recalling Eliot's concept of
free verse as a variable pattern the poet can approach and
retreat from at creative will. Grieve uses lines of differing
lengths and occasional rhymes and sometimes breaks into the
full iambic pentameter for grandiloquent statements: 'My
hollow loins acknowledge whom thou art.' (11) The two re-
maining poems in *Annals* are in the nature of footnotes to
'Spanish Girl'. 'Consummation' describes the orgasmic ecstasy of a satisfactory sexual encounter and 'A Last Song' has
the poet's words scattering in space. Grieve realises that the
source of creativity can be found rooted in the earth or scattered in 'The heavens' (14) so he is becoming equally at home
on the earth or adventuring, imaginatively, in space.

Before *Annals* appeared in print, Grieve had invented Hugh
MacDiarmid and had embarked on the most far-reaching
literary experiment in twentieth-century Scottish literature.
MacDiarmid's lyrics showed a new kind of Scots poetry and
lifted the Scottish poetic spirit out of a post-Burnsian depression. Scots had become synonymous with metrical triviality.
The comic connotations of the vernacular had been developed
to the exclusion of all other linguistic properties the language
possessed. As soon as a Scottish poet turned to Scots he
assumed a sentimental approach and generally fitted the sentiments into the Standard Habbie stanza (which I suggest be
renamed the Standard Rabbie in honour of its most accomplished exponent). Stevenson's Scots poems in *Underwoods*

(1887) were pseudo-Burnsian. Even George Douglas Brown, whose *The House with the Green Shutters* (1901) drastically altered the character and range of the Scottish novel, could turn out a typical product in the Language Burns called Lallans (Lowland Scots) and Stevenson singularised as Lallan. Brown's poem 'The Dying Covenanter' was published on 9 August 1900 in *The Examiner* and was an attempt to do into verse the deathbed sentiments of John Montgomerie (d. 15 May 1732) that 'I would like to dee where the wind blaws and the whaup skirls.' Here is Brown's closing quatrain:

> And whaups may skirl i' the lanely sky,
> And the sun shine miles aroun',
> And quately the far-off ships gae by,
> But I'll be sleepin' soun'.

By the 1920s Scots verse was a homemade product cultivated in the kailyard and handled by amateurs. Its recent history was one of decline as witness the work produced by the Whistlebinkie school of versifiers who flourished in Victorian Glasgow. When a more obviously talented poet, like Charles Murray, came along he used Lallans (or Braid Scots or the vernacular) for homely domesticated poems. Grieve despised such verse as hopelessly inadequate and felt that the idiom itself was an instrument unable to play the tunes a new Scotland needed. He referred to Charles Murray as a man 'constitutionally incapable' of writing poetry (Studies, 6) and felt that the Scots revivalist work of the Vernacular Circle of the London Burns Club was a conspicuous waste of time and energy since 'the English language is an immensely superior medium of expression' to dialect Scots.[3] Grieve had no time at all for the dialect Scots of Murray and his imitators; he was, however, impressed by the Middle Scots experiment of Lewis Spence. Spence was a formidable character, a forceful journalist who had a formative influence on Scottish Nationalist politics (founding the Scottish National Movement in 1926, helping to found the National Party of Scotland in 1928, and becoming the first Scottish Nationalist to stand for Parliament in 1929). As early as 1888 he had written poetic imitations using Middle Scots in an attempt 'to modernize that phase of Scots in such a manner as would make it serviceable for use at the present time in prose and verse'.[4] Grieve noted the experiment with approval.

In February 1922 a more momentous linguistic experiment reached its climax when Shakespeare and Co. published one thousand numbered copies of Joyce's *Ulysses*. Christopher Grieve was astonished by the linguistic presence of the novel and felt that Joyce had, in effect, issued a challenge for what an Irishman could do a Scotsman ought at least to be able to attempt. In August the first issue of Grieve's new magazine *The Scottish Chapbook* appeared. On the cover there was the provocative slogan 'Not Traditions – Precedents' and inside there was a pseudonymous contribution in English by Hugh M'Diarmid. About this time Grieve had written 'The Water-gaw' since he cited it in an article (in *Dunfermline Press* of 30 September) as the work of an anonymous friend who had produced his poem in response to a book on the Lowland Scots spoken in Perthshire. Grieve's favourite critical book, frequently mentioned approvingly in *The Scottish Chapbook*, was G. Gregory Smith's *Scottish Literature* and Smith had poured scorn on the practice of digging poems out of dictionaries:

> ['Braid Scots'] may be taken as seriously by us as most of the Latin prose of our classrooms must be by the shade of the long-suffering Cicero. We know how it is made, how our poeticule waddles in good duck fashion through his Jamieson, snapping up fat expressive words with nice little bits of green idiom for flavouring. It is never literature, and it is certainly not Scots.[5]

Grieve produced his Scots poems by precisely this method and he began by being on the defensive about it since he wanted to avoid being thought either reactionary (as he supposed the Vernacular Circle of the London Burns Club to be) or ridiculous (as G. Gregory Smith suggested any dictionary-derived Scots poetry must be). In October the third issue of *The Scottish Chapbook* published, on its first page, 'The Watergaw' which was now attributed to Hugh M'Diarmid. Grieve's editorial Causerie was given over to an explanation of his reasons for supporting a new style of poetry in the vernacular. Thus special pleading was done on behalf of a single poem, 'The Watergaw', and a prose monologue in the vernacular, 'Following Rebecca West in Edinburgh', also attributed to M'Diarmid:

> One of the objects of *The Scottish Chapbook* is to supplement the campaign of the Vernacular Circle of the London Burns Club for the revival of the Doric [but] I do not support the campaign for the revival of the Doric where the essential Scottish diversity-in-unity is forgotten, nor where the tendencies involved are anti-cultural.
>
> The work of Mr Hugh M'Diarmid, who contributes a poem and a semi-dramatic study to this issue, is peculiarly interesting because he is, I think, the first Scottish writer who has addressed himself to the question of the extendability (without psychological violence) of the Vernacular to embrace the whole range of modern culture – or, in other words, tried to make up the leeway of the language. . . Stripping the unconscious form of the Vernacular of the grotesque clothes of the Canny-Sandy cum Kirriemuir Elder cum Harry Lauder cult, he has shown a well-knit muscular figure that has not been seen in Scottish Literature for many a long day. . . It is an achievement which I hope Vernacular enthusiasts will not be the last to recognise.[6]

To give a revolutionary ring to his experiment MacDiarmid used the phrase 'a great Scottish Literary Renaissance' and the idea of a movement was amplified by the poet's friend Denis Saurat who, in 1924, published an article on 'Le groupe de "la Renaissance Écossaise" '.[7] To distinguish his experimental Scots from dialect Scots, MacDiarmid coined the term Synthetic Scots writing, for example, as if there was a whole host of MacDiarmids on the horizon:

> It is certain, at all events, that all the best poets of to-day

and to-morrow who write in Scots must be out to obtain
effects which were not within the compass of Burns or of
the instrument of Scots he fashioned. . . The true line is
. . . a synthetic Scots gathering together and reintegrating
all the *disjecta membra* of the Doric and endeavouring to
realise its latent potentialities along lines in harmony at
once with distinctive Scots psychology and contemporary
cultural functions and requirements. (Studies, 61)

MacDiarmid's polemical terminology was often misleading
and Scottish Renaissance was only apposite as a reference to
a one-man campaign. Synthetic Scots, however, is an accurate
description of the language MacDiarmid used. The linguistically synthetic Scots was an almost Hegelian coalescence of
a literary, dictionary-derived thesis and an oral antithesis. To
take the first element, MacDiarmid claimed his primary
source was Jamieson's *Etymological Dictionary of the Scottish
Tongue* and there is ample evidence that MacDiarmid did
indeed extract from the dictionary the words he wanted. Yet
the great MacDiarmid poems do not sound artificial and the
experiment would not have succeeded unless the poet had
been in command of an instinctive appreciation of the possibilities of the language. MacDiarmid's cerebral conception
took shape in its emotional matrix and it is immediately
apparent that the Scots he used was not only found but felt.
He was absolutely adamant on this issue. In 1941 he said:

There has been much debate in many quarters during the
past decade as to the artificiality – the dictionary-dredged
character – of the Scots in which most of my poetry is
written; but the fact is that Scots was my native tongue –
I can still speak it as easily as I speak English, and with
far greater psychological satisfaction; while all my
subsequent education and life in England and abroad
have never robbed me of my strong Scots accent. (LP,
17)

More than thirty years later he still felt this was a point worth
pursuing even though it involved the admission of the sin-

gularity of the Scottish Renaissance movement. MacDiarmid
felt his disciples simply hadn't a feel for the language:

> Now all these poets who followed my example, who
> looked up Scots words in dictionaries and so on, they've
> all faded out. They hadn't got it natively and that's
> where I had the advantage. I was born into a Scots-
> speaking community and my own parents and all those
> round about spoke Scots. But these poets hadn't that
> advantage and, of course, I have antagonised them –
> politically and otherwise. I don't think that any of them
> has really followed my example – certainly not
> technically. Their poetry has no resemblance to mine
> except at the mere level of vocabulary and in some uses
> of the language. (Metaphysics, [16–17])

It is as well, at the outset, to establish that MacDiarmid's
Scots was not quite so dictionary-based as his early propaganda suggested. He did, after all, grow up in the Borders
where many of the great traditional ballads had been preserved in oral transmission and had coloured the local speech
with rich images and expressions. Moreover, Border Scots
was unusually vivid because the Borderers liked to underline
their differences from their English neighbours. Another Scottish writer remembered her Border childhood and the earthy
vocabulary of a farmworker:

> Some of Jessie's words were difficult to translate into
> plain English, but they were so expressive that their
> meaning was easily guessed. A chatterbox was a
> bletherskite, a tell-tale a clype, a round-shouldered person
> was humphy-backit, a throat was a thrapple, a turkey-
> cock a bubblyjock, upside-down was tapsulteerie, and
> dumfoonert meant astonished. It was far better fun than
> a dead language like Latin.[8]

Thrapple, bubblyjock, tapsulteerie, dumfoonert: these are
words MacDiarmid effortlessly absorbed into his poetry.
Later in the same book about Jessie, the phrase 'The hale
clamjamfry'[9] appears and there, quite casually, is the last line

of the first lyric printed in *Sangschaw*, 'The Bonnie Broukit Bairn' with its memorable image of the weeping earth

> *– But greet, an' in your tears ye'll droun*
> *The haill clanjamfrie!* (17)

Thus MacDiarmid began with a reservoir of Scots words he had learned in his Border childhood; his development of this familiar speech into Synthetic Scots was motivated by a desire to bring Scottish culture into the mainstream of contemporary modernism but also by a pleasure in words that took him 'out of the world and into Langholm'.

Grieve's creation of MacDiarmid was not, then, a Pauline conversion to Scots. He had grown up with Scots and had been converted to a literary English because of a desire to dissociate himself from the kailyard productions and to avail himself of the international range of poetry in English. What persuaded him to return to Scots was the realisation that the language could be shaken to its linguistic roots by the application of modernist theory. Taking as his poetic ingredients oral Scots, literary Scots and a shrewd contemporary mentality he self-consciously constructed an idiom that would be so alive with modern thought that it could not be construed as either reactionary or escapist.

An experiment is an exploration of a possible world; MacDiarmid's 'The Watergaw' is an experiment that succeeded triumphantly enough to look like the pinnacle of a long tradition rather than the renewal of a lost language:

> Ae weet forenicht i' the yow-trummle
> I saw yon antrin thing,
> A watergaw wi' its chitterin' licht
> Ayont the on-ding;
> An' I thocht o' the last wild look ye gied
> Afore ye deed!

There was nae reek i' the laverock's hoose
That nicht – an' nane i' mine;
But I hae thocht o' that foolish licht
Ever sin' syne;
An' I think that mebbe at last I ken
What your look meant then. (17)

We have already seen how MacDiarmid aspires upwards to
heavenly light though he is anxious to avoid the pious connotations of such an aspiration. Here he observes an actual
manifestation and brings it suddenly down to earth by intro-
ducing an image of the last light glinting from his dying
father. It is typical of MacDiarmid that, in discussing the
poem, he should attempt to obscure its autobiographical
element:

Take 'The Watergaw'. That was supposed by one writer
to be a poem for my first wife . . . and it was also
supposed to be my father's death. These sort of
speculations have got to be wede awa. (Conversation,
[17])

Actually it *is* a memory of the death of the poet's father, and
there is no doubt about that since the incident is also alluded
to in the poem 'Kinsfolk':

Afore he dee'd he turned and gied a lang
Last look at pictures o' my brither and me
Hung on the wa' aside the bed, I've heard
My mither say. I wonder then what he
Foresaw or hoped and hoo – or gin – it squares
Wi' subsequent affairs. (1148)

However synthetic the language the experience is a basic
one and it is MacDiarmid's evocation of the mystery of reality
that makes the poem so powerful. He uses imagery for speculative purposes, takes a symbol and invests it with a spiritual
significance. In the second stanza MacDiarmid refuses to
elaborate further on the vital light that is both watergaw and

life itself. Instead he lets the conclusion, like the symbol, hang in the air. By bringing the two images into creative conflict MacDiarmid persuades the reader that there is a visionary unity to be perceived. What he achieves is, to borrow a term from Arthur Koestler, 'the fusion or *bisociation* of previously unconnected cognitive structures.'[10]

Structurally the poem is a demonstration of contrast and counterpoint and MacDiarmid builds on the tension created by his bisociation of concepts. The basic *abcbdd* stanza (which is simply a couplet tacked onto a quatrain) is a welcome departure from the Standard Rabbie stanza. Stylistically MacDiarmid has introduced a new note to Scots poetry in 'The Watergaw'. He has evolved a fluid form for an expansive imagination, has intellectualised Scots poetry by isolating a particular image and then seeking out its cosmic implications. The movement of the verse is both formal and conversationally plausible (as the lines progress in pairs by means of enjambement). The 'mebbe' in the penultimate line, for example, is not inserted only in the interests of prosodic regularity; its hesitant delicacy suggests human fallibility and the possibility that there might be a perspective that transcends the three-dimensional world suggested by the five senses. It is often asserted that the essence of great poetry is its untranslatability. With this critical commonplace in mind MacDiarmid challenged his earliest readers to translate the first stanza of 'The Watergaw':

Doric economy of expressiveness is impressively
illustrated in the first four lines of ['The Watergaw'].
Translate them into English. That is the test. You will
find that the shortest possible translation runs something
like this: 'One wet afternoon (or early evening) in the
cold weather in July after the sheep-shearing I saw that
rare thing – an indistinct rainbow, with its shivering
light, above the heavily-falling rain.' Not only so; but the
temper of the poem is modern and the Doric is adequate
to it. It is disfigured by none of the usual sentimentality.

It has a distinctively Scottish *sinisterness* for which
expression is too seldom found nowadays.[11]

Reading that translation it is obvious that the poem is much,
much more than the sum of its etymological parts.

'The Watergaw' led to an exceptionally productive period
of writing for MacDiarmid who always wrote at great speed
and often obtained the effect he wanted at the first attempt
so that there was little revision. The romantic notion of
inspiration as a creative myth MacDiarmid regarded with
scepticism; however he acted like a man inspired. In the
period between the composition of 'The Watergaw' and the
publication of *A Drunk Man Looks at the Thistle* – that is, from
September 1922 to November 1926 – the poems seemed to
come to him in the spontaneous Keatsian sense of leaves
coming to trees (a notion that Grieve had, after all, incorporated into 'A Moment in Eternity'). He was certainly inspired
by the latent energy he was about to unleash in the language:

> The Scottish Vernacular is the only language in Western
> Europe instinct with those uncanny spiritual and
> pathological perceptions alike which constitute the
> uniqueness of Dostoevski's work, and word after word of
> Doric establishes a blood-bond in a fashion at once
> infinitely more thrilling and vital and less explicable than
> those deliberately sought after by writers such as D. H.
> Lawrence in the medium of English which is inferior for
> such purposes because it has entirely different natural
> bias which has been so confirmed down the centuries as
> to be insusceptible of correction. . . The Vernacular is a
> vast unutilised mass of lapsed observation made by minds
> whose attitudes to experience and whose speculative and
> imaginative tendencies were quite different from any
> possible to Englishmen and Anglicised Scots to-day. It is
> an inchoate Marcel Proust – a Dostoevskian debris of
> ideas – an inexhaustible quarry of subtle and significant
> sound.[12]

MacDiarmid was a man possessed by the certainty that he

had actually discovered the source of creativity and could
reproduce it in Scots. The terrible crystal of creativity was
buried, like a treasure, in the suppressed Scottish consciousness. To reach it MacDiarmid had dug into the pages of
Jamieson and tapped the resources of the Scots acquired as
a child in Langholm. All his explorations led to the terrible
crystal which shifted from the earth to the sky and back again.
MacDiarmid realised that it was elusive enough to change
location and forms but he was also sure that he could only
reach it through Scots:

> Just as a glass can be shattered by striking a certain note
> on the fiddle or – if an alleged American case is authentic
> – a suspension bridge can be broken down in the same
> way . . . so it is only in the Scots language I can achieve
> or maintain if not, in certain senses, integrity of
> expression, at least 'the terrible crystal'; its sounds . . .
> bring me fully alive. (LP, 35)

MacDiarmid's first book of lyrics, *Sangschaw*, was published
in 1925 with a perceptive preface by John Buchan who observed that

> My friend, the author of this book, has set himself a task
> which is at once reactionary and revolutionary. . . He
> would treat Scots as a living language and apply it to
> matters which have been foreign to it since the sixteenth
> century. Since there is no canon of the vernacular, he
> makes his own, as Burns did, and borrows words and
> idioms from the old masters. He confines himself to no
> one dialect, but selects where he pleases between
> Aberdeen and the Cheviots. This audacity may make
> some of the pieces difficult for the reader, and it may be
> that he does not always succeed, for a man with a new
> weapon rarely hits the mark at the first shot.[13]

That is more revealing than MacDiarmid's own comments
on his early lyrics (which he tended to disparage, anyway, to
emphasise what he took to be more ambitious work):

[64]

> It's the association of music and poetry that I was
> concerned with, particularly in those early lyrics, and
> after all I was writing them for a composer [F. G. Scott].
> (Conversation, [53])

MacDiarmid is, and not for the first or last time, being misleading. He did not write the lyrics for Scott in the first
instance. What happened was that Grieve's former teacher in
Langholm, William Burt, read *The Scottish Chapbook* and made
the necessary connexion between contributor MacDiarmid
and editor Grieve. He imparted this intelligence to his former
colleague F. G. Scott and this led to a reunion. Scott immediately began setting MacDiarmid lyrics and this in turn
greatly encouraged the poet since he set great value by such
impressive encouragement. But it would be wrong to assume
that MacDiarmid conceived the lyrics as words for music;
especially as the poems in *Sangschaw* and *Penny Wheep* are
distinguished by a conceptual depth and pictorially vivid
quality.

Some of the finest pieces in *Sangschaw* are two-stanza affairs,
like 'The Watergaw'. They pack the maximum of contrast
and counterpoint into the minimum space; they hover between earthiness and eternity and are always ready to take
what MacDiarmid liked to call the 'mad leap . . . Into the
symbol'. (389) Often MacDiarmid will begin with an image
of great pictorial clarity, then subject it to creative pressure
by insisting on an astonishing comparison that leads to a
conclusion that has the philosophical quality of folklore. The
poems sound as if they expressed the eloquence of a community rather than the opinion of one poet. MacDiarmid is,
quite intentionally, speaking for Scotland. 'The Frightened
Bride' is an example of his ability to generate what seems like
a collective concern, a communal value judgment. Although
the poem opens with a reference to the bride's apprehension
it turns on the paradox that fear creates courage:

> Seil o' yer face! Ye needna seek
> For comfort gin ye show yer plight.

[65]

To Gods an' men, coorse callants baith,
A fleggit bride's the seilfu' sicht. (28)

Even when the two stanzas seem to amount to little more
than rural scene-setting (as with 'Country Life' or 'Reid
E'en') the thought is usually contrived to carry a sting in its
tail and the longer the poem is the more liable the concluding
lines are to have a verbal density since the speculative weight
is suddenly resolved and crushed into the final exclamation.
In 'Farmer's Death', a five-quatrain poem, MacDiarmid sets
up a splendid picture of abundant life on the farm as the hens
and the pigs act independently of the ominous atmosphere.
In the final quatrain the previous lines are clarified in a
revelational instant by information withheld until the last
moment:

Hen's cries are a panash in Heaven,
And a pig has the warld at its feet;
But wae for the hoose whaur a buirdly man
Crines in a windin' sheet. (34)

It is part of MacDiarmid's creative strategy to spring a surprise on the reader.

Sangschaw, like later books by MacDiarmid, does not intro-
duce many recognisable individuals. The poet's sympathy is
grandly larger than life and is magnanimously extended to
the earth itself. MacDiarmid, a countryman with a cosmic
consciousness, plays on the double meaning of earth as planet
and soil, takes a God's-eye view of the earth he feels he can
hold in his hands. In 'The Bonnie Broukit Bairn' the earth
is a weeping child surrounded by beautiful but indifferent
planets. In the third part of 'Au Clair de la Lune' the earth
is eerily lost in space:

The moonbeams kelter i' the lift,
An' Earth, the bare auld stane,
Glitters beneath the seas o' Space,
White as a mammoth's bane. (24)

MacDiarmid isolates the image of the earth, emphasises the insecurity of the planet that sustains human life as the poet perceives it. In 'The Eemis Stane' this concept is raised to a stark depiction of the planet as a stone wobbling in the sky of a harvest night. Under the influence of the poet the stone then dissolves into the image of a tombstone with a message obscured by a snowstorm. Paradoxically the poet claims that even without the blinding snowstorm the message would have been indecipherable because it is buried beneath 'the fug o' fame/An' history's hazelraw'. (27) As clearly as he can the poet is making inroads into the ineffable and the integrity of the poetic idiom ensures that the message cannot be easily read. There is always an other-worldly quality about Mac-Diarmid's stony imagery. It is associated, in his mind, with the symbol of resurrection. Such an ostensibly sacred subject is crucial to MacDiarmid's poetic strategy and it is to his tactical advantage that he approaches it from every possible angle. So serious poems almost collide with humorous ones. MacDiarmid places, just before 'The Eemis Stane' his poem on an irreverent resurrection in Langholm. 'Crowdieknowe' is full of incident and pictorial clarity. There is the colloquial reference to the dead 'loupin' owre/The auld grey wa's' and the precise visual formulation of 'Muckle men wi' tousled beards' who indignantly 'glower at God an' a' his gang/O' angels.' And, as usual, there is the compression of the specu-lative gist of the poem into the final flourish:

> Fain the weemun-folk'll seek
> To mak' them haud their row
> – *Fegs, God's no blate gin he stirs up*
> *The men o' Crowdieknowe!* (27)

On the evidence of the poems in *Sangschaw* MacDiarmid's most urgent poetic concern is to discover earthly evidence of eternity which is conceived as a metaphysical extension of poetic immortality. To particularise this general interest Mac-Diarmid brings in the figure of Christ and approaches it in his multi-angular, or multi-faceted, manner. 'O Jesu Parvule'

shows the poet's characteristic use of the two-stanza counterpoint. Here the contrast is between the reader's expectation
of tenderness and the poet's insistence on an intellectual
toughness. Naturally the first glimpse of the subject is homely
and comforting as the baby Jesus listens to a lullaby. Having
thus lulled the reader into a false sense of security MacDiarmid unleashes his subversive secondary image and presents
the mildly blasphemous icon of the precocious child with his
head on his mother's breast and already formulating the
future:

> 'Fa' owre, ma hinny, fa' owre, fa' owre,
> A' body's sleepin' binna oorsels.'
> She's drawn Him in tae the bool o' her breist
> But the byspale's nae thocht o' sleep i' the least.
> *Balloo, wee mannie, balloo, balloo.* (31)

'The Innumerable Christ' begins with a quotation from a
man MacDiarmid had publicised, in *The Scottish Chapbook* and
elsewhere (SE, 38–43) as a Scottish Solovyov. Professor J. Y.
Simpson is quoted as saying 'Other stars may have their
Bethlehem, and their Calvary too.' MacDiarmid enlarges the
idea and gives, in the penultimate stanza, an image so
strongly pictorial that the poem has the force of an altarpiece
by Grünewald:

> I' mony an unco warl' the nicht
> The lift gaes black as pitch at noon,
> An' sideways on their chests the heids
> O' endless Christs roll doon. (32)

Evidently MacDiarmid's cosmic consciousness has a spiritual dimension that encourages him to speak not simply of,
but for, God. In 'I Heard Christ Sing' MacDiarmid begins
with a ballad introduction to Christ as a man among men
though the experienced MacDiarmid reader will be wary of
taking anything in a three-page-long poem at its face value.
Christ stands in the centre of a circle formed by the twelve

disciples and, with the metaphorical angularity that is synonymous with his developed style, MacDiarmid illustrates
the situation by shifting images. Christ surrounded by disciples is like a maypole or like the centre of a compass or the
fixed point of a clock. Christ is, literally, defined by the
satellites that spin around him as he sings 'the bonniest sang
that e'er/Was sung sin' Time began.' (19) Christ addresses
God directly in his song and his greatest wish is for a human
renaissance to accompany his resurrection:

> *And when I rise*
> *Again from the dead,*
> *Let me, I pray,*
> *Be accompanied*
> *By the spirit of man.* (20)

MacDiarmid's interest in resurrection-renaissance-rebirth is
only equalled by his certainty that the saviour (be he Christ
or a Scottish poet) has to undergo a form of martyrdom. Seen
in this light the interests of Christ and Judas coincide: this
conforms to MacDiarmid's belief that opposites attract and
extremes meet. With a beautiful display of verbal dexterity
MacDiarmid ends the poem on a deliberate note of ambiguity
that leaves the reader to decide whether the 'he' of the penultimate line refers to Judas or Christ:

> Judas and Christ stude face to face,
> And mair I couldna' see,
> But I wot he did God's will wha made
> Siccar o' Calvary. (21)

The longest poem in *Sangschaw*, 'Ballad of the Five Senses'
is also the most metaphysical and shows MacDiarmid re-
working some of the philosophical material he had explored
in 'A Moment in Eternity'. In this poem, as in the earlier
poem in English, the movement is towards a universal unity
and an insight into the creative principle so that the poet is
granted a divine vision and is transfigured as a man made in

the image of God. In the first part of the poem MacDiarmid
introduces his subject by acknowledging that the world as
perceived by the five senses is substantial. In part II he uses
the image of the tree of life in paradise as an emblem for the
dawning of the spiritual world. As in 'A Moment in Eternity'
the poet is identified with the tree on this 'First Day'. (37)
Again MacDiarmid combines this biblical image with the
neoplatonic notion that the world we perceive through the
senses is but an imperfect copy of an ideal and eternal world:

> O I wist it is a bonny warl'
> That lies forenenst a' men,
> But it's naething but a shaddaw-show
> To the warl' that I saw then. (37)

It is not enough, MacDiarmid feels, to be aware of the
phenomenal world; it is necessary to transcend it and to
reach, by means of an intellectual vision, to eternity in order
to stand face to face with the creator. To attain to this metaphysical realm MacDiarmid simulates a phenomenological
and spiritual rebirth. In part III of the poem he has entered
eternity – 'a place where there/Seemed nocht but naething-
ness'. (38) In this eternal world extremes meet and contradictions are united in a spiritual harmony:

> Water for stane micht weel be ta'en
> Or Heaven and Hell seem yin,
> A' differences men's mind can mak',
> Maun end or ye begin. . . . (39)

MacDiarmid holds on to this notion until it gives on to a pun
on 'lie' (which is fairly typical of a poet who enjoys puns as
condensed paradoxes):

> For the warl' is like a flourishing tree,
> And God is like the sun,
> But they or I to either lie
> Like deid folk i' the grun'. (39)

He considers (in part IV) that death might be an escape from the five senses into eternity; and that God might turn out to be an idealisation of the individual. The poem closes with the poet willing for the appearance of a new star and the growth of a new tree. Such hopes have mystical overtones and show that MacDiarmid's personal ambitions were predominantly spiritual at this time.

Like *Sangschaw*, *Penny Wheep* is a collection that mixes comic and serious, lyrical and anecdotal, narrative and philosophical poems and sometimes MacDiarmid becomes his unique self by bringing all the elements together in the one poetic performance. Both collections of early lyrics seem the product of the one sustained creative impulse though there are signs in *Penny Wheep* that MacDiarmid wants to move from texture to structure in order to explore a large theme in a way that will stretch all his powers. Throughout the collections he is careful to avoid classification and reject labels. He is not to be thought of as a regional, or even narrowly national, poet. One of the poet's defensive ploys is the parade of international names: in the two collections he derives poems from the German (of Stefan George in ' "You Know Not Who I Am" ' and Rudolf Leonhardt in 'The Dead Liebknecht'); from the Russian (of Dmitry Merezhkovsky in 'The Last Trump'), from the Cretan ('Under the Greenwood Tree', 'The Three Fishes', 'The Robber') and from the French (of Gustave Kahn in 'On the Threshold'). He also writes a sonnet to Anna Akhmatova (' "U Samago Moria" ') and composes a poem in French ('La Fourmilière') for his friend Denis Saurat.

Most of the poems in *Penny Wheep* are short pieces in either a lyrical or a light anecdotal mode. Confident enough in his poetic manner to treat both his sense of humour and his earthy sensuality to the spiritual qualities he discerned in Synthetic Scots (though at times the Scots is only colloquial), MacDiarmid goes further afield in the thematic territory already covered in *Sangschaw*. In a predominantly amorous mode are poems such as 'Wheesht, Wheesht', 'The Currant Bush', 'Cloudburst and Soaring Moon', 'Feery-o'-the-Feet', 'Focherty', 'Sabine', 'The Love-sick Lass', 'Wild Roses', 'The

Widower', 'In Mysie's Bed', 'Servant Girl's Bed', 'Empty
Vessel', 'The Bonnie Lowe', 'The Quest'. Given that theme,
though, MacDiarmid varies the treatment of it enormously.
This can be seen to advantage by contrasting two of the best
poems. 'Wheesht, Wheesht' comprises a statement that contains its own contradiction. The poet speaks to his heart,
telling it to be still lest the whole sexual cycle begin again.
Yet to acknowledge desire is to succumb to it so that the tug
between determination and desire is caught in MacDiarmid's
facetious fusion of apparent opposites:

> It's guid to see her lie
> Sae snod an' cool,
> A' lust o' lovin' by –
> *Wheesht, wheesht, ye fule!* (45)

'Feery-o'-the-Feet' plays verbal and conceptual games with
MacDiarmid's obsessive interest in resurrection and spiritual
rebirth. It uses the classic MacDiarmid format, the two-
stanza poem comprising confident assertion and creative re-
futation. The comedy is both modernistically amoral and
gravely Gothic and the coalescence (or bisociation) is
spectacular:

> 'A deid man's never
> Feery o' the feet,
> Jock, five years buried
> Maun be far frae fleet,
> Sae, lad ye needna worry,
> He'll no' hae's in a hurry.'

> Aye, lass! but Resurrection's
> The danger that dings a',
> We maun up braw an' early
> Gin we're to win awa',
> Else sune's the trumpet's blared
> *There'll be twa daiths in oor kirkyaird.* (47)

In such poems MacDiarmid celebrates sexuality. However, he is equally capable of coping lyrically with tragedy, of imparting to his verse a timeless quality of human endurance. 'Empty Vessel', as the poet George Bruce noted (Festschrift, 58–61), is a redaction of an anonymous song which begins

> I met ayont the cairnie
> Jenny Nettles. Jenny Nettles
> Singin' til her bairnie
> Robin Rattles bastard

MacDiarmid appropriates the first and third lines, replaces the alternate lines with informative phrases then takes the tragedy out of time and space by persuading the reader to compare the woman nursing a dead child with God's indifference to his creations. It is an audacious image, a MacDiarmidian ascent from the earthly to the eternal:

> I met ayont the cairney
> A lass wi' tousie hair
> Singin' till a bairnie
> That was nae langer there.

> Wunds wi' warlds to swing
> Dinna sing sae sweet,
> The licht that bends owre a' thing
> Is less ta'en up wi't. (66)

As so many of the poems in *Penny Wheep* confirm, MacDiarmid's interests compel him to specialise in the distance – or lack of it – between the earthly and the eternal, the physical and the metaphysical, the natural and the supernatural, the real and the spiritual. In 'The Quest', for instance, he goes beyond physical desire towards universal unity through sexual harmony which is therefore seen as a means to a speculative end:

[73]

And och! for your beauty
And och! for your braith
Gin you're the wumman I want
On the yon side o' Daith! (72)

Other poems come together in clusters as they are linked
by intention and imagery. 'Trompe l'oeil', 'Blind Man's Luck'
and 'Jimsy: an Idiot' all connect eyes with eggs in a grotesque
visual comedy. MacDiarmid was probably thinking in sequences rather than in isolation. The poems for children, for
example, are linked by their transformational power. 'Hungry
Waters', written for William Burt's three-year-old son Billy,
anthropomorphises the sea. The two songs for the poet's
infant daughter Christine have the same metamorphic agility.
In 'The Bubblyjock' the turkey becomes a transformational
law unto itself:

Syne it twists its neck like a serpent
But canna get oot a richt note
For the bubblyjock swallowed the bagpipes
And the blether stuck in its throat. (71)

These short poems constantly hit the grace notes in a mode
that is limited in length but imaginatively expansive. Mac-
Diarmid wanted to go further than that, though, and all
through his career he was unkind about what he took to be
the limited and restricted tonality of the lyric. Euphony could
not be an end in itself, he felt; nevertheless as MacDiarmid's
love of contradictions had been sharpened into a credo of
contrariness he was willing to respond 'To One Who Urges
More Ambitious Flights' (doubtless himself since he enjoyed
internal argument):

Wee bit sangs are a' I need,
Wee bit sangs for auld times' sake!
Here are ferlies nae yin sees
In a bensil o' a bleeze. (57)

[74]

Even in the context of *Penny Wheep* that sentiment does not bear examination. Not only was he engaged on *A Drunk Man Looks at the Thistle* when the defence of 'Wee bit sangs' appeared but three poems in *Penny Wheep* move, with some determination, beyond the confines of the song. MacDiarmid wanted to shake Scotland to its linguistic roots, wanted to set the heather on fire with a blaze of creative glory. Three poems – 'Bombinations of a Chimaera', 'Sea-Serpent' and 'Gairms-coile' – show the way his imagination was shaping up for an endeavour that extended him as never before. 'Bombinations of a Chimaera', a ten-part poem mainly in quatrains, is a return to what is by this time a favourite theme: the poet as an individual made in the special image of God the creator. In discussing the work of his friend William Soutar, Mac-Diarmid pointed out that 'he thought he was following the ballad tradition when in fact he was only following the trad-ition of our hymns.' (Company, 225–6) To make such a point so forcefully MacDiarmid must have been aware of the danger – especially as so many of his references are theological and christological. Fortunately this poem, despite some dubious moments when the poet is caught flatfooted, has a communal rather than a congregational quality.

It opens with a series of MacDiarmidian contrasts, as if to show (by analogy with a scientific principle) that each crea-tive action has an equal and opposite reaction:

> And Poverty and Daith
> I need them as Earth needs
> The winter's bitter braith
> To lowse the simmer's seeds. (61)

As an envoi to that thought MacDiarmid *qua* Chimaera re-members that while men can easily imitate God's destructive energy it requires an extraordinary talent to emulate God's ability to create. The creative individual has to do, in fact, what Christ did and escape from an infernal environment:

> But he didna bide in Hell,
> Didna turn a Deil Himsel',
> And gin we'd wun through it tae
> We maun try to find His way. (62)

This task has its own heroism as MacDiarmid is conscious of
the self-sacrifice and martyrdom involved. As his quatrains
unroll, in a routine manner despite his attempt to vary the
stanzaic pattern in part V, the heroic quality is increasingly
important:

> The meek may inherit
> The Earth, but till then
> We maun ha'e spirit
> Gin we're to be men. (63)

Spirit can be both insubstantial and alcoholic and MacDiarmid is already fascinated by a pun that has a prominent place
in *A Drunk Man Looks at the Thistle*. At the conclusion of the
poem MacDiarmid turns to another biblical image and fuses
it with a philosophical concept. He, the saviour-poet, will free
himself of the burden of mere being by rising, Christ-like, to
a new challenge. This challenge will issue from the mouth of
the poet as he lifts himself up from the darkness that is both
Christian sepulchre and Platonic cave of creation:

> The wecht o' my body,
> The wecht o' my soul,
> Like the stane frae the mooth
> O' the sepulchre roll.
>
> *This is the tune*
> *Fu' o' elation*
> *That'll wauken the giants*
> *In the cave o' creation.* (64)

This clash of concepts exhilarates the poet who senses he has the power to respond to the challenge he is excitedly enunciating.

In *Sangschaw* there is a three-stanza lyric, 'God Takes a Rest', which is headnoted as a fragment from 'A Sea Suite'. In the lyric God speaks in the first person and considers returning to man's original element:

> For I sall hie me back to the sea
> Frae which I brocht life yince,
> And lie i' the stound o' its whirlpools, free
> Frae a' that's happened since. (33)

'Sea-Serpent' in *Penny Wheep* is also derived from 'A Sea Suite' and takes up the story where the earlier lyric left it. This time the poet takes over the first-personal role and regards God as a third person, a subject under consideration. God's creations, in fact, are surveyed by a poetic creator who regards himself as an astute critic of the divine art. MacDiarmid's angular approach sees the serpent as a singular creation, something uncoiling in God's wayward imagination; a creature shaped like a spiral galaxy in 'the cantles o' space' or submerged in God's subconscious 'Like a ca' o' whales'. (49) The serpent is an offspring of the creative principle, it is a malleable form that God considered before creating more rigid beings. Contemplating this serpentine form in all its glory MacDiarmid despairs of the physical limitations placed on man and longs for metaphysical harmony with the universe. The poet wants to follow his imagination beyond the world of the five senses and into the timelessness of eternity:

> Whiles a blindin' movement tak's in my life
> As a quick tide swallows a sea.
> I feel like a star on a starry nicht,
> A'e note in a symphony,
> And ken that the serpent is movin' still,
> A movement that a' thing shares,
> Yet it seems as tho' it twines in a nicht
> When God neither kens nor cares. (50)

Carrying through his multi-faceted imaginative insight MacDiarmid dwells on the serpent's symbolism which links Adam to Christ in a subtle way that recalls God's deviousness. MacDiarmid now addresses the principle of divinity and directly sounds out the source of creation, the force that unites the earthly and the eternal, the cosmic matrix wherein universal harmony is present like an infinite ocean of amniotic fluid:

O Thou that we'd fain be ane wi' again
Frae the weary lapses o' self set free,
Be to oor lives as life is to Daith,
And lift and licht us eternally.
Frae the howe o' the sea to the heich o' the lift,
To the licht as licht to the darkness is,
Spring fresh and fair frae the spirit o' God
Like the a'e first thocht that He kent was His. (50)

In writing that stanza MacDiarmid doubtless thought of Solovyov's Sophia, the feminine personification of God's wisdom, who reappears at a crucial passage of *A Drunk Man*. Thus 'Sea-Serpent' fits into the larger pattern of MacDiarmid's work, the pattern that finally found its own idiosyncratic form in *A Drunk Man*.

'Gairmscoile' is the most prophetic poetic statement in *Penny Wheep*: a linguistic credo that actually demonstrates the theory it enunciates. It is, thus, both principle and proof. It is also, as one critic realised, 'the missing link between the Lallans lyrics, the experimental poems of *Penny Wheep*, and . . . *A Drunk Man Looks at the Thistle*.'[14] Originally, on receipt of a letter from Edwin Muir suggesting that 'a long poem in the language you are evolving would go tremendously' (1234) MacDiarmid began work on 'a long poem which was to have contained twelve Sections, each consisting of four or five eight- or ten-line verses, with a Prologue and an Epilogue.' (1234) The plan of the long poem was given in *The Scottish Chapbook*, after the appearance of the prologue and three sections:

The other sections of this poem, which it is hoped to publish later, are as follows: – IV., The Voice of Scotland; V., Invocation to the Old Makars; VI., Scotland as Mystical Bride; VII., Braid Scots and the Sense of Smell; VIII., Braid Scots, Colour, and Sound; IX., Address to the World-Poets of To-day; X., Edinburgh; XI., Glasgow; XII., Sunrise Over Scotland and an Epilogue. Each section consists of four or five eight- or ten-line verses.[15]

A Drunk Man incorporates some aspects of this plan with 'Scotland as Mystical Bride' becoming the section beginning 'O Wha's the bride', 'Address to the World-Poets of To-day' becoming the address to Dostoevsky, and 'Sunrise Over Scotland' becoming the thematic dawning of a new consciousness on the Drunk Man. 'Gairmscoile' is, thus, a rehearsal of some of the themes taken up so decisively in *A Drunk Man*. It is also an impressive poem in its own right.

MacDiarmid's evolutionary ideal projected the poetic individual as a Christ-like figure of perfection but also acknowledged his animal origins. Man, as he currently existed was the missing link between the social ape and the artistic angel. In order to pass from one extreme to the other it was necessary to contemplate the sort of impulsive imaginative leap that MacDiarmid had raised up into a poetic principle. In contemplating creation MacDiarmid inevitably turns to sexuality since it can be both physically compelling and metaphysically satisfying. It involves both the ape and the angel. In discussing this concept MacDiarmid goes for an image that is both subtle and spectacular. He puns on the twin meaning of 'herts' (so using Scots in an imaginative manner) and invokes the sexual connotations of 'i' themselves' and 'stan's' so that there is always the possibility of a metamorphosis from ape to angel or vice versa:

Aulder than mammoth or than mastodon
Deep i' the herts o' a' men lurk scaut-heid
Skrymmorie monsters few daur look upon.

Brides sometimes catch their wild een, scansin' reid,
Beekin' abune the herts they thocht to lo'e
And horror-stricken ken that i' themselves
A like beast stan's, and lookin' love thro' and thro'
Meets the reid een wi' een like seevun hells.
. . . . Nearer the twa beasts draw, and, couplin', brak
The bubbles o' twa sauls and the haill warld gangs
    black. (72)

There is a sweep and swagger to that that shows MacDiarmid
growing impatient with the stanzaic brevity of the lyrics. He
is anxious to expand, to achieve something grandiose.

Sustaining the pun on 'herts' as hearts and harts Mac-
Diarmid brings his opening climax to a vision of the symbolic
stag of Scotland, 'that pure white stag with great branching
horns the appearance of which, tradition says, will betoken
great good luck for Scotland at long last.' (SE, 127) Mac-
Diarmid's love of images that beget other images adds to the
rich texture of this poem. The horns on the hart are likened
to 'a croon o' thorns' (72) which leads to a Christological
identification. So much for the prelude. In part I of the poem
MacDiarmid addresses Henrik Wergeland, the Norwegian
revivalist poet whose Landsmaal experiments adumbrated
those of the Scottish Renaissance. MacDiarmid, intent on a
creative evolution, feels that modern man has buried himself
in the present by building urban concentrations that cut him
off from his animal origins and also distance him from visionary evolutionary aspirations. Thus MacDiarmid declares war
on cities, imagines them invaded by mutations from man's
evolutionary past:

And, sudden, on the hapless cities linked
In canny civilisation's canty dance
Poor herds o' heich-skeich monsters, misbegotten,
. . . . Streets clear afore the scarmoch advance:
Frae every winnock skimmerin' een keek oot
To see what sic camsteerie cast-offs are aboot. (73)

Far from accepting Darwin's contention that only the fittest
survive – 'The best survive there's nane but fules contend'
(73) – MacDiarmid suggests there is a linguistic link in common between the social ape and the artistic angel:

> Mony's the auld hauf-human cry I ken
> Fa's like a revelation on the herts o' men
> As tho' the graves were split and the first man
> Grippit the latest wi' a freendly han'
> . . . . And there's forgotten shibboleths o' the Scots
> Ha'e keys to senses lockit to us yet
> – Coorse words that shamble thro' oor minds like stots,
> Syne turn on's muckle een wi' doonsin' emerauds lit.
> (73–4)

The language that transcends the limitations of the present
by forging a new link between the past and the future is,
naturally, Synthetic Scots which MacDiarmid justifies in a
tribute to the onomatopoeic qualities of words:

> *It's soon', no' sense, that faddoms the herts o' men,*
> *And by my sangs the rouch auld Scots I ken*
> *E'en herts that ha'e nae Scots'll dirl richt thro'*
> *As nocht else could – for here's a language rings*
> *Wi' datchie sesames, and names for nameless things.* (74)

In part II MacDiarmid tells Wergeland that he endorses his
opinion of the worthlessness of 'Maist folk' (74) and joins
with him in holding that the creative artist must be a saviour
ready, willing and able to battle with the Philistines. The
poetic saviour leads by example, brings social apes on the
upward ascent to the level of the artistic angel. The poetic
saviour accepts the past and embraces the future but has little
use for the inadequacies of the present:

> For we ha'e faith in Scotland's hidden poo'ers,
> The present's theirs, but a' the past and future's oors.
> (75)

[81]

With an irony that is to be expected from MacDiarmid this resounding declaration of faith in Synthetic Scots is followed, two poems later, by the final piece in *Penny Wheep*. It is a satirical piece about the Burns cult and, it is in English. 'Your Immortal Memory, Burns!' is another rehearsal of a notion developed in *A Drunk Man*. MacDiarmid's masterpiece quickly moves into an assault on the Burns cult and this English poem is the first stage in the attack. MacDiarmid's attitude to Burns was ambiguous. He thought of him as a great songwriter but an overrated poet whose cult had been erected as an obstacle to excellence in Scotland. To Mac-Diarmid, the mindless worship of Burns was comparable to the adulation of Sir Harry Lauder. It was a grotesque mis-representation of the Scottish character, a travesty that re-duced everything to a backslapping bonhomie that disappeared along with the inevitable hangover. Burns is thus fit subject for MacDiarmid's satirical talent which emerges strongly in this poem. When MacDiarmid wrote the poem Burns had the status of a deity in Scotland and had been marketed as a profitable item in the tourist industry. In re-nouncing this ersatz Burns as a false God, MacDiarmid is not being destructive. He believes presbyterian Scotland is about to be visited by a more formidable figure, nothing less than 'A greater Christ, a greater Burns.' (86) That the spokesman for this poetic saviour should stagger in the guise of a drunk man is only to be expected in Scotland where all men are assumed to be equally inebriated since this was the immor-tality granted to Burns:

> Only thy star
> Falls from afar
> To swim into the ken
> Of countless masses of befuddled men,
>
> In their hearts' skies
> Like barmaids' eyes
> Glabrous to glitter till
> Their minds like rockets shoot away and spill

These vivid clots
Of idiot thoughts
Wherewith our Scottish life
Is once a year incomparably rife! (78)

MacDiarmid's immortal Drunk Man was about to change all
that once and, perhaps, for all.

Chapter Three

TO PROVE MY SAUL IS SCOTS

To prove my saul is Scots I maun begin
Wi' what's still deemed Scots and the folk expect,
And spire up syne by visible degrees
To heichts whereo' the fules ha'e never recked.
        A Drunk Man Looks at the Thistle (83)

Montrose, that small town on the east coast of Scotland, may
not immediately spring to mind as a likely setting for the
most celebrated poetic experiment in twentieth-century Scottish literature yet it was there that Christopher Murray
Grieve, town councillor and local reporter with *The Montrose
Review*, created Hugh MacDiarmid and invented a modernistic idiom known as Synthetic Scots. The sentimental kailyard standards came to grief in Montrose and it was there
that MacDiarmid had the creative time of his life. One facet
of the complex symbolism he created during the 1920s was
clearly Christian in origin and the poet saw himself as a
saviour who happened to be in the right place at the right
time:

And in the toon that I belang tae
– What tho'ts Montrose or Nazareth? –
Helplessly the folk continue
To lead their livin' death! (88)

So MacDiarmid's immortal Drunk Man addressed the Thistle. By the same irrational logic that combines the contradic-

[84]

tions in the poem (a dialectic in dialect) MacDiarmid anticipated a Montrosian resurrection. The new Scottish saviour was to be crucified on the thistle and Calvary was a hillside in Montrose from the tragic height of which Mac-Diarmid would observe the insensitivity of his natural enemies:

> Aye, this is Calvary – to bear
> Your Cross wi'in you frae the seed,
> And feel it grow by slow degrees
> Until it rends your flesh apairt,
> And turn, and see your fellow-men
> In similar case but sufferin' less
> Thro' bein' mair wudden frae the stert! (134)

A Drunk Man Looks at the Thistle is MacDiarmid's masterpiece; it is the poem he was apparently destined to write for all his interests and artistic talents merge in this poem. It is the poem in which the Synthetic Scots experiment proves amenable to an extended visionary treatment, the poem in which the subject is big enough to be the target for sustained assault by MacDiarmid, the poem in which he creates a persona idiosyncratic enough to suit himself, the poem in which MacDiarmid's staggering range of reference produces thematic variety rather than confusion. *A Drunk Man* was published on 22 November 1926, but the poet had probably been contemplating it since the publication of Joyce's *Ulysses* in February 1922. On account of the following reference there is a case to be made for reading the poem as Scotland's aggressive answer to the defeatist mood of Eliot's *The Waste Land* which appeared in October 1922:

> T. S. Eliot – it's a Scottish name –
> Afore he wrote 'The Waste Land' s'ud ha'e come
> To Scotland here. He wad ha'e written
> A better poem syne – like this, by gum! (94)

However, it is Joyce, not Eliot, that MacDiarmid wishes to

emulate and the formal difference between Joycean prose and MacDiarmidian poetry is not so important as the similarity between a diurnal odyssey through Dublin and a nocturnal odyssey over a Scottish hillside. Joyce's urban example of contemporary heroism becomes MacDiarmid's rural example of spiritual resurrection and both Bloom and the Drunk Man win home to the woman of their dreams. It was MacDiarmid's repeated contention that Synthetic Scots was a linguistic idiom particularly suited to a modernist consciousness. He frequently made this the point of his propaganda in *The Scottish Chapbook*. In the monologue 'Following Rebecca West in Edinburgh' the English narrator refers to the 'stupendous uprising of the *vis comica*' in *Ulysses* and the Scots speaker insists that 'Scottish literature . . . needs an almark like Joyce.'[1] In a 'Causerie' of 1923 MacDiarmid returned to the Joycean implications of Synthetic Scots with an enthusiasm that reads like a prelude to the composition of *A Drunk Man*:

> We have been enormously struck by the resemblance –
> the moral resemblance – between Jamieson's
> Etymological Dictionary of the Scottish language and
> James Joyce's Ulysses. A *vis comica* that has not yet been
> liberated lies bound by desuetude and misappreciation in
> the recesses of the Doric: and its potential uprising would
> be no less prodigious, uncontrollable, and utterly at
> variance with conventional morality than was Joyce's
> tremendous outpouring.[2]

The notion of the interrupted voyage, so central to *A Drunk Man*, served both Homer and Joyce and MacDiarmid's Drunk Man is, initially, an unsteady Ulysses who compares his predicament to the complacently comfortable members of Scottish social clubs:

> Nae doot they're sober, as a Scot ne'er was,
> Each tethered to a punctual-snorin' missus,
> Whilst I, puir fule, owre continents unkent
> And wine-dark oceans waunder like Ulysses. . . . (95)

As Homer's Ulysses sails home to Penelope and Joyce's
Bloom walks home to Molly, so MacDiarmid's inebriated
Ulysses-Bloom figure staggers home to the arms of his Jean.
One of the triumphs of the poem is the original combination
of different artistic modes; the Homeric and Joycean associations are integrated into a Burnsian atmosphere for the
Drunk Man's bedmate Jean has a distinct resemblance to
Tam o'Shanter's Kate. Burns's offstage heroine is a 'sulky
sullen dame' and MacDiarmid's Jean 'maun natter, natter,
natter' (88) although she is conspicuous by her physical
absence from the poem. MacDiarmid's Drunk Man is aware
of the similarity between his predicament and that of Tam
O'Shanter though he is more rooted than Tam:

> 'Noo Cutty Sark's tint that ana',
> And dances in her skin – Ha! Ha!
>
> I canna ride awa' like Tam,
> But e'en maun bide juist whaur I am.' (109)

What MacDiarmid wanted to do was to write a Scottish
modernist masterpiece that would, by a series of culture
shocks, shake the nation out of its linguistic and cultural
preconceptions and thus renew the indigenous tradition. After
the publication of the book he wrote to his old teacher Ogilvie:

> I set out to give Scotland a poem, perfectly modern in
> psychology, which could only be compared in the whole
> length of Scots literature, with Tam o'Shanter and
> Dunbar's Seven Deidly Sins. And I felt I had done it by
> the time I had finished – despite all the faults and flaws
> of my work.[3]

MacDiarmid's poem combines narrative elements with
Symbolism, epic with anecdote, lyricism with satire. Yet the
original idea of the poem may have been to produce an
exercise in what G. Gregory Smith defined as the quintessential contrariness of Scottish literature. It is worth recalling
that Smith's book on *Scottish Literature* was used by MacDiar-

[87]

mid as a scholarly sourcebook of the Scottish Renaissance and he may have noted the following passage in particular since it delineates principles subsequently articulated in *A Drunk Man*:

> The Scot is not a quarrelsome man, but he has a fine sense of the value of provocation, and in the clash of things and words has often found a spiritual tonic. . . Does literature anywhere, of this small compass, show such a mixture of contraries as his in outlook, subject, and method; real life and romance, everyday fact and the supernatural, things holy and things profane, gentle and simple, convention and 'cantrip', thistles and thistledown? . . . There is more in the Scottish antithesis of the real and fantastic than is to be explained by the familiar rules of rhetoric. The sudden jostling of contraries seems to preclude any relationship by literary suggestion. The one invades the other without warning. They are the 'polar twins' of the Scottish Muse. . . We are dull indeed if we do not see in [references to alcohol in Scottish literature] a quizzing of those prosaic and precise persons who must have that realism which presents everything as sober fact, within an ell of their noses. The poet seems to say: 'Here is fantasy strange enough; if you, drunkard of facts, must explain it, do so in the only way open to you, or to any 'auld carlin.' Be satisfied, if you think it is we who are drunk. As for us, let the contrast be unexplained, and let us make merry in this clash of strange worlds and moods.' It is beside the point to hint at or deny John Barleycorn's aid to the poetic imagination, and unnecessary to consider the ingenious view of a recent writer on Celtic literature, that bardic intemperance is not the satisfying of a sordid appetite but proof of the 'cravings for the illusion of an unreal world.'[4]

During the making of *A Drunk Man* MacDiarmid must have recalled that passage to support his plan to create a modernistic work that yet had precedents in a distinctively Scottish tradition.

Such is the power of the poem that it has attracted to itself a literary legend and can be made to sound like a sacred book with an apocryphal genesis. *A Drunk Man* was written in Montrose and apparently put together at the house at 16 Links Avenue where Christopher and Margaret Grieve lived in the 1920s. MacDiarmid's former teacher and close friend, the composer Francis George Scott, took much credit for the final shape of the poem and supplied Maurice Lindsay with a colourful account of an urgent summons to Montrose:

> It was late at night when I reached Montrose and after his wife and youngsters went off to bed, we sat down to a table, a great heap of scribbled bits of paper and a bottle of whisky. I can still see Christopher's face when I was indicating the shape the poem, or for that matter a musical composition, ought to take – he was literally flabbergasted either by the extent of my knowledge or by the whisky – it's anybody's guess! We spent until day-break sorting out the items worth keeping, Christopher arranging them on the table like a pack of cards in the order that I indicated as likely to give the best sequences, climaxes, etc. My plans necessitated a pianissimo close, after so much bustle ('The Stars like Thistle's Roses flower') to be followed by ('Yet hae I Silence left, the croon o' a' ') and I'm pretty certain I supplied the last two lines to bring the thing to some kind of conclusion.[5]

Such was Scott's claim in 1946 though he is not to be accepted as a totally reliable witness. Before he produces that anecdote he claims, in the same letter, that MacDiarmid 'never had any sense of form'[6] which is a charge difficult to reconcile with the shapely progress of the lyrics; moreover in 1926, when *A Drunk Man* was completed, MacDiarmid had one daughter and not 'youngsters', so Scott's memory can be faulted there. Scott also changed the setting when he told the story to his cousin, the painter William Johnstone, who wrote:

Francis told me that Christopher arrived one evening at
Jordanhill with a collection of poems written on the backs
of envelopes, odd scraps of paper and reporters'
notebooks. Francis placed a bottle of whisky on the table
between them and they spread out *Drunk Man*. Taking
drams from the bottle, Christopher soon fell fast asleep
on the sofa, not stirring until the morning when Mrs
Scott brought in tea, but Francis worked all night, and
was still hard at work in the morning. The bottle was
empty but Christopher's fragments had been edited and
placed in order. The poem needed a conclusion, but they
were stuck and Francis in the end wrote the final lines.[7]

It is an entertaining story but should be treated with extreme
caution. Fortunately there is epistolary evidence – letters to
George Ogilvie and J. K. Annand – to show that neither
MacDiarmid nor even Francis George Scott put the poem
together in one convivial night but that the poet worked
carefully on the composition for the better part of a year.

There is no doubt whatsoever about Scott's importance in
encouraging the author of *A Drunk Man*. As the Author's Note
of 1926 explains:

This gallimaufry is dedicated to my friend, Francis
George Scott, the composer, who suggested it and to
whom, in the course of writing it, I have been further and
greatly indebted for cooperative suggestions and for some
of the most penetrating and comprehensive of modern
European criticism. (Thistle, vii)

Forty years later MacDiarmid was equally generous in giving
due credit to Scott:

I remember, as illustrating our deep community of
insight, that when I wrote the *Drunk Man* working on my
own I had got to the point when I had ceased to be able
to see the forest for the trees. I found the necessary
imaginative sympathy in F. G. Scott and handed over the
whole mass of my manuscript to him. He was not long in
seizing on the essentials and urging the ruthless

discarding of the unessentials. I had no hesitation in taking his advice and in this way the significant shape was educed from the welter of stuff and the rest pruned away. (Company, 96)

Scott, in other words, provided MacDiarmid with assistance when it was needed. Though the poem describes a drunken night it should not be inferred from that, and Scott's story, that it was put together in the same circumstances. As J. K. Annand shows, MacDiarmid worked steadily on the poem throughout 1926. On 25 May 1926 he was integrating into the structure of the poem 'a long "Ballad of the General Strike" which I think will rank as one of the most passionate cris-de-coeur in contempoary literature', on 2 June he had 'just written' the closing lyric of *A Drunk Man*, and on 6 August he wrote to Ogilvie with a sense of creative urgency:

[*A Drunk Man Looks at the Thistle*] will either make or finish me so far as Braid Scots work, and Messrs. Blackwood's are concerned. I dare not let them down with a work of such magnitude. As it now stands it'll be at least six times as big a book as 'Sangschaw' – some risk for any publisher these days. I've let myself go in it for all I'm worth. My friend Scott, (the composer) and I afterwards went over the whole thing with a small tooth comb. But we both felt that the section I've been re-writing – which comes about midway in the book and should represent the high water mark, the peaks of highest intensity, could be improved by being recast and projected onto a different altitude of poetry altogether – made, instead of a succession of merely verbal and pictorial verses, into a series of metaphysical pictures with a definite progression, a cumulative effect – and that is what I've been so busy with. It's infernally intractable material: but I've spared no pains and put my uttermost ounce into the business. I'm out to make or break in this matter. There are poems in the book (which is really one whole although many parts are detachable) of extraordinary power, I know – longer and far more

powerful and unique in kind than anything in
'Sangschaw' or 'Penny Wheep'; but that's not what I'm
after. It's the thing as a whole that I'm mainly concerned
with, and if, as such, it does not take its place as a
masterpiece – sui generis – one of the biggest things in
the range of Scottish literature, I shall have failed.[8]

A Drunk Man Looks at the Thistle is a mould into which
MacDiarmid pours all his cerebral conceptions, all his personal insights, all his philosophical conclusions, all his political passions. Little wonder, then, that the mould threatens to
shatter under so much poetic pressure. As MacDiarmid is
interested in visionary unity rather than psychological fragmentation this persistent attempt to find a form flexible
enough to carry all MacDiarmid's ideas becomes a subject of
comment throughout the poem:

> I doot I'm geylies mixed, like Life itsel',
> But I was never ane that thocht to pit
> An ocean in a mutchkin. As the haill's
> Mair than the pairt sae I than reason yet. (87)

and

> O ilka man alive is like
> A quart that's squeezed into a pint
> (A maist unScottish-like affair!) (122)

and again

> And liquor packed impossibly
> Mak' pint-pot an eternal well (125)

So MacDiarmid is aware that the form has to emerge from
the poetic experience and not vice versa; his reliance on couplets, quatrains and tercets in a modernist composition is his
way of investing the familiar with the unexpected. The most
familiar form that came to hand in Scotland was the ballad

measure, especially appropriate in view of MacDiarmid's Border origins in Langholm. In one sense *A Drunk Man* is the biggest Border Ballad the world has ever seen. If we think of a ballad as a narrative poem intended for oral circulation then we must give MacDiarmid credit for taking this traditional technique and extending it into a speculative infinity. In the traditional ballad, story is raised to the musical level of song; in MacDiarmid's poem the narrative notion is enlarged into a rich compositional pattern capable of great variation. The poem presents a theme with its own variants and with metaphysical variations. Still, the essential rhythm is reassuring as MacDiarmid emphasised (in an 85th birthday broadcast on Radio Scotland on 11 August 1977):

> Largely, the engine that motivates the whole poem and keeps it going is the ballad measure, of course. It varies – there's a lot of variation of metre and so on in the *Drunk Man* – but underlying all the variations there's that continuing ballad metre. It comes back to the ballad all the time.

The poem unfolds on several levels of significance; it is a basic notion raised to a complex issue by the intensity of MacDiarmid's vision of a Scotocentric universe. On a purely narrative level the poem is the first-personal account of a Drunk Man's nocturnal adventures as he wakens from a hard-drinking session to find himself on a hillside confronted by the formidable flora of Scotland. The Drunk Man, as protagonist, is a representative Scot whose inviolable individuality gradually dawns on him. In this sense *A Drunk Man* is a demonstration of MacDiarmid's evolutionary idealism in action since the hero begins as a stereotypical Scottish drunk who, by a process of cerebration and emotional identification with the destiny of Scotland, moves away from the influence of alcoholic spirit into a unity with a universally creative spirit. In the beginning the Drunk Man looks at the thistle and he ends by tapping the wordless eloquence of the universe. MacDiarmid's great triumph is in allowing the spiritual aspects of the poem to develop, persuasively, from a convincing situation. As the poem opens the hero is exhausted, like Scotland. Punning on the associations of the word 'waun'ert' MacDiarmid then sets the Drunk Man on a hillside where he is ready to hold an argument with himself:

> But that's aside the point! I've got fair waun'ert.
> It's no' that I'm sae fou' as juist deid dune,
> And dinna ken as muckle's whaur I am
> Or hoo I've come to sprawl here 'neth the mune.
>
> That's it! It isna me that's fou' at a',
> But the fu' mune, the doited jade, that's led
> Me fer agley, or 'mogrified the warld.
> – For a' I ken I'm safe in my ain bed.
>
> *Jean! Jean!* Gin *she*'s no' here it's no' *oor* bed,
> Or else I'm dreamin' deep and canna wauken,
> But it's a fell queer dream if this is no'
> A real hillside – and thae things thistles and bracken!
> (86)

It is, indeed, a strange dream that makes such spectacular advances on reality.

This Drunk Man is partially made in the image of his creator since he makes references to Montrose, (88) where the poem was executed; to the Muckle Toon of Langholm (97) where the poet was born; and to

> that upheaval in which I
> Sodgered 'neth the Grecian sky
> And in Italy and Marseilles (159)

Such autobiographical allusions are incidental since the main purpose of the poem is not self-portraiture but the creation of a new visionary unity that begins by being rooted in Scotland (like a thistle) and ends by reaching out into the stars. The process involves a startling metamorphosis for the Drunk Man is, ostensibly, a typically Scottish drunk – an argumentative creature who knows he must eventually creep home shamefacedly to his nagging wife. Yet, in the course of the poem, he becomes something that is both unique and exemplary. When, having left his boozing cronies Cruivie and Gilsanquhar, the Drunk Man introduces himself his individuality is merely an assertive orthodoxy, a tiresome wha's-like-us affair:

> I'll bury nae heid like an ostrich's,
> Nor yet believe my een and naething else.
> My senses may advise me, but I'll be
> Mysel' nae maitter what they tell's (87)

With the slow dawning of sober spirituality the Drunk Man realises it is not enough to claim uniqueness since individuality is a quality that transcends a feeling of self-importance. It is a state of mind that enables the representative individual to project himself as an ideal embodiment of a national ideal:

> And let the lesson be – to be yersel's,
> Ye needna fash gin it's to be ocht else.
> To be yersel's – and to mak' that worth bein'.
> Nae harder job to mortals has been gi'en. (107)

As he acquires philosophical responsibility the Drunk Man understands that evolutionary idealism requires a creativity that transcends the domestic routine of reproduction:

> I dinna say that bairns alane
> Are true love's task – a sairer task
> Is aiblins to create oorsels
> As we can be – it's that I ask. (113)

So the Drunk Man wills himself upwards into a mystical union with the universe, this being the direction MacDiarmid himself wanted to take:

> The general (as beyond the particularly Scottish) theme
> of *A Drunk Man Looks at the Thistle* is to show 'a beautiful

soul in the making' – to trace, that is to say, its rise through all struggle and contradiction till its stands out a self-conscious, self-directing personality – a purified person.[9]

MacDiarmid's own intellectualism is integrated into the cerebral texture of the poem which is ingeniously explained by a reference to the scholastic tradition of Scotland. The erudition of the Drunk Man is taken as a positive part of the Scottish educational heritage:

> Gin you're surprised a village drunk
> Foreign references s'ud fool in,
> You ha'ena the respect you s'ud
> For oor guid Scottish schoolin'. (97)

This village drunk translates from the Russian of Alexander Blok (88) and Zinaida Hippius (94), from the French of George Ramaekers (92) and Edmond Rocher (102) and from the German of Else Lasker-Schüler (95); or rather he adapts to his own ends extant English translations.[10] He also cites various intellectual and Scottish historical figures in the interests of contrast and counterpoint: Jascha Heifetz, Sir Harry Lauder, Mary Garden, Duncan Grant (84), G. K. Chesterton (85), Robert Burns (85), Sigmund Freud (93), T. S. Eliot (94), Arnold Schönberg (96), Leopold von Masoch, Marquis de Sade (99), William Dunbar, Oswald Spengler, Dostoevski, Nietzsche (106), Mallarmé (117), Herman Melville, Nathaniel Hawthorne (135), Tolstoi (153), Plato (157), Euclid, Einstein (159), Knox, Clavers, Mary Queen of Scots, Wallace, Carlyle (164). The display of booklore is part of the general assault on the reader's complacency for MacDiarmid makes it clear that he intends to lift up the reader's spirit and also brutally bring him down to the earth that sustains him. So he explains in a two-quatrain parenthesis:

> (To prove my saul is Scots I maun begin
> Wi' what's still deemed Scots and the folk expect,

And spire up syne by visible degrees
To heichts whereo' the fules ha'e never recked.

But aince I get them there I'll whummle them
And souse the craturs in the nether deeps,
– For it's nae choice, and ony man s'ud wish
To dree the goat's weird tae as weel's the sheep's!) (83)

The Thistle *qua* thistle and Drunk Man *qua* drunk man are
intellectually provocative items in their own right. To extend
the Thistle and the Drunk Man from physical objects to
metaphysical emblems MacDiarmid uses a multi-referential
approach that leads to a Synthetic Symbolism (to match his
Synthetic Scots). The eclecticism is energetic and the poetic
synthesis of all the elements is MacDiarmid's triumph. From
Socrates he takes the idea of a dynamically unfolding dialectic; from Plato the concept of earthly objects as imperfect
copies of eternal Ideas; from biblical Christianity the figure
of the saviour and the notions of crucifixion and resurrection;
from neoplatonism the three hypostases of Soul, Mind and
One; from Solovyov he borrows the figure of Sophia, the
feminine personification of the wisdom of God; from Nietzsche
the belief in an evolutionary idealism; from Freud the importance of phallic symbolism and lunar cycles. The Drunk
Man tends ever upwards towards a union, through the mystical bride (or Sophia), with the universe which is the source
of all creativity, the object of MacDiarmid's poetic search.
This intellectual vision is a cerebral conception developed in
an emotional matrix in aid of a metaphysical nativity. At the
end of the poem the Drunk Man, who has already seen the
eternal feminine principle assume the shape of both Sophia
and the Virgin Mary, goes back to his earthly mate. At the
beginning of the poem he is physically exhausted, at the end
he has attained a Silence which is abruptly broken by Jean
who closes the poem by speaking for the first time. The Drunk
Man's odyssey is also an obsessive quest, as references to
Moby-Dick (108) and The Flying Dutchman (111) confirm,
and from all the internal evidence we are made to realise that

the coming of 'A greater Christ, a greater Burns' (86) announced at the beginning of the poem has been accomplished by the end of it.

MacDiarmid concentrates a mass of conceptual, artistic and symbolic material into this poem of 2,685 lines and does so with reference to a small country whose visions are, proverbially, alcoholically induced nightmares. It is MacDiarmid's ability to make preconceptions rebound on the reader that provides the poem with its enduringly novel quality. At one point, aware of investing his native land with a universal importance, the Drunk Man asks a rhetorical question:

> Is Scotland big enough to be
> A symbol o' that force in me,
> In wha's divine inebriety
> A sicht abune contempt I'll see? (145)

The answer is in the affirmative. Scotland, in this poem, is as big as the mind of the man who describes it. It is a world in itself but also a crucial part of the cosmos; in MacDiarmid's imaginative vision the universe is Scotocentric. Scotland's traditional symbol is the thistle and in looking at one the other is involved. At various points in the poem the thistle is described as something fundamentally alien and apart: it is 'Gurly' (90), 'Gothic' (93), 'Shudderin'' (105), 'nervous' (128), 'Infernal' (132), 'monstrous' (147), 'rootless' (147), 'epileptic' (149), 'Presbyterian' (152), 'grisly' (153), 'Grugous' (156). These epithets conjure up a series of metamorphoses. MacDiarmid's thistle is clearly not the picture-postcard symbol of Lauderesque Scotland. At least, not by the time MacDiarmid has finished with it. It has a constantly changing quality as it seems to alter before the Drunk Man's eyes which are bleary before the vision comes. It carries the traditional connotations of defiance and austerity and its thorns relate it, figuratively, to the passion of Christ. MacDiarmid's Drunk Man is a saviour anxious to recreate Scotland in a spiritually appropriate image, aware that such an effort involves self-sacrifice on the altar of Scotland's defeatist history:

> '*A Scottish poem maun assume*
> *The burden o' his people's doom,*
> *And dee to brak' their livin' tomb.*' (165)

which is a tragic, though ultimately triumphant, consequence of the situation prefigured at the beginning of the poem:

> A greater Christ, a greater Burns, may come.
> The maist they'll dae is to gi'e bigger pegs
> To folly and conceit to hank their rubbish on.
> They'll cheenge folks' talk but no their natures, fegs!
> (86)

The Christian symbolism does not, however, exhaust the poem which has layers and layers of meaning as it expands outwards from an explosive centre. For example the Christian concept of the saviour involved in spiritual struggle is complicated by being overlaid with the Nietzschean belief in the artist-as-redeemer. MacDiarmid isolates 'the Scots aboulia' (93) and proposes to deal with it by means of a Nietzschean will to (creative) power:

> Or gin ye s'ud need mair than ane to teach ye,
> Then learn frae Dostoevski and frae Nietzsche. (106)

In the propagandist period leading up to the composition of *A Drunk Man*, MacDiarmid showed an enthusiastic interest in Freud who is undoubtedly an important figure in the structural and symbolic interpretation of the poem. From the Freudianism rampant in the art of the 1920s MacDiarmid derived two important ideas for application to *A Drunk Man*: the principle of free association (*freier Einfall*) developed by Freud in the 1890s to describe the preconscious shaping of human thought; and the psychological relevance of sexual symbolism. From the Freudian viewpoint, *A Drunk Man* can be seen as an enormous free association session as the fertile symbol of the thistle provokes multiple associations in the mind of the poet. MacDiarmid once referred to his own method of composition in these terms:

> As keen students of the Vernacular will appreciate, he was making scores of little experiments in Doric composition and style even as he spoke – subtle adaptations of ancient figures of speech to modern requirements, finding vernacular equivalents for Freudian terminology – all infinitely difficult work but infinitely necessary if the Doric is again to become a living literary medium.[11]

In *A Drunk Man* he refers to how '*This* Freudian complex has somehoo slunken/Frae Scotland's soul'. (93) Throughout the poem the thistle, personifying Scotland as a thrusting aggressive force, becomes a phallic symbol of great power. Just as the full moon, the mystical bride (Sophia), and the conspicuously absent Jean represent the feminine principle of receptivity and creative congress, the thistle stands (phallically) for the masculine principle of thrust and procreation. This strong sexual image is sustained throughout the poem as the Drunk Man's spirit rises to the occasion, falls as the alcoholic spirit wears off, then rises again under the influence of a metaphysical spirit. Having found himself on the hillside under the full moon (and how MacDiarmid enjoys punning on the moon being 'fu' ' in the Scottish colloquial sense of being full of drink), the Drunk Man is aware of stirrings that link him to Jean who is his own moon goddess and earthly representative of the eternal feminine ideal personified as Sophia, the mystical and universal bride:

> Or doest thou mak' a thistle o' me, wumman? But for thee
> I were as happy as the munelicht, withoot care,
> But thocht o' thee – o' thy contempt and ire –
> Turns hauf the warld into the youky thistle there. (91)

After brooding, in the 'fickle licht' (92), on the intimate appearance of the thistle the Drunk Man thinks back on his childhood days in Langholm, 'the Muckle Toon', (97) when the Common Riding celebrants carried an 'aucht-fit thistle' (97) through the Walligate. This memory of vitality provokes a memory of his wife Jean as she was on her wedding day and, at the erotic thought, the thistle seems to rise sexually before his eyes:

> Nerves in stounds o' delight,
> Muscles in pride o' power,
> Bluid as wi' roses dight
> Life's toppin' pinnacles owre,
> The thistle yet'll unite
> Man and the Infinite! (98)

It is the contention of the poem that the thistle can penetrate deep space, shoot out seeds like stars into the universe, and thus create a new metaphysical nativity, a Scottish spirit that comes back to the earth in a beautiful gesture of unity. So many images and allusions blend in MacDiarmid's poem that the symbols begin to acquire an autonomous power and at two sections – the climactic and miraculous nativity (101–6) and the closing triumph of Silence (166–7) – no amount of paraphrase or interpretation can detract from the element of mystery MacDiarmid creates.

MacDiarmid's ability to shift swiftly from the ridiculous to the sublime, from the earthly to the seemingly far-fetched, provides *A Drunk Man* with its power; the poem has a depth that contains a wealth of implications. The long evocation of a modern miracle of nativity must be the section MacDiarmid referred to as 'the high water mark' of the poem in his letter of 6 August 1926 to George Ogilvie (see above, p. 91). In this sequence the poet uses the thistle as both phallic symbol and emblem of the Christian passion; in the same way the mystical bride is both Solovyov's Sophia and the Virgin Mary. Substantiating the complex symbolism is the reality that is forever in MacDiarmid's grasp: the thistle is always a real plant and the sexual references have an impressive physicality. Early on in the poem MacDiarmid has prepared the reader for the notion of a miraculous nativity since he cites the possible coming of 'A greater Christ, a greater Burns'. (86) By a process of evolutionary idealism a new kind of being is coming into existence. In the context of MacDiarmid's Scotland he is conceived as a poetic saviour whose spirituality contrasts so cruelly with the vicious materialism rampant in the nation that there is an inexorable progress towards martyrdom. In Scotland the thistle can be a sacrificial cross or fertility symbol or both in a fusion that is both pregnant and procreative. Approaching the central mystery of his poem, MacDiarmid stages an annunciation in bed where an unholy trinity of forces is represented by Jean and the duality that is the Drunk Man:

> Said my body to my mind,
> 'I've been startled whiles to find,
> When Jean has been in bed wi' me,
> A kind o' Christianity!' (101)

This kind of Christianity has its genesis in passion, in physical intimacy that affirms life in a way that institutional Christianity can deny. MacDiarmid's strongest work always, we have noted, places a cerebral conception in an emotional matrix and in a series of couplets he broods on the prospect of a sexual synthesis since it illuminates his poetic method and enunciates the theme of *A Drunk Man*:

> I wish I kent the physical basis
> O' a' life's seemin' airs and graces.
>
> It's queer the thochts a kittled cull
> Can lowse or splairgin' glit annul.
>
> Man's spreit is wi' his ingangs twined
> In ways that he can ne'er unwind.

A wumman whiles a bawaw gi'es
That clean abaws him gin he sees.

Or wi' a movement o' a leg
Shows'm his mind is juist a geg.

I'se warrant Jean 'ud no' be lang
In findin' whence this thistle sprang.

Mebbe it's juist because I'm no'
Beddit wi' her that gars it grow! (101–2)

The rampant spectacle of the masculine principle of pen-
etration provokes tender consideration (suggested by the
French of Edmond Rocher) of the capacity of women to
encourage the procreative impulse in men. As if enchanted
men are compelled to act in accordance with the eternally
feminine principle of creation. MacDiarmid has now reached
the point of consummation and, by a brilliant twist of emphasis, produces a poetic climax that contains a narrative
anticlimax for the reader is told a poignant story of apparent
infidelity in a ballad of betrayal:

O wha's the bride that cairries the bunch
O' thistles blinterin' white?
Her cuckold bridegroom little dreids
What he sall ken this nicht. (102)

That quatrain contrasts a rhetorical question with an ominous
conclusion. In fact at this point of the poem the whole verbal
atmosphere pulsates with paradox and glows with counter-
pointed images of 'blinterin' white' purity and sexual indis-
cretion. To answer MacDiarmid's leading question is difficult:
the bride is not only a real woman in a passionate ballad but
the imperfect earthly copy of an eternal feminine ideal who
is, according to philosophical choice, both Sophia and the
Virgin Mary. Her fertility is universal and she has been
impregnated by a man that died before she was born. (103)

This paradox suggests an eternal process of recurrence so that each woman enacts a perpetual passion that transcends earthly events. Jean, Sophia and Mary amount to the eternally feminine as experienced by the Drunk Man as he begins to ascend to the universal. This coalescence of all female fertility in an endless and eternal process explains the presence of the oxymoronic image in this beautifully mysterious quatrain:

> *And on my lips ye'll heed nae mair,*
> *And in my hair forget,*
> *The seed o' a' the men that in*
> *My virgin womb ha'e met* (103)

The bridegroom is not cuckolded by another individual but by humanity; the bride is about to conceive a universal saviour fathered by 'a' the men'.

There is a particularly Scottish aspect of this nativity. Impregnated by the spirit of the thistle the eternal bride is obligated, in this instance, to bear a Scottish saviour:

> *Wull ever a wumman be big again*
> *Wi's muckle's a Christ? Yech, there's nae sayin'.* (103)

According to the biblical evidence, Christ was born in the image of divine perfection. The Scottish saviour is not destined to conform to such flawlessness but to carry within him grim reminders of his country past, to appear like 'This skeleton-at-the-feast'. (104) The Drunk Man now connects the image of a forlorn Virgin Mary with the sight of the Moon who is asked to accept responsibility for tempting the phallic thistle and thus encouraging the new arrival on earth:

> *Prood mune, ye needna thring your shouder there,*
> *And at your puir get like a snawstorm stare,*
> *It's yours – there's nae denyin't – and I'm shair*
> *You'd no enjoy the evenin' much the less*
> *Gin you'd but openly confess!* (104)

So the fullness of the moon was not, as the Drunk Man originally thought, insobriety but pregnancy. In such circles does his confused mind run. It is interesting to notice that the Scottish saviour is described as 'an eaten and a spewed-like thing' (104) for when the baby Christopher Murray Grieve was born his own mother called him 'an eaten' an' spewed lookin' wee thing.'[12] So the poetic saviour is made in the image of his creator, the poet Hugh MacDiarmid who now changes the metaphor of birth into one of growth and considers how difficult it is for anything to blossom in the unyielding soil of Scotland:

> The roots that wi' the worms compete
> Hauf-publish me upon the air.
> The struggle that divides me still
> Is seen fu' plainly there. (104)

At this stage in the poem we have a saviour born of a union between the thistle and the moon, Scotland and infinity, spirit and substance. The result is hardly believable, an 'impossible truth'. (105) Yet the biblical Christ worked miracles and a miracle is what Scotland urgently needs in order to rise to resurrection:

> *Pu' Scotland up,*
> *And wha can say*
> *It winna bud*
> *And blossom tae.*
>
> *A miracle's*
> *Oor only chance.*
> *Up, carles, up*
> *And let us dance!* (106)

As soon as he has conceived the possibility of a Scottish miracle the Drunk Man's thoughts turn automatically to Burns 'wha's bouquet like a shot kail blaws'. (106) Throughout the poem the pressure of evolutionary idealism prompts the Drunk Man to consider the distance between Everyman, as represented by his intoxicated self, by his cronies Cruivie and Gilsanquhar; and the visionary Superman as represented by Christ, Burns, Dostoevsky and the reborn Drunk Man on whom the consciousness of eternity has gradually dawned. The Drunk Man's first heroic triumph is to win through to an internationalism that is the essential stage towards universalism:

> He's no a man ava',
> And lacks a proper pride,
> Gin less than a' the warld
> Can ser' him for a bride! (114)

Implicit in that quatrain is the presence of Sophia and the Drunk Man is always able to affirm the potency of the creative life force through its sexual expression on earth:

> Whisky mak's Heaven or Hell and whiles mells baith,
> Disease is but the privy torch o' Daith,
> – But sex reveals life, faith! (114)

What holds the poem together, however, what combines the many ideas in a neoplatonic unity-in-diversity is the impression imposed on the reader that the Drunk Man is a real Scotsman before he is a representative of the evolutionary ideal in action. Although destined for a spiritual rebirth and a familiarity with universalism he is distinctively Scottish in his drunkenness, his contrariness and his obsession with national symbols such as the thistle.

As a Scotsman, the Drunk Man can cite only two products that have proved so amenable to export that they are known internationally: whisky and the 'star of Rabbie Burns'. (85) First and foremost there is whisky which allows MacDiarmid to extend the pun on spirit into an epic conceit. Whisky is a spirit whose price on earth is too high:

It's robbin' Peter to pey Paul at least. . . .
And a' that's Scotch aboot it is the name,
Like a' thing else ca'd Scottish nooadays
– A' destitute o' speerit juist the same. (83)

Everything, at any rate, is destitute of spirit in Scotland where
the national drink is indissolubly associated with the national
bard. Parodying Wordsworth's call to the spirit of Milton –
as, later, he parodies Eliot's 'Sweeney Among the Nightin-
gales' (150–1) – the Drunk Man invokes the alcoholic spirit
of Burns:

Rabbie, wad'st thou wert here – the warld hath need,
And Scotland mair sae, o' the likes o' thee!
The whisky that aince moved your lyre's become
A laxative for a' loquacity. (85)

The Drunk Man now addresses Burns as an equal and explains to him exactly how his name has been taken in vain in
the Scotland he loved. This enables MacDiarmid to develop,
with great satirical power, the theme of cultural betrayal.
Burns's poetic gift to Scotland has been grotesquely abused
so that the bard has become synonymous with alcoholic and
gastronomic over-indulgence. Worse still, the poetry is reduced to a few set-pieces and the Drunk Man savagely denounces the spectacle of Burns Clubbers through the world
proclaiming:

Burns' sentiments o' universal love,
In pidgin English or in wild-fowl Scots,
And toastin' ane wha's nocht to them but an
Excuse for faitherin' Genius wi' *their* thochts. (84)

The parallel with Christ is carefully explained which makes
the reader alert to the perpetual possibility of the appearance
in the poem of 'A greater Christ, a greater Burns'. (86) As
sobriety and a new kind of spirit descend on the protagonist
he roams the earth for evidence of a mind creative enough to

be thought of as 'A greater Christ, a greater Burns'. He finds such a man in Dostoevsky.

   Long before he joined the Communist Party in 1934, Mac-Diarmid was fascinated by the transformation of Russia from a peasant to a revolutionary economy. He felt that political events had confirmed ideas expressed by Russia's most creative thinkers. MacDiarmid's pantheon included three Russians: Leo Chestov, 'my favourite philosopher', (LP, 28) Vladimir Solovyov and Dostoevsky. Though MacDiarmid did not study these writers in a scholarly or systematic fashion, he was able to lift from each of them an idea that corresponded with his own intuition. Chestov, for example, celebrated the element of risk-taking in philosophy and MacDiarmid's use of chiaroscuro in *A Drunk Man* – 'Darkness comes closer to us than the licht,/And is oor natural element' (148) – is influenced by Chestov's remark that 'To grasp and admit absolute freedom is infinitely hard for us, as it is hard for a man who has always lived in darkness to look into the light'. (LP, 67) Solovyov provided MacDiarmid with the universally fertile figure of Sophia and the notion of *vse-chelovek* (134): the All-Man or Pan-Human organism that unites humanity. With even greater enthusiasm MacDiarmid responded to 'Dostoevsky's Russian Idea . . . a great creative idea – a dynamic myth'. (SE, 67) Just as Russia has risen to revolution, which MacDiarmid regards as a political resurrection or renaissance, on an intellectual foundation built by such as Chestov, Solovyov and Dostoevsky, so Scotland can be reconstructed from ruin:

> But even as the stane the builders rejec'
> Becomes the corner-stane, the time may be
> When Scotland sall find oot its destiny,
> And yield the *vse-chelovek*
>
> – At a' events, owre Europe flaught atween,
> My whim (and mair than whim) it pleases
> To seek the haund o' Russia as a freen'
> In workin' oot mankind's great synthesis. (134–5)

The Drunk Man approaches Dostoevsky by way of the honorary Scotsman Herman Melville, whose *Moby-Dick* is cited as another obsessive quest relevant to the symbolism of the poem since

> *– The mune's the muckle white whale*
> *I seek in vain to kaa!*
>
> *The Earth's my mastless samyn,*
> *The thistle my ruined sail.* (108–9)

MacDiarmid felt Melville had anticipated him in making a masterpiece from monomania. Melville is, unlike Dostoevsky, a kinsman:

> Melville (a Scot) kent weel hoo Christ's
> Corrupted into creeds malign,
> Begotten strife's pernicious brood
> That claims for patron Him Divine. (135)

The reference here is to Melville's narrative poem *Clarel: A Poem and Pilgrimage in the Holy Land* (1876) in which the hunchback renegade Catholic, Celio, defies Christ.[13] The Drunk Man notes this since he is interested in the coming of 'A greater Christ' (86) and supposes that the Scot, reinforced with a knowledge of Melville, will change his attitude to the Christ of the presbyterian Kirk:

> And never mair a Scot sall tryst,
> Abies on Calvary, wi' Christ,
> Unless, mebbe, a poem like this'll
> Exteriorise things in a thistle,
> And gi'e him in this form forlorn
> What Melville socht in vain frae Hawthorne. (135)

What Melville sought from Hawthorne was an insight into darkness, 'that Calvinistic sense of Innate Depravity and Original Sin, from whose visitations in some shape or other,

no deeply thinking mind is always and wholly free.'[14] The
Drunk Man is, in the beginning, a product of presbyterianism
so conditioned by guilt-edged insecurity that he can refer (in
an adaptation from the Russian of Hippius) to his soul as
'this deid thing, whale-white obscenity'.(94)

Seeking an affirmative answer to the doubts that darken
his nocturnal odyssey the Drunk Man turns to Dostoevsky in
an address that begins and ends with uncharacteristic humility: he begins by asking Dostoevsky for 'a share o' your/
Appallin' genius' (138) and later looks up to the Russian 'As
bairn at giant'. (145) The Drunk Man considers the depths
of his own soul and then the 'flegsome deeps/Whaur the soul
o' Scotland sleeps'. (138) This reference to oceanic quest
brings Melville and his Leviathan back into the reckoning.
With the assistance of Melville, the Drunk Man is able to
perceive the significance of Dostoevsky who is perhaps the
'greater Christ' (86) predicted at the beginning of the poem:

> '*Melville, sea-compelling man,*
> *Before whose wand Leviathan*
> *Rose hoary-white upon the Deep,*'
> *What thou has sown I fain 'ud reap*
> *O' knowledge 'yont the human mind*
> *In keepin' wi' oor Scottish kind,*
> *And, thanks to thee, may aiblins reach*
> *To what this Russian has to teach,*
> *Closer than ony ither Scot,*
> *Closer to me than my ain thocht,*
> *Closer than my ain braith to me,*
> *As close as to the Deity*
> *Approachable in whom appears*
> *This Christ o' the neist thoosand years.* (139)

What Dostoevsky teaches the Drunk Man is the ability to rise
imaginatively above the most intractable obstacles. Dostoevsky, handicapped by a 'baggit wife' (139) and epilepsy (140)
nevertheless created works of genius. In the same way the

Drunk Man feels he can lift himself above the immediate environment:

> Lowsed frae the dominion
> O' popular opinion,
> And risen at last abune
> The thistle like a mune
> That looks serenely doon
> On what queer things there are
> In an inferior star
> That couldna be, or see,
> Themsel's, except in me. (141)

The Drunk Man wants to 'be free/O' my eternal me' (142); he cannot accept that his quest for individuality ends with the afterlife of theological orthodoxy though the sentence also carries the sense of a longing for liberty from an oppressive earthly identity. The Drunk Man wants to go beyond convention in order to remake himself in the spiritual image of his own country:

> Thou, Dostoevski, understood,
> Wha had your ain land in your bluid,
> And into it as in a mould
> The passion o' your bein' rolled,
> Inherited in turn frae Heaven
> Or sources fer abune it even. (144)

Simultaneously the Drunk Man is interested in emancipating Scotland from its ugly image of itself, an image determined by a history of defeatism and what the poet thinks of as English oppression. The spiritual liberation depends on Scotsmen breaking away from stereotypes, refusing to behave like drunken caricatures and aspiring to an astonishing individuality. The Drunk Man determines to do for Scotland what Dostoevsky has done for Russia:

For a' that's Scottish is in me,
As a' things Russian were in thee,
And I in turn 'ud be an action
To pit in a concrete abstraction
My country's contrair qualities,
And mak' a unity o' these
Till my love owre its history dwells,
As owretone to a peal o' bells. (145)

Dostoevsky and, to a lesser extent, Burns are examples the Drunk Man is inclined to follow as he wishes to 'let my soul increase in me'. (125) He is painfully aware of his physical mortality and there is a hint in the poem that he is not simply weary, in a state of exhaustion corresponding to the sorry state of Scotland, but actually ill. MacDiarmid, who died of cancer more than fifty years after the publication of *A Drunk Man*, uses the disease as a metaphor for cultural atrophy in 'Ex-Parte Statement on the Project of Cancer' (444–9) and suggests its pathological presence in *A Drunk Man*. In his usual rejection of urbanisation and the mindless chatter of 'maist folk', MacDiarmid contrasts his neurotic quest for the source of creativity with the robust indifference of his friends Cruivie and Gilsanquhar:

And Edinburgh and Glasgow
Are like ploomen in a pub.
They want to hear o' naething
But their ain foul hubbub. . . .

The fules are richt; an extra thocht
Is neither here nor there.
Oor lives may differ as they like
– The self-same fate we share.

And whiles I wish I'd nae mair sense
Than Cruivie and Gilsanquhar,
And envy their rude health and curse
My gnawin' canker. (108)

This 'gnawin' canker' could be pathological or psychosomatic or metaphorical; still, its existence leads the Drunk Man to moments of despair which the poet expresses through a verbal simulation of insobriety. In his essay on *A Drunk Man*, David Daiches observes that 'drunkenness serves for MacDiarmid the same purpose that the medieval poet found in the dream'. (Thistle, 106) MacDiarmid certainly enthusiastically researched the altered consciousness caused by intoxication and parts of the poem are hallucinatory in nature. One section (109–13) presents a mind on the edge of *delirium tremens*. It opens, appropriately enough, with a plea for endless boozing:

> Clear keltie aff an' fill again
> Withoot corneigh bein' cryit,
> The drink's aye best that follows a drink.
> Clear keltie aff and try it. (109)

MacDiarmid's Symbolist moon now assumes nightmarish proportions, seems like the barmaid at a Gothic bar, the Craidle-and-Coffin, (109) tempting the Drunk Man with siren signals to reproduce himself in her. MacDiarmid's metrical units are generally self-contained but by a clever use of enjambement he infers that this reproduction would be pointlessly repetitive and not the spiritual rebirth he is seeking:

> You needna fash to rax and strain.
> Carline, I'll *no'* be born again
>
> In ony brat you can produce.
> Carline, gi'e owre – O what's the use? (109)

Mechanical sex depresses the Drunk Man and, no doubt steeped in the supernatural, he remembers Tam o'Shanter's pursuit of a witch. His imagination now begins to run riot and he associates his penis with a fertile spigot on a beer barrel:

> My belly on the gantrees there,
> The spigot frae my cullage,
> And wow but how the fizzin' yill
> In spilth increased the ullage! (110)

All MacDiarmid's seminal images lead to the one notion of an upwards expression of creative force which explodes climactically like stars in a universal womb; or, anticlimactically here, like froth falling on barren ground. Developing the concept the Drunk Man imagines himself as the source of a new flood (of ale) that will wash away the world. However the world does not so easily evolve into a new Eden (110) and drink is seen as a poor spiritual substitute. In despair the Drunk Man is haunted by the persistence of the real world and begins to experience it in macabre nightmarish visions of his own imminent death:

> As the worms'll breed in my corpse until
> It's like a rice-puddin', the thistle
> Has made an eel-ark o' the lift
> Whaur elvers like skirl-in-the-pan sizzle (111)

Such morbid thoughts are unbearably depressing but the Drunk Man cannot shake them off, cannot sleep for fear of the hallucinogenic consequences. His mind, attempting to stabilise itself, is invaded with the thought of a necrophiliac embrace between corpses:

> Gin my thochts that circle like hobby-horses
> 'Udna loosen to nightmares I'd sleep;
> For nocht but a chowed core's left whaur Jerusalem lay
> Like aipples in a heap! . . .
>
> It's a queer thing to tryst wi' a wumman
> When the boss o' her body's gane,
> And her banes in the wund as she comes
> Dirl like a raff o' rain.

> It's a queer thing to tryst wi' a wumman
> When her ghaist frae abuneheid keeks,
> And you see in the licht o't that a'
> You ha'e o'r's the cleiks. . . . (112)

Appalled by this image the Drunk Man contrasts the skull-like emptiness of the earth with his own teeming mind. He longs for some relief from the darkly sinister thoughts that visit him and asks for assistance from above:

> Bite into me forever mair and lift
> Me clear o' chaos in a great relief
> Till, like this thistle in the munelicht growin',
> I brak in roses owre a hedge o' grief. . . . (113)

Recovering from his delirium the Drunk Man, now considerably more sober (and the development of the poem as a dramatic monologue is always relevant), comes back to earth to survey some recent events. His pessimism increases when he considers the failure of a heroic attempt at political renewal. Though a 'village drunk' (97) the Drunk Man's sympathies are, despite all his misgivings, with 'maist folk'. (86) He therefore recalls his joy at the prospect of a popular victory in a Ballad of the General Strike (119–22) which begins with a leaping movement:

> I saw a rose come loupin' oot
> Frae a camsteerie plant.
> O wha'd ha'e thocht yon puir stock had
> Sic an inhabitant? (119)

MacDiarmid conveys the hope of the General Strike in a soaring simile that sees the rose 'Like a ball o' fire' (120) carried upwards by the thistle. Alas, the heroic effort ends in agony and the diffidence of 'maist folk' destroys a great opportunity:

> – The thistle like a rocket soared
> And cam' doon like the stick. (121)

In the traditional ballad the rose and the briar are intertwining images denoting the survival of love after death. MacDiarmid alters the folksy implications of this convention, invests the rose-and-briar symbol with Christian connotations and produces a pictorially vivid description of the working people of Scotland pathetically acquiescing in their own crucifixion:

> The orderin' o' the thistle means
> Nae richtin' o't to them.
> Its loss they ca' a law, its thorns
> A fule's fit diadem.
>
> And still the idiot nails itsel'
> To its ain crucifix,
> While here a rose and there a rose
> Jaups oot abune the pricks.
>
> Like connoisseurs the Deils gang roond
> And praise its attitude,
> Till on the Cross the silly Christ
> To fidge fu' fain's begood! (121–2)

Such martyrdom is a central thematic issue in the poem and the Drunk Man realises that he will have to accept a measure of it if he is to transform himself. So the Drunk Man stands up for himself and Scotland and – with 'thocht o' Christ and Calvary' (122) – reaches out to grasp the thistle which is metamorphosed into a tree:

> And still the puzzle stands unsolved.
> Beauty and ugliness alike,
> And life and daith and God and man,
> Are aspects o't but nane can tell

> The secret that I'd fain find oot
> O' this bricht hive, this sorry weed,
> The tree that fills the universe,
> Or like a reistit herrin' crines.
>
> Gin I was sober I micht think
> It was like something drunk men see! (126)

Eternity, like sobriety, is slowly dawning on him. The Drunk Man remembers his 'mither's womb' and his 'Faither in heaven' (126) by way of a metaphysical prelude to another miraculous nativity. He is about to give birth to himself; or, at least, to renew himself in a spiritual dimension. His self-sacrifice is a renunciation of earthly indifference and an acknowledgment of eternity for he tells the thistle his universalist intentions:

> Thou art the facts in ilka airt
> That breenge into infinity,
> Criss-crossed wi' coontless ither facts
> Nae man can follow, and o' which
> He is himsel' a helpless pairt,
> Held in their tangle as he were
> A stick-nest in Ygdrasil! (129)

He sees that the thistle has expanded, like his consciousness. It is Ygdrasil, the 'Celtic Tree of Life' (1458): the mighty ash, the evergreen, the fountain of eternal life and immortality. It is also the tree Christ was crucified on:

> What is the tree? As fer as Man's
> Concerned it disna maitter
> Gin but a giant thistle 'tis
> That spreids eternal mischief there,
> As I'm inclined to think. (131)

The point MacDiarmid forcefully makes is that the Drunk Man *is* now 'inclined to think' and, as the poet suggested at

the beginning of the poem, it is thought that liberates man
and operates the process of evolutionary idealism:

> Juist as man's skeleton has left
> Its ancient ape-like shape ahint,
> Sae states o' mind in turn gi'e way
> To different states, and quickly seem
> Impossible to later men,
> And Man's mind in its final shape,
> Or lang'll seem a monkey's spook,
> And, strewth, to me the vera thocht
> O' Thocht already's fell like that! (131)

The Drunk Man moves to a new level of consciousness,
exists as an equal with Dostoevsky, and rises to a resurrection
in eternity:

> I tae ha'e heard Eternity drip water
> (Aye water, water!), drap by drap
> On the a'e nerve, like lichtnin', I've become,
> And heard God passin' wi' a bobby's feet
> Ootby in the lang coffin o' the street (147)

As he increases his consciousness of his rebirth he links the
earth he stands on with the eternity he aspires to. He himself
has roots, branches, and blossoms, is a tree and a thistle and
any form his imagination enables him to assume. He glows
with the terrible crystal of creativity:

> A mony-brainchin' candelabra fills
> The lift and's lowin' wi' the stars;
> The Octopus Creation is wallopin'
> In coontless faddoms o' a nameless sea.
>
> I am the candelabra, and burn
> My endless candles to an Unkent God.
> I am the mind and meanin' o' the octopus
> That thraws its empty airms through a' th'Inane.
> (147–8)

The Drunk Man's unsteady odyssey is almost over for he has found his direction and it is eternally upwards. Before he finally wins home to Jean, the Drunk Man has a vision of the Great Wheel. (157–66) Having passed from arrogant inso-briety to sober spirituality he regards the galaxy and his own light-emitting position on it. Throughout the poem the Drunk Man has been breaking away from the Scottish stereotype to become a fully developed individual. In order to make this transformational principle a precedent for all Scots he attempts a synthesis of the contradictions he has encountered. He seeks resolution and projects the problem of duality into a universal context. Earthbound man is convinced that the body is the opposite of the spirit just as truth is contrasted with beauty:

> Beauty is a'e thing, but it tines anither
> (For, fegs, they never can be f'und thegither),
> And 'twixt the twa it's no' for me to swither.
>
> As frae the grun' sae thocht frae men springs oot,
> A ferlie that tells little o' its source, I doot,
> And has nae vera fundamental root. (157)

In a cosmic context the individual is a microcosmic world tending towards a universal unity-in-diversity. Since 'Man's mind is in God's image made', (158) the individual can con-tain the universe imaginatively; by realising his own spiritual potential he makes a contribution to a national unity which leads to a global unity which merges in a universal unity. Every creative act of will is instrumental in altering the universe:

> I've often thrawn the warld frae me,
> Into the Pool o' Space, to see
> The Circles o' Infinity. (159)

Thus self-realisation is the first step to a oneness with the world and a universal union. Although art has been frequently earthbound – 'to the Earth confined' (160) – new human creations can explode ecstatically upwards and penetrate the deep space of eternity. First there must be a firm earthly foundation and the Drunk Man therefore arranges his renaissance (as MacDiarmid did) in Scotland:

> Whatever Scotland is to me,
> Be it aye pairt o' a' men see
> O' Earth and o' Eternity
>
> Wha winna hide their heids in't till
> It seems the haill o' Space to fill,
> As t'were an unsurmounted hill.
>
> He canna Scotland see wha yet
> Canna see the Infinite,
> And Scotland in true scale to it. (161–2)

Evolutionary idealism ends in universal unity and harmony. The Drunk Man, knowing this, is able to dissociate himself from the defeatist history of his country for the burden of defeat has been the cross every Scot has carried. By assuming it all the Drunk Man removes the burden and gives Scotland a new image. Ever since the obsessive study of the thistle began at the beginning of the poem the Drunk Man has been fascinated by the idea of the saviour, 'A greater Christ, a greater Burns'. (86) Now he is ready to take this challenge seriously. He will speak for Scotland as a poetic saviour though he realises that to do so is to invite martyrdom:

> *'A Scottish poet maun assume*
> *The burden o' his people's doom,*
> *And dee to brak' their livin' tomb.*
>
> *Mony ha'e tried, but a' ha'e failed.*
> *Their sacrifice has nocht availed.*
> *Upon the thistle they're impaled.'* (165)

This time the sacrifice will be worth the effort; such is the poetic conclusion the Drunk Man comes to after exhaustively exploring the spiritual and cultural map of Scotland.

There is nothing more to add and the Drunk Man ends with an image of his resurrection as a personified Silence:

> No' her, withooten shape, wha's name is Daith,
> No' Him, unkennable abies to faith
>
> – God whom, gin e'er He saw a man, 'ud be
> E'en mair dumfooner'd at the sicht than he
>
> – But Him, whom nocht in man or Deity,
> Or Daith or Dreid or Laneliness can touch,
> *Wha's deed owre often and has seen owre much.* (167)

He is the evolutionary ideal, the creative spirit, the source of poetry and is eternally renewed though he has 'deed owre often and has seen owre much' even since he appeared earlier in the poem as 'A man that deed or I was born'. (103) The Drunk Man has achieved the ineffable and finally turns to Jean who, the voice of the eternally feminine principle of creativity, speaks for the first and last time in the poem:

> O I ha'e Silence left,
>
>   – 'And weel ye micht,'
> Sae Jean'll say, 'efter sic a nicht!' (167)

Resurrection, rebirth, renaissance all come together in MacDiarmid's great work which is both universal in theme and insistently Scottish in origin:

> The thistle rises and forever will,
> Getherin' the generations under't.
> This is the monument o' a' they were,
> And a' they hoped and wondered. (152)

Chapter Four

FRAE BATTLES, MAIR THAN BALLADS

Reivers to weavers and to me. Weird way!
Yet in the last analysis I've sprung
Frae battles, mair than ballads
    'Kinsfolk' (1150)

In 1929 MacDiarmid exchanged the comparative security he
enjoyed in Montrose for the bigger opportunities he thought
would be available in London. He felt it was time for a
change. His wife Peggy did not care for the smalltown atmosphere of Montrose and MacDiarmid thought the job Compton Mackenzie offered him as editor of the radio magazine
Vox promised a big financial improvement on his position
and, moreover, represented a worthwhile journalistic challenge. He had come to feel that conditions in Montrose were
no longer in his creative interests; that, at any rate, is the way
he portrayed the situation in *To Circumjack Cencrastus* (1930),
the long poem that was planned as a worthy successor to *A
Drunk Man*. Unfortunately it was nothing of the kind. In *A
Drunk Man*, as we have seen, MacDiarmid portrayed the
thistle-crucified Scot rising to resurrection – in Montrose,
coincidentally – as 'A greater Christ, a greater Burns'. (86)
In *Cencrastus* the saviour-poet has too many local difficulties
and virtually acknowledges defeat:

Thrang o' ideas that like fairy gowd
'll leave me the 'Review' reporter still
Waukenin' to my clung-kite faimly on a hill

O' useless croftin' whaur naething's growed
But Daith, sin Christ for an idea died
On a gey similar but less heich hillside.
Ech, weel for Christ: for he was never wed
And had nae weans clamourin' to be fed! (237)

MacDiarmid exhibits a defeatist despair throughout the poem. At one point he recalls the noble theme of *A Drunk Man*:

> For freedom means that a lad or lass,
>   In Cupar or elsewhaur yet
> May alter the haill o' human thocht
>   Mair than Christ's altered it. (257)

In this poem, however, he rejects the idea as being unattainable in modern Scotland:

> A'e thing's certain: Christ's Second Comin'
> 'll no' be to Scotland whaurever it is. (258)

In the circumstances MacDiarmid could no longer believe in himself as the bearer of an evolutionary idealism. From the internal evidence of *Cencrastus*, which is full of bitter complaints, it is obvious that MacDiarmid was going through a difficult and disturbing period. Francis George Scott was summoned to Montrose to set the seal of approval on *Cencrastus* but could not respond as before:

Christopher's next call for a visit was before the *Cencrastus* MS was sent off to Blackwood's. Again I went through to Montrose but he was very disappointed that I couldn't give my approval of the poem and he was still more disappointed when the MS was returned to him. I know that for some time after this he was very unsettled and gladly went off to London to assist Compton Mackenzie in running . . . *Vox*, pottered on the *Cencrastus* MS for a few months and it finally appeared in 1930, but

Blackwood's dropped him, I fancy after completing the contract, and when he wrote me from London enclosing the book, he asked me never to discuss it with him.[1]

From this epistolary record it seems that *Cencrastus* was given its final form in London which might account for the virulence of the passages concerning the hopelessness of contemporary Scotland. Certainly 1929 was a bad year. MacDiarmid's marriage was disintegrating, *Vox* collapsed through under-capitalisation, and in December MacDiarmid sustained severe concussion falling from the top of a London double-decker bus. The poet's personal misfortunes insinuate themselves into the poem:

> Even my wife whiles fails to see
> – And wha can blame her? Fegs no' me! –
> What ails me that I canna win
> Wi' a' my brains the comfortin'
> Security that maist folk hae
> (*Folk in oor station, that's to say*)
> But aye on ruin's brink maun away,
> And risk her and the bairns tae
> – It's no' as if I could be shair
> My verse at last'll be worth mair. . . (251)

MacDiarmid is not being entirely facetious in these lines; his doubts were deeply felt and his distress over the breakdown of his family life was profound.

Whereas *A Drunk Man* is triumphant, *Cencrastus* is defeatist. This is revealed in the hit-and-miss structure of the poem and the inability to aim at a rich central symbol. In *A Drunk Man* the symbol of the thistle integrates all the incidental elements; in *Cencrastus* the symbol only occasionally rises to the surface as a loose point of reference. *To Circumjack Cencrastus* is not a meditative poem with a visionary basis; it is an autobiographical essay in verse on the difficulty of being a serious poet in a Philistine Scotland. Writing under the pseudonym 'Pteleon'

MacDiarmid drew attention, in *The Scots Observer* of 1930, to the abusiveness of the poem:

> it is impossible to condone an Ishmaelitism which has its hand against everybody . . . Knox, Burns, Lord Rosebery, Neil Munro, Sir Harry Lauder, Will Fyffe, J. J. Bell, Dr Lauchlan Maclean Watt, are only a few of the targets of his wholesale abuse. (Uncanny, 135)

Half a century later it is difficult to see why MacDiarmid bothered with some of his enemies but the hitlist suggests the pettiness that disfigures *Cencrastus*. The defeatist tone vitiates the verse overall, so that brilliant setpieces are separated by passages that simply mark time and fill space with ephemeral affairs and expressions of spite. MacDiarmid even descends, in places, to the level of the Scots he attacks. He shows, for example, a love of childish puns: he speaks of 'A tea-change into something rich and Scots', (239) relates 'anglin'-mania' to 'anglo-mania' (256) and plays with the aural similarity of 'Bourbons and baboons'. (258)

It would be a mistake, however, to dismiss *Cencrastus* as a total failure; the problem is the indifferent execution of an inspired concept. When the autonomous items incorporated into the poem are considered out of the context of *Cencrastus* they take their place among the finest things MacDiarmid published. 'The Parrot Cry' (192–4) is a strong satire on the 'auld, auld story' of the supposed benefits of parliamentary Union; the adaptation of Rilke's Requiem for Paula Modersohn-Becker (197–202) is a sublime piece of translation, probably MacDiarmid's finest stretch of sustained writing in English; the reprinted 'A Moment in Eternity' (276–81) is worthy of inclusion in any book; the quatrains beginning 'I'm the original/Plasm o' the ocean' (242) exude good humour; and the lyric 'Lourd on my hert' (204–5) is one of MacDiarmid's poignant meditations on the darkness Scotland imposes on its citizens. Compressed into three stanzas is the poetic vision of the light that eludes the majority ('a' the stupid folk'), the notion of the Platonic dream which MacDiarmid connects with the Gaelic 'Brightness o' Brightness',

(224), and (emphasising the metaphysical pattern) the physical reality of a bleak Scottish winter:

> *Nae wonder if I think I see*
> *A lichter shadow than the neist*
> *I'm fain to cry: 'The dawn, the dawn!*
> *I see it brakin' in the East.'*
> > *But ah*
> > *– It's juist mair snaw!* (205)

MacDiarmid condenses a whole cluster of concepts into these
lines. As, in fact, he invariably does when in full possession
of his poetic faculties, something that only happens intermit-
tently throughout *Cencrastus*.

MacDiarmid is unable to concentrate on the symbolism or
theme of his poem because of personal matters. So the poem
falls into name-calling, diatribes against the indifference of
'maist folk' (*passim*), 'the foul mob', (285) 'the mass o' men'.
(287) When the spite is particularised the victim is liable to
be a caricature like MacDiarmid's portrait of the man who
employed him to produce *The Montrose Review*:

> Curse his new hoose, his business, his cigar,
> His wireless set, and motor car
> Alsatian, gauntlet gloves, plus fours and wife,
> – A'thing included in his life;
> And, abune a', his herty laughter,
> And – if he has yin – his hereafter. (235)

Against that we can set the retrospective irony of the complaint MacDiarmid makes in the following lines:

> Losh! They'd ha' put me a brass plate up
> In Langholm Academy,
> And asked me to tak' the chair
> At mony a London Scots spree.
> They'd a' gien me my portrait in oils
> By Henry Kerr, and the LL.D.,

And my wife and weans 'ud been as weel aff
As gin I'd been a dominie,

    If I'd only had hokum, hokum,
      Juist a wee thing common hokum! (253)

There are plaques marking MacDiarmid's home in the Library Buildings in Langholm and his place of work with *The Montrose Review* in Montrose; his portrait, commissioned by the Scottish National Portrait Gallery, was executed in oils by R. H. Westwater, R.S.A.; and Edinburgh University awarded him the LL.D. In 1929, when he wrote those lines lamenting his lack of hokum, MacDiarmid felt intolerably isolated and neglected. As *A Drunk Man* shows he was prepared for a grand spiritual martyrdom; what he could not accept was being made to suffer by petty economic circumstances.

The Drunk Man can always sober up to his serious theme so that the asides are always relevant; in *Cencrastus* MacDiarmid makes so much of his personal predicament (lack of money, lack of prospects, lack of hokum) that there is no metamorphosis of himself into a transfigured individual. Instead the poet is reduced to mocking his earlier aspirations and portraying himself as a ridiculous figure:

Noo in synoptic lines
A Scot becomes a God
– A God in Murray tartan
To whom nae star's abroad. . .

He looks wi' equal een
On a'thing deid and livin'
His bauchles in the Zeitgeist,
His bonnet cocked in Heaven! . . . (246)

That self-disparagement is just not MacDiarmid's style, artistic or otherwise. In *A Drunk Man* he had articulated the deliberately blasphemous (and Nietzschean) notion of himself as a spiritual redeemer; in *Cencrastus* he dropped from the eternally sublime to the occasionally ridiculous. The title of *To Circumjack Cencrastus* can be translated, with the aid of Jamieson, as 'to square the circle' but the erratic performance of the poet makes the poem too one-sided to be truly paradoxical. The MacDiarmidian metaphysic depends on bringing abstract ideas down to earth and allowing earthbound ideals to soar; in *Cencrastus* the poet never really squares up to his subject and the overall effect is confused.

Cutting across the spurious element in *Cencrastus* it is possible to admire the idea that activated the poem. MacDiarmid began by synthesising a classical Celtic image with an Edenic memory of Langholm. In Celtic art the serpent swallowing its tail is a symbol of eternity; in choosing it, therefore, MacDiarmid continued his quest for universal unity and did so with reference to a culture he increasingly accepted as his own. MacDiarmid wants to substitute for the Drunk Man's Scottish paradise regained an image of 'Gaeldom regained'. (188) The pantheon of *Cencrastus* comprises Gaelic poets – Aodhagán Ó Rathaille (224) with his vision of 'the Brightness o' Brightness', Alasdair MacMhaighstir Alasdair (209–12) with his 'endless ecstasies', Mary Macleod (256–8) with 'a new sang in her mooth' – who, collectively, take the place Dostoevsky occupied in *A Drunk Man*. MacDiarmid seems dissatisfied with the vulgarity of dialect Scots and with the impurity of Synthetic Scots and longs to forge a linguistic link with the great Gaelic poets:

> *O wad at least my yokel words*
> *Some Gaelic strain had kept* (225)

Although *Cencrastus* contains two lyrics – 'There's owre mony killywimples' (250) and the four stanzas beginning 'At dawn at the heid o' Clais Linneach' (209–10) – which were contributed to a book of tributes to Mrs Marjory Kennedy-Fraser,[2] MacDiarmid is determined to dissociate his Gaelic Idea from the nostalgic notion of the Celtic Twilight:

It's no Missus Kennedy Fraser's sangs,
A' verra weel for Sasunnachs and seals,
That'll voice the feelin's movin' amang's
To whom the sicht as to men appeals.
Let's hear nae mair o' Tir nan Og
Or the British Empire! See the fog
Is liftin' at last, and Scotland's gien,
Nae bletherin' banshee's, but Europe's een... (223)

What MacDiarmid wants is a 'dynamic myth' that will do
for Scottish literature what the Russian Idea did for Dostoevsky and he feels that 'Only in Gaeldom can there be the
necessary counter-idea to the Russian idea ... the Gaelic
commonwealth with its aristocratic culture – the high place
it gave to its poets and scholars.' (SE, 67) Much of Mac-
Diarmid's poetry has a cerebral conception as a consequence
of some *ad hoc* theory and when he is inspired the poetry soars
above the theory. At pedestrian moments the poetry fails to
materialise and only the theory remains which is why the
Gaelic Idea, as presented in *Cencrastus*, is so mechanical and
mundane:

> If we turn to Europe and see
> Hoo the emergence o' the Russian Idea's
> Broken the balance o' the North and Sooth
> And needs a coonter that can only be
> The Gaelic Idea
> To mak' a parallelogram o' forces,
> Complete the Defence o' the West,
> And end the English betrayal o' Europe.
> (Time eneuch then to seek the Omnific Word
> In Jamieson yet.
> Or the new Dictionary in the makin' noo,
> Or coin it oorsels!) (222–3)

In *A Drunk Man* the idea of eternity gradually dawns on the
individual; in *Cencrastus* it is more readily available to those

who are touched by the serpent in the service of the Gaelic Idea.

The symbol of the serpent had other connotations for Mac-Diarmid whose childhood in Langholm frequently led him to a serpentine path called The Curly Snake which he had good cause to remember as 'It has always haunted my imagination and has probably constituted itself the ground-plan and pattern of my mind.'³ Significantly, *Cencrastus* is subtitled The Curly Snake. Cencrastus was therefore pictured as a Celtic serpent familiar with Langholm which is invoked in the poem through the obligatory mention of 'the Muckle Toon' (216), the description of gathering hines in the Langfall (271) and the reference to 'Tree-trunks, sheep, bee skeps and the like/ On the bible-black Esk' (283). Just as the knowledge of the serpent cast Adam out of Eden, so MacDiarmid has been expelled from Langholm into his miserable state of domestic martyrdom:

> Up to the een in debt I stand
> My haill life built on shiftin' sand
> And feel the filthy grit gang grindin'
> Into my brain's maist delicate windin'.
> And gin a' Thocht at sicna time
> Is present to me what's the use?
> It's bad eneuch to droon in slime
> And no' rive a' Eternity loose (252)

Cencrastus, in MacDiarmid's poem, becomes a symbol of the will. It is the poet's contention that the feminine and masculine principles of creation are represented by the receptive ocean and the penetrating snake. In a single stanza, almost lost in the massive expanse of the poem, MacDiarmid explores this concept with perception:

> An image o' the sea lies underneath
> A' men's imaginations – the sea in which
> A' life was born and that cradled us until
> We cam' to birth's maturity. Its waves bewitch

Us still or wi' their lure o' peacefu' gleamin'
Or hungrily in storm and darkness streamin'.
The imagination has anither poo'er – the snake,
He who beats up the waters into storm
Wha's touch electrifies us into action;
In th' abyss o' their origin, their basic form,
A' oor imaginations partake
O' ane or th'ither – the sea or the snake. (289–90)

By the time this thematic exposition appears, at the end of
the poem, the central symbol has been almost forgotten. Mac-
Diarmid moves towards his conclusion slowly but in doing so
he does not convincingly come to terms with the serpent that
lies coiled intestine-like inside him. If he is a man invaded by
the serpent he seems hardly aware of it and, instead, anxious
to apportion blame to nameless Scots:

> *The way that maist men think*
> *And feel's beneath contempt*
> *And frae a' that seems established*
> *We canna be owre quick exempt* (221)

Against the apathy of 'maist men' MacDiarmid sets his
evolutionary idealism which has now acquired an economic
programme. He feels that economic reorganisation can be
easily achieved through Social Credit:

> I'm oot for shorter oors and higher pay
> And better conditions for a' workin' folk
> But ken the hellish state in which they live's
> Due maistly to their ain mob cowardice.
> Yet tho' a' men were millionaires the morn
> As they could easily be
> They'd be nae better than maist rich folk noo
> And nocht that maitters much 'ud be improved
> And micht be waur. (228–9)

Politics, as ever, is only a means to MacDiarmid's great

spiritual end. The quest is for the fully evolved individual aspiring towards eternity and uttering the Gaelic Idea in a 'truly classical' (261) form. Encouraged to preach his evolutionary gospel by the realisation that 'Maist men are prehistoric still!' (268) and that 'Christianity's . . . no' been tried' (260) MacDiarmid reinstates his vision of universal unity. It is not an easy doctrine as the poet's exclamation 'To hell wi' happiness!' (281) recognises – but it claims to lift man out of his original element into an appreciation of eternity:

> Up frae the slime, that a' but a handfu' o' men
> Are grey wi' still. There's nae trace o't in you.
> Clear withoot sediment. Day withoot nicht.
> A' men's institutions and maist men's thochts
> Are tryin' for aye to bring to an end
> The insatiable thocht, the beautiful violent will,
> The restless spirit of Man, the theme o' my sang (285)

Still, the flaws in *Cencrastus* coincided with the cracks in MacDiarmid's personal life and if he was to write his way out of the impasse he would have to begin again.

In building his poetry on the basis of a cerebral conception (which required an emotional matrix in order to give birth to a great poem) MacDiarmid ran the risk of using so many ideas and secondary sources that concepts neither collided provocatively nor coalesced creatively but simply resisted integration into the intellectual vision. When that happened the reader was offered only vicarious ideas and derivative fragments and both occur in *Cencrastus*. MacDiarmid's poetry, which needs both cerebration and celebration, had moved too far in the speculative direction and he needed an emotional renewal. He had literally lost his sense of direction when *Cencrastus* appeared; he was in England in pursuit of a career when clearly he wanted to be in Scotland in search of an ideal. In *Cencrastus* he had announced the Gaelic Idea which placed him in a predicament for if the poetry of the future was to be written in Gaelic then MacDiarmid would be a prophet though not a participant. He was showing some signs of impatience with Synthetic Scots and *Cencrastus* alternates that idiom with eloquent English and racy colloquial Scots. As a poet MacDiarmid needed a basic idea he could articulate with enthusiasm and he realised this would mean an imaginative return to Langholm.

Having failed, albeit honourably, in *Cencrastus* MacDiarmid was particularly anxious to explore a theme big enough to contain all the poems that continued to pour out of him. He still wanted to avoid any suggestion that his talent was primarily lyrical and he hoped to write something monumental, something that would convey the philosophical size and referential range of his Scottish vision. In this spirit he conceived a poem with the collective title *Clann Albann*. The scope of the new project surfaced when, in the *Modern Scot* of July 1931, MacDiarmid published (under the title 'From Work in Progress') the poem 'Kinsfolk'. This is both a tribute to the beauty of MacDiarmid's native place and an honest appraisal of his personal position. The poem is written in a six-line stanza rhyming *abcbdd* concluding with a couplet containing a long and short line. Each stanza operates as a paragraph, with a premiss and an argumentative advance. Such stanzaic autonomy is perhaps the poet's way of granting independence to small notions, for this is poetry that progresses gradually and not explosively in the manner of *A Drunk Man*. It is meditative poetry and shows MacDiarmid in a seriously reflective mood.

'Kinsfolk' was written in Liverpool (as the fifteenth stanza reveals) where MacDiarmid was working after his separation from his wife Peggy and his children Christine and Walter. Psychologically it was a wretched time for the poet who looked personal failure in the face and attracted bitter hostility on account of *Cencrastus* (though Edwin Muir praised the poem's occasional brilliance and power). In an essay published in 1931 MacDiarmid acknowledged his need to return to the emotional source of his poetry, the Muckle Toon of Langholm:

In all my published poetry there is, I think, but one lyric

in *A Drunk Man* and a few lines of allusion in *To Circumjack Cencrastus* devoted to [Langholm]. And yet, within the past year or two I have found myself increasingly caught up in happy recollections of it and speculations as to what divided me so early and so completely from all the tastes and tendencies of my relatives and other early friends. One of the main reasons for this, probably, is the fact that my own children are domiciled in London [so] it is not for myself that I crave any renewed experience of its delights, but for my children, whose city-sted lives seem to me attenuated and glamourless in comparison. I would have their lives enriched by a similar colourful and diverse contact with nature [though] if I ever go 'out of the world and into Langholm' again, it will only be in dreams or in my poet's craft in which, perchance, I may yet find words for some of the felicities I remember and to which (despite all my subsequent divergence of interest and effort) the texture of my spirit must owe incomparably more than I can ever repay or acknowledge. (SE, 53–5)

'Kinsfolk' shows MacDiarmid in the process of repossessing Langholm in his poetry. It is, of course, the Eden he has been ejected from but it is also a community he was once glad to belong to. What MacDiarmid wants to explore is the distinctive quality that separates him from his fellow men for he is aware of how special he is and wants to know in what way his uniqueness relates to his immediate ancestors and his offspring:

> Foreseein' in Christine's or in Walter's mind
> A picture o' mysel' as in my ain
> My mither rises or I rise in hers
> Incredible as to a Martian brain
> A cratur' o' this star o' oors micht be
>   It had nae point o' contact wi'.

Daith in my faither's case. I ha'e his build,
His energy, but no' his raven hair,
Rude cheeks, clear een. I am whey-faced. My een
Ha'e dark rings roon' them and my pow is fair.
A laddie when he dee'd, I kent little o'm and he
      Kent less o' me. (1148)

MacDiarmid's evolutionary ideal owes more to Lamarck
and Nietzsche than to Darwin and Spencer; the poet, as
creative force of nature, employs his strength of will before he
accepts the consequences of a genetic inheritance. At the same
time MacDiarmid grants that the poet is partly the product
of an environment, an especially important factor when there
exists a uniquely inspirational location such as Langholm.
With its 'maze/O' waters' (314) Langholm confronts the native with reminders of man's original element; with its pro-
fusion of natural beauty it evokes Eden. The Langholmite
who is also a poet is therefore able to overcome blind instinct
and organise his own ecstasy by an act of will:

    To mind and body I ha' nae sic clue,
    A water flowin' frae an unkent source
    Wellin' up in me to catch the licht at last
    At this late break in its hidden course,
    Yet my blin' instincts nurtured in the dark
        Sing sunwards like the lark. (1150)

When 'Kinsfolk' appeared in *The Modern Scot* a note placed
it in the context of a large work in progress:

['Kinsfolk' comprises] the first few stanzas of Part I of
Mr M'Diarmid's big new poem, 'Clan Albann,' the
complete scheme of which is as follows: – Dedicatory
Poem, Prologue; Part I. The Muckle Toon, First
Interlude; Part II. Fier Comme un Ecossais, Second
Interlude; Part III. Demidium Anima Meae, Third
Interlude; Part IV. The Uncanny Scot, Fourth Interlude;
Part V. With a Lifting of the Head, Epilogue.[4]

This was to be an even bigger project than *A Drunk Man* or *Cencrastus*. MacDiarmid's next three collections of poetry were projected as parts of *Clan Albann* since a note to *Scots Unbound and Other Poems* (1932) explained that:

> The poems in this volume, like those in my *First Hymn to Lenin and Other Poems* (Unicorn Press, 1931) and *Second Hymn to Lenin* (Valda Trevlyn, Thakeham, 1932) are separable items from the first volume of my long poem 'Clann Albann' now in preparation.[5]

As it survives *The Muckle Toon* sequence – that is, the first volume of *Clan Albann* – consists of *First Hymn to Lenin and Other Poems* (1931), *Second Hymn to Lenin* (1932), *Scots Unbound and Other Poems* (1932), 'Envoi: On Coming Home' from *Scottish Scene* (1934) and such poems as 'By Wauchopeside' and 'Whuchulls' collected in *A Lap of Honour* (1967) and 'Bracken Hills in Autumn' collected in *Selected Poems* (1970). Seen as a small part of this grand plan the 'First Hymn to Lenin' justifies the wilful idiosyncrasy of the oxymoronic title since Lenin is one of many figures from the pantheon to be introduced in a poem that is 'a study in the evolution of my mentality and development as a poet, and, in particular, my knowledge of and attitude towards Scotland.'[6] MacDiarmid's 'First Hymn to Lenin' is not, then, a political poster-poem like the didactic slogans Mayakovsky wrote in the white heat of the Russian Revolution. Instead MacDiarmid sees political change as a practical necessity to be entrusted to a strategist such as Lenin who can sweep away political and economic problems and leave the poet, as custodian of creativity, to establish the spiritual shape of the new society. Poetry is to be respected as the verbal embodiment of the creative source which is a mightier matter than politics. 'First Hymn to Lenin' is not, despite its title, a poem a theoretical Marxist could endorse. Discussing all three Hymns to Lenin, the Marxist critic David Craig wrote:

> If we consider MacDiarmid as a Communist and a Communist poet, some very odd things come to light

even in the 'Hymns to Lenin'. In the 'Second Hymn'
MacDiarmid confides to Lenin that 'politics is bairns'
play' to what poetry must be – a claim difficult to
reconcile with responsible Communism. . . . Again, in the
finely outspoken lyric from the 'Hymn', 'Oh, it's
nonsense, nonsense, nonsense' [the simple assertions
suggest that] the poet here is no Marxist, no historical
materialist. He is using Marxism to license an almost
maniacal wish to escape from the necessities of existence
as we know it. In the 'Third Hymn' [the claim that
'thought is reality – and thought alone'] is the most
arrant idealism – treating the mental processes that
depend on material existence as somehow higher than it,
more 'real'. It is what the great thinkers in the Marxist-
Leninist tradition have specifically fought against time
and again. (Festschrift, 95–6)

That is an interesting example of MacDiarmid's ability to
evade classification: his nationalism offends nationalists, his
Marxism appals Marxists. Once again we realise that Mac-
Diarmid selfconsciously thought of himself as a being individual enough to soar above any orthodoxy.

With an irony typical of MacDiarmid, 'First Hymn to
Lenin' is dedicated to a Russian prince, D. S. Mirsky. It
follows the stanzaic pattern of 'Kinsfolk' and this *abcbdd*
format was obviously earmarked by the poet as the Muckle
Toon Stanza since its shape is imposed on many of the poems
in the sequence. Always attracted to radicalism, MacDiarmid
sought in Communism a political equivalent of what he held
literature to be, namely (in Hardy's declaration) 'the written
expression of revolt against accepted things.' (LP, 67) Communism, to the poet, is a mercifully rapid method of settling
political issues and abruptly bringing into operation the classless society. It is not an end in itself; merely a means to an
end. The poet has (so the poem suggests) little time for
day-to-day politics and even less for the limitations of the
proletariat; 'Maist men' (298) are moronic and thus unfit for
poetry. MacDiarmid is not at all concerned with niceties like

Lenin's New Economic Policy and was, in fact, glad to call himself a Marxist while enthusiastically accepting C. H. Douglas's Social Credit system. It is an important part of MacDiarmid's nature to display impatience with theoretical details and when he mentions political ideology he is always liable to colour it with a remark as apparently incongruous as his statement that 'I entirely agree with Pound on economics.' (Conversation, [22]) He joined the Communist Party in 1934, was expelled in 1937, then reinstated only to be expelled again in 1938 and then he rejoined in 1956 when other intellectuals were leaving in protest against the Russian invasion of Hungary. He insisted that 'I totally lack – and detest – the Puritanism that goes with most so-called Communism or Socialism' (LP, 239) and felt that 'Communism is a stage on the way to Anarchism – a necessary and indispensable stage; the only entrance to the promised land.' (LP, 67) That reference to the promised land is apposite: Communism, to MacDiarmid, is ultimately idealistic. It promises to deliver the future in a revolutionary instant. Norman Mac-Caig, one of MacDiarmid's closest friends, has said (in conversation) that the poet's Communism was not so much an ideology as a convenient mythology, something as mythical as Yeats's gyres or Graves's White Moon Goddess. Mac-Diarmid's hagiographical regard for Lenin centred on the Russian's strategic brilliance; he was a man with the vision to be 'A greater Christ, a greater Burns' (86) and with the organisational ability to bring the vision into sharp focus so that the plan could be implemented. In his prosaic references to Lenin MacDiarmid emphasised the Russian's intellectual credentials and cited his remark that the Communist is 'a mere bluffer, if he has not worked over in his consciousness the whole inheritance of human knowledge.' (LP, 153)

After comparing Lenin's stature to lesser men MacDiarmid is anxious to categorise the Russian as a greater Christ:

> Christ's cited no' by chance or juist because
> You mark the greatest turnin'-point since him
> But that your main redress has lain where he's

Least use – fulfillin' his sayin' lang kept dim
That whasae followed him things o' like natur'
    'Ud dae – and greater! (297)

This greater Christ is equipped with the means to work miracles on a massive scale. According to MacDiarmid Lenin
the miracle-worker has an imagination similar to that of
nameless oral poets; as the ballad singers articulated the voice
of the people, so Lenin announces the aspirations of the mob.
Lenin has a duty to act in the name of artistic integrity and
an evolutionary obligation to lift men from their present stage
of infantilism and force them to face the future in one revolutionary moment. This task is so urgent that it transcends
narrow morality. Lenin is to deliver mankind to the future
which will, in turn, be shaped as a spiritual end by the poetic
imagination. And this spiritual end justifies any political
means, or so MacDiarmid argues in a stanza whose savagery
is unmatched by anything in Western poetry at that period:

As necessary, and insignificant, as death
Wi' a' its agonies in the cosmos still
The Cheka's horrors are in their degree;
And'll end suner! What maitters't wha we kill
To lessen that foulest murder that deprives
    Maist men o' real lives? (298)

To find a precedent for such poetic ferocity it is necessary to
go back to one of MacDiarmid's favourite poets, Milton,
whose sonnet 'On the late Massacre in Piedmont' calls on the
vengeance of God in much the same way as MacDiarmid
invokes the ruthlessness of Lenin. What MacDiarmid admires
in Lenin is his apparent grasp of the future, the swift con-
spirational mind exhibited in *What Is To Be Done?* (1902). He
is able to impose his 'real will' on 'the crood' (299) at a
crucial moment in history.

It is MacDiarmid's intention, in other poems in this sequence, to project himself as a biological and spiritual advance on Lenin; to show how he, the poet, has evolved into

a unique individual in touch with the ultimate source of creativity. Using the Muckle Toon Stanza in 'Prayer for a Second Flood', 'Charisma and My Relatives', 'The Burning Passion', and 'Water of Life', MacDiarmid meditates on the quality of life glimpsed in Langholm with its ubiquitous trinity of rivers. 'Prayer for a Second Flood' is a comic account of a divine downpour in the little town. In this poem Mac-Diarmid's chosen enemies are the Unco Guid, the hypocrites who pay lip service to a God whose spirit is far above them. Just as MacDiarmid seriously expects Lenin to impose his will on 'the crood' (299) so he, jokingly, wants God to take his revenge in a flood that will flush hypocrisy away. Mac-Diarmid's chummy familiarity with God imparts a lively linguistic exuberance to the poem:

> O arselins wi' them! Whummle them again!
> Coup them heels-owre-gowdy in a storm sae gundy
> That mony a lang fog-theekit face I ken
> 'll be sooked richt doon under through a cundy
> In the High Street, afore you get weel-sterted
>   And are still hauf-herted!

> Then flush the world in earnest. Let yoursel' gang,
> Scour't to the bones, and mak' its marrow holes
> Toom as a whistle as they used to be
> In days I mind o' ere men fidged wi' souls,
> But naething had forgotten you as yet,
>   Nor you forgotten it. (300)

In a more earnest mood 'Charisma and My Relatives' recalls the proverbial Border spirit and how it has, ironically, given rise to a poet whose belligerent quality seems out of place in the modern Borders where MacDiarmid is 'a man sae shunned'. (302) The poet as a man alone is the subject of 'The Burning Passion' which considers the obligations imposed on poetic genius. Without false modesty, MacDiarmid considers how arbitrary the birth of genius appears and looks forward to a day when evolutionary idealism is attainable on earth and the genius (such as himself) does not have to work his way upwards from a culturally backward base:

> Juist as frae ony couple genius springs,
> There is nae tellin' save wi' folk owre auld
> Or impotent. The stupidest pair on earth
> Are still as likely to strike in the blin'fauld
> Maze o' manseed upon the vital spark
>   As folk o' merit, means, or mark.

> Wanted a technique for genius! Or, at least,
> A means whereby a' genius yet has done
> 'll be the stertin' point o' a' men's lives,
> No' zero, as if life had scarce begun,
> But to owrecome this death sae faur ben in
>   Maist folk needs the full floo'er o' Lenin. (305)

There is a disinterested quality, an artistic integrity, in such verse. In projecting himself as an evolutionary miracle, a cultural superman, MacDiarmid is not idly flattering himself but drawing attention to his status as a specimen of creative evolution. What one Langholmite can do, MacDiarmid implies, all men can do by superhuman effort of will. 'Water of Life', the longest and last poem in *First Hymn to Lenin and Other Poems*, brings the poet's evolutionary idealism to bear on the concept of man as a being caught 'twixt sun and slime'. (316) The poem therefore takes up some of the themes sounded by the watery environment of Langholm. Looking at a woman (MacDiarmid reflects) reminds the poet of the biological genesis of each man as a foetus in the amniotic fluid. Cradled in the watery womb and raised in a town where three rivers meet the poet feels amphibious, a man equally at home in any element. Coincidentally this leads him to an allusion 'Frae Sodom or Gomorrah wi' yon Eastern whore' (315) and a description of an intense affair. As always with MacDiarmid's imagery sexual passion is treated as a biological expression of creativity. Similarly the inevitability

[141]

of physical death should be seen as the basis of a consideration of spiritual immortality:

> A man never faced wi' death kens nocht o' life.
> But a' men are? But micht as weel no' be!
> The ancient memory is alive to few
> And fewer when it is ken what they see,
> But them that dae fear neither life nor death,
> > Mindin' them baith. (315)

Rising (literally) to his theme MacDiarmid considers the variety of life, catalogues some key contraries – 'vice and innocence, peace and war,/Culture and ignorance, humility and pride' (316) – and raises the Blakean possibility that there is an infinity in each drop of water

> > aye, and ilka drap a world
> > Bigger than a' Mankind has yet unfurled. (317)

At this critical stage MacDiarmid departs from the Muckle Toon Stanza and introduces some quatrains dedicated to the life force and its eternally upward direction

> *And aye the force that's brocht life up*
> *Frae chaos to the present stage*
> *Creates new states as ill for us*
> *As oors for eels to gauge.* (317)

Such evolutionary speculation is put aside for the moment by an abrupt MacDiarmidian return to the everyday reality of life as it is lived in the Muckle Toon with its Factory Gullets, Skipper's Pool and The Buck and Croon Hotels where the most familiar liquid is contained in a measure of whisky, 'A wee hauf wi' the emphasis on the wee' (318). In this poem the poet describes an evolutionary arc that begins in Langholm, shoots upward towards the evolutionary ideal, then comes back to earth in the Muckle Toon which is liquid enough to remind the poet of the oceanic origins of life.

The shorter poems in *First Hymn to Lenin and Other Poems*
are also connected to the overall thematic obsession with
evolutionary idealism. 'At My Father's Grave' describes, in
stately lines, what quality of mind separates the poet from his
father who lies buried in the earth of Langholm; 'It is my
mind, nae son o' yours' (299). It is part of MacDiarmid's
general argument that, though physical characteristics can be
transmitted from father to son, creative evolution is a matter
of will:

> A livin' man upon a deid man thinks
> And ony sma'er thocht's impossible. (299)

'Museum Piece' turns to the maternal influence and claims
that the creation of poetry is a more responsible task than the
routine reproduction of a child because 'Poetry bears mair
than the womb'. (300). Some anecdotal interludes show Mac-
Diarmid shaking off the influences he was exposed to as a
child in Langholm: in 'Pedigree' he chooses his own outrageous Border ancestors, in 'Religion and Love' and 'The
Church of My Fathers' he dismisses the local kirk as inimical
to the spirit of Christ, in 'The Prostitute' he lifts up the
proverbially fallen woman, and in 'Country Folk' he comments on the low expectation of the locals he knew as a child.

In three related poems – 'The Hole in the Wall', 'Another
Turn of the Screw', 'The Seamless Garment' – the poet mo-
mentarily drops his poetic elitism in an attempt to appeal to
his fellow Borderers on a popular level. Though, he contends
in 'The Hole in the Wall', the individual can transcend his
physical features, there is also a collective concern that sur-
passes any individual effort:

> Individual glory is little.
> We're sodgers. Let each
> Dae his duty, not care wha makes
> – Sae lang as it's made – the breach. (309)

That goes against the grain of all MacDiarmid's expressions

of evolutionary idealism and it is apparent that the poet is
making a conscious effort to write in a popular easily accessible manner. 'Another Turn of the Screw' is an internal
dialogue on poetic courage which prepares the reader for 'The
Seamless Garment' where, in an uncharacteristically patient
mood, the poet offers a simplified statement of his beliefs. In
spelling out the Leninist (or, rather, MacDiarmidian) message to a cousin working in a Langholm mill, the poet poses
as a homely expositor of important ideas. Although this role
is not really suited to MacDiarmid's personality, the integration of weaving imagery into the texture of the poem is impressive since metaphorical density is a rather rare and
neglected technique in modernist poetry. What makes the
poem such an unusual item in this poet's repertoire is the
willingness to acknowledge an area of ignorance. The poet
who so frequently and confidently quotes Rilke's statement
that 'the poet must know everything' (LP, 67) humbly defers
to the practical expertise of the millworker:

> The haill shop's dumfoonderin'
>> To a stranger like me.
> Second nature to you; you're perfectly able
>> To think, speak and see
> Apairt frae the looms, tho' to some
> That doesna sae easily come. (311)

Having granted cousin Wullie his trade and introduced him
to Lenin and Rilke, MacDiarmid turns inquisitor and corners
his cousin with rhetorical questions:

> Are you equal to life as to the loom?
>> Turnin' oot shoddy or what?
> Claith better than man? D'ye live to the full,
>> Your poo'er's a' deliverly taught?
> Or scamp a'thing else? Border claith's famous.
> Shall things o' mair consequence shame us? (312)

Without abandoning any of his evolutionary idealism Mac-

Diarmid was evidently at least considering the possibility of a populist poetry. He felt, at any rate, in a unique position to articulate the aspirations of the working class:

> My coming to Communist membership was not the resolution of a conflict, but the completion, as it were, of a career. . . For it had never been my aim to rise above the class into which I was born . . . and my regression to Scots was, in fact, the counter-process to the usual course; where others were concerned to rise, I, on the contrary, was determined to strengthen and develop my organic relationship to the Commons of Scotland by every means in my power, not to get back to the people – for I had never allowed myself to get away from them – but to get right under the skin, to get deeper and deeper into their innermost promptings, their root-motives. The tremendous proletarian virtue of the Langholm I knew as a boy saved me – despite the religiosity, the puritanism, of both my parents, and the ambitious gentility of my mother, and despite my own literary gifts – from . . . the extremely difficult ordeal of getting back to the people, of rising again to proletarian integrity, of becoming once more organically welded with the working-class. (LP, 232)

That theory is tested in 'The Seamless Garment' and, more provocatively, in 'Second Hymn to Lenin' which appeared in Eliot's journal *The Criterion* in July 1932 (before being pub-lished, as a limited edition, by the poet's second wife Valda Trevlyn in September of that year when an author's note described the poem as part of *Clann Albann*). This is a genu-inely dialectical poem that seeks to reconcile contradictory issues. MacDiarmid sets up an internal argument and asks the reader to participate by considering, as thesis, the notion that poetry is the only force with a sufficient spiritual purity to lift humanity towards a pinnacle of evolutionary idealism; and, as antithesis, the populist insistence that when art fails to 'win through to the man in the street' (323) it is hopelessly

elitist and escapist. The solution to the argument will, Mac-
Diarmid implies, amount to a visionary synthesis.

'Second Hymn to Lenin' opens conversationally with Mac-
Diarmid putting his point of view to Lenin:

> Ah, Lenin, you were richt. But I'm a poet
> (And you c'ud mak allowances for that!)
> Aimin' at mair than you aimed at
> Tho' yours comes first, I know it. (323)

The humility of the last line of that quatrain is more apparent
than real for the meaning is underpinned with a pun; the
'comes first' is meant literally and the new society will be
achieved in order to clear the way for a new poetry. In moving
from the Muckle Toon Stanza, as employed in *First Hymn to
Lenin and Other Poems*, to a basic *abcb* quatrain MacDiarmid
squares up to himself. He condemns the current state of
poetry. The poet who has, in previous works, dismissed 'the
feck' and 'Maist folk' and 'the crood' now speaks on behalf
of the culturally underprivileged majority:

> *Are my poems spoken in the factories and fields,*
> *In the streets o' the toon?*
> *Gin they're no', then I'm failin' to dae*
> *What I ocht to ha' dune.* (323)

This inner voice demands an answer and MacDiarmid, whose
poetic art has been cerebral and modernist, admits there is
a sense in which the contemporary intellectual and aesthete
has foolishly isolated himself from his fellows by his sheer
indifference to the majority. The artist has cultivated the
minority and the majority have reciprocated with hostility to
the artistic community. Poetry, in particular, has been the
entertainment of the elite and MacDiarmid calls for a revolutionary change:

> Poetry like politics maun cut
> The cackle and pursue real ends,

> Unerringly as Lenin, and to that
> Its nature better tends. (324)

In acknowledging that poetry has so far failed the majority MacDiarmid deliberately raises the argument to a new level. Change must be both evolutionary and revolutionary; poetry and the people must come together in a way that displays the subtlety of the one and the strength of the other. As a demonstration of this synthesis MacDiarmid offers a poetry whose language is a dialect Scots accessible to the majority(of Scots anyway) and whose theme is a reiteration of the poet's evolutionary idealism:

> *Oh, it's nonsense, nonsense, nonsense,*
> *Nonsense at this time o' day*
> *That breid-and-butter problems*
> *S'ud be in ony man's way.*
>
> *They s'ud be like the tails we tint*
> *On leavin' the monkey stage;*
> *A' maist folk fash aboot's alike*
> *Primaeval to oor age.*
>
> *We're grown-up folk that haena yet*
> *Put bairnly things aside*
> *– A' that's material and moral –*
> *And oor new state described.* (325)

Having proved his point to his own satisfaction MacDiarmid divests poetry of its exclusively literary connotations. It is not primarily a metrical affair, he reveals, for that is simply a technical matter of verbal organisation relating to padding like 'I wis' (327) and *ad hoc* rhymes like 'wash-tub' and 'hub' (328). Poetry is, the poet claims, 'The greatest poo'er amang men' (326). It is certainly the closest thing on earth to the source of creativity (the same source that is glimpsed in sexuality and in the strategic brilliance of a Lenin). This creative

force has the power to alter humanity in a way that politics
cannot:

> Unremittin', relentless,
> Organized to the last degree,
> Ah, Lenin, politics is bairns' play
> To what this maun be! (328)

As these lines suggest MacDiarmid was actively contemplating a new approach to the experimental possibilities of
language in the hope of evolving an idiom that was both
complex and comprehensible. The result was exhibited in
poems such as 'Scots Unbound' and 'Depth and the Chthonian Image' in the collection *Scots Unbound and Other Poems*
which appeared in 1932 as (so a prefatory note explained)
part of *The Muckle Toon* volume of *Clann Albann*. The ostentatiously experimental poems in this book used a language
MacDiarmid called Aggrandised Scots which was designed
to deal with abstruse scientific and philosophical matters. It
seemed imperative to MacDiarmid that he devise a form of
Scots capable of moving beyond the lyrical confines of Synthetic Scots and this had to be built up on the basis of extant
scientific terminology and *ad hoc* neologisms.[7] To make the
new experimental pill more palatable MacDiarmid offered it
alongside some of his most attractive compositions in Synthetic Scots. 'Milk-Wort and Bog-Cotton' is an exquisite lyric
whose genesis has been entertainingly described in an anecdote. In 1932 MacDiarmid was living in the village of Thakeham where he adopted, as his local, the White Lion pub:

> During a convivial evening here C.M.G. was inspired to
> write and Valda produced the only paper available from
> the ladies' toilet. In a matter of minutes C.M.G. wrote
> the poem 'Milk-Wort and Bog-Cotton'.[8]

In this lyric MacDiarmid uses his euphonic and his pictorial
gifts in sounding out the spiritual qualities of chiaroscuro.
The contrast between physical and metaphysical darkness is
suggested in the stanzaic division. In the first stanza the earth

is seen at its most fragile when deprived of the sustaining light of the sun 'And frae the lift nae shadow can fa' '; the mood of resignation provokes a tender response from the poet. In the second stanza the poet compares his own situation with that of the earth since both are regularly plunged into darkness; 'deep surroondin' darkness I discern/Is aye the price o' licht.' In this state both the earth and the poet generate an inner light. The poem is a remarkable example of elemental empathy and reveals MacDiarmid's fundamental identification with the earth and his rural roots. Technically the poem is masterly; Norman MacCaig has pointed out (in conversation) that the third line of the first stanza – 'When the shy spirit like a laich wind moves' (331) – is an iambic pentameter that defies conventional prosodic notation since its rhythm is entirely oral. MacDiarmid has described himself as 'an inferior technician' (Conversation, [22]) but there is no evidence of inferiority in this poem as witness the internal rhyming on 'licht' and 'nicht' and the proximity of the pararhymes 'nicht nocht' in the last lines.

A more spectacular display of metrical virtuosity is to be seen, and heard in 'Water Music'. This, the poet's most joyful showpiece in Synthetic Scots, is addressed (appropriately enough) to James Joyce. As the Irishman sang so eloquently of the Liffey (as Anna Livia Plurabelle) so the Scotsman sings of the three rivers that merge in his native Langholm. The alliteration of the successive stanzas may have been determined by a perusal of Jamieson but the mechanism of the poem is of little consequence in comparison to its stunning onomatopoeic eloquence. It ripples with light, reduces Langholm to the sound and sight of its rivers, and regards the rivers themselves as shimmering sources of vitality:

They ken a' that opens and steeks,
    Frae Fiddleton Bar to Callister Ha',
And roon aboot for twenty miles,
    They bead and bell and swaw.

Brent on or boutgate or beshacht
    Bellwaverin' or borne-heid,
They mimp and primp, or bick and birr,
    Dilly-dally or show speed. (334)

'Milk-Wort and Bog-Cotton' and 'Water Music' show that MacDiarmid was still bubbling with lyrical impulses. That, though, was not enough for him since the lyric did not fit into his artistic programme. He had to discover something different. 'Tarras', like 'Milk-Wort and Bog-Cotton' and 'Water Music', was also written at Thakeham but it exists on another level of creativity. Tarras Moss is a boggy wasteland in Langholm so MacDiarmid used it as a fitting symbol for the element the new society would emerge from. In his previous evolutionary poems MacDiarmid had described the source of life surfacing from the primordial ocean; now a new kind of life is to rise to the surface from 'This Bolshevik bog'. (337) MacDiarmid delights in the diversity of life-forms in the bog and wills an evolutionary miracle. As a prelude to the revolutionary birth in the bog MacDiarmid describes Tarras Moss as a more seductive sight than a beautiful woman:

Ah, woman-fondlin'! What is that to this?
Saft hair to birssy heather, warm kiss
    To cauld black waters' suction.
    Nae ardent breists' erection
But the stark hills'! In what dry-gair-flow
Can I pillow my lowin' cheek here
Wi' nae paps' howe below?
What laithsome parodies appear
O' my body's secrets in this oorie growth
Wi' its peerieweeries a' radgie for scouth
And the haill ratch and rive o' a world uncouth? (338)

The poem ends with an envoi on becoming a Scottish Nationalist in response to the infinite challenges available in a Scotocentric universe. MacDiarmid has delivered up his new poetic style and justifies it as an idiom in the interests of evolutionary idealism, cerebral stylishness, international communism and Scottish nationalism. In his Synthetic Scots poems MacDiarmid always used an oral element to aural effect. The Aggrandised Scots attempts to impose on the vernacular a scientifically advanced vocabulary.

Eric Linklater's comic novel *Magnus Merriman* (1934) has a description of MacDiarmid as he was at the time of writing poems like 'Tarras', 'Scots Unbound' and 'Depth and the Chthonian Image'. Moreover, the fictional Hugh Skene was thoroughly approved of by MacDiarmid himself who said 'That's me to a T.' (LP, 230) Skene is described as author of *The Flauchter-spaad* which is a reference to a line in 'Tarras' – 'Nor wi' their flauchter-spades ettle to play' (339). Bearing in mind the poet's enthusiasm for the fictional portrait and the fact that Linklater was on friendly terms with MacDiarmid, the following passage reads like an authorised version of the artistic gospel according to MacDiarmid in 1933:

> In Scotland the chief exponent of literal revolution was Hugh Skene, and he . . . attempted to revive the ancient Scottish forms of speech. They had this advantage, at least, that they were fully as obscure as Joyce's neologisms or the asyntactical compressions of the young English poets. But as Skene's genius matured he discovered that the Scots of Dunbar and Henryson was insufficient to contain both his emotion and his meaning, and he began to draw occasional buckets from the fountains of other tongues. At this time it was not uncommon to find in his verse, besides ancient Scots, an occasional Gaelic, German, or Russian phrase. The title-poem of his new volume, *The Flauchter-spaad*, was strikingly polyglot, and after three hours' study Magnus was unable to decide whether it was a plea for Communism, a tribute to William Wallace, or a poetical rendering of certain prehistoric fertility rites.[9]

That describes the impact of Aggrandised Scots accurately enough.

Two poems in particular, 'Depth and the Chthonian

Image' and 'Scots Unbound', embody the language MacDiarmid was putting forward as the voice of the future (in Scotland certainly). As we have seen, 'Depth and the Chthonian Image' contained a credo of MacDiarmid's perpetual quest for the source of creativity. 'Scots Unbound' is a lighter poem, a more playful composition as the poet acknowledges by subtitling it 'Divertissement Philologique'. It is dedicated to Robin and Margaret Black at whose Edinburgh home MacDiarmid lived for a period in 1932. Black published, with the financial assistance of Dr Stanley Robertson, a Social Credit weekly *The Free Man* and MacDiarmid agreed to work on the journal for a nominal salary. Although the poem has a clear purpose it does not rise above the level of an exercise designed to edify the converted. In bypassing the colloquial present and dragging Scots from the past and thrusting it into a theoretical future MacDiarmid was depriving himself of the rhythmic source that had sustained his greatest verse and came through sufficiently in 'Depth and the Chthonian Image' to make the reading of that poem a rewarding experience. 'Scots Unbound' is a programme without the backup of a demonstration and its theme is simply the theoretical extent of the programme:

> And the words you want,
> Oorie and nesh eneuch, I fear,
> 'll tak' an unco gettin' thegither
> As you get a youk frae some broc-faced place
> Or the world gangs a' knedeuch in your face;
> And, certes, it's only in Scots you'll find,
> Tho' few can use them, words o' the kind. (342)

In 'Scots Unbound' MacDiarmid is careful to insist that 'through my separate works I see/Their underlyin' unity' (343) and he is enough of a showman to shower a variety of effects on the reader. Although the showpiece poems in *Scots Unbound and Other Poems* advance a philological argument the occasional poems generally test the central theory on a tentative basis and with a down-to-earth empiricism. 'The Back o' Beyond' and 'Lynch Pin' convey the Langholm sunshine in sensuous Scots; 'An Apprentice Angel' (with its satirical portrait of MacDiarmid's old enemy Lauchlan Maclean Watt) and 'Dytiscus' have in common the entomological imagery that distinguishes a key passage of 'Depth and the Chthonian Image'; 'Cheville' and 'Antenora' continue the discussion of the place of water in Langholm (and, by extension, life); and three literary poems – on John Davidson, Sir Walter Scott and Goethe – divulge MacDiarmid's personal taste in poetry. John Davidson, as we have already seen, was a poetic hero. 'The Scott Centenary' is a four-line footnote to 'The Oon Olympian' in recognition of the fact that the centenary of the deaths of both Scott and Goethe fell (flat in the case of Scott) in 1932. In 'Second Hymn to Lenin' MacDiarmid had mentioned Goethe as a great poet whose work was nevertheless inaccessible to the majority of men; here he continues the dialectical argument with 'dialectic logic workin' at aince/In coontless coonter ways' (356). MacDiarmid denounces Goethe's elitism as a betrayal of the people and suggests that his own evolutionary idealism is fundamentally different from Goethe's Olympian affectations because he, MacDiarmid, is rooted in the reality of Langholm and so can speak for the people as one of them, albeit an exalted one:

> *And I am richt in ga'en back*
> *In like wise to the Muckle Toon;*
> *And dungarees are better wear*
> *For a man than a scarlet goon.*
>
> *Nae poet can be nocht but that;*
> *But man, freend, citizen, as weel.*
> *Let him tak' tent he disna tine*
> *Sicht o' a' that in poet's zeal.* (359)

That is a warning issued by MacDiarmid to himself. He clearly felt he had to come to a working arrangement to accommodate both the demands of experimental poetry and the obligations of the decent human being.

The poems that MacDiarmid contributed to *Scottish Scene*, the book he and Lewis Grassic Gibbon collaborated on, are evidently part of the *Clan Albann* concept. In his plans for *Clann Albann* he thought of beginning with Langholm and extending outwards to describe every aspect of the Scotocentric universe. In 'Scotland' he parades his knowledge of the country then claims to diversify in the interests of a universal unity:

> Nor is the whole lost in the parts,
> All Scotland seen save Scotland yet;
> He sees his land as a unity too,
> And Creation in terms of it. (367)

Fascinated by the paradox of the poet of the people who writes poetry for a small minority of intellectuals MacDiarmid comes up with his only extended narrative poem. 'Tam o' the Wilds and the Many-Faced Mystery' is an exhibit designed to show what the poetry of the future could be since this poem is both entertaining *and* edifying. It reads like a metrical novel about the sort of man MacDiarmid would have been had he been untouched by poetic genius. In his Muckle Toon, MacDiarmid had brooded on problems in an obsessive way that cut him off from other folk; from parents, relatives, friends. The eponymous Tam is as individualistic as the poet; he is a 'common workin' man' (368) with an insatiable passion for knowledge. Written in a compact eight-line stanza, the poem details Tam's life and his amateur interests in entomology, ornithology, ichthyology and helminthology. His life on the grey coast of Morayshire becomes meaningful as a quest for the vital source of biological being. Tam's interests draw him increasingly towards the microstructure of life:

> A cod's stomach for the smaller fry
> Was aye his happiest huntin' grund
> For testaceous and crustaceous rarieties
> – Mony new to Scotland, or even science, he fund –

Fish lice, sea mice, Deid Men's Paps, actinias,
And algae and zoophytes yont number
Were rescued thence and ta'en in triumph
His humble wee but-and-ben to cumber. (374)

Having described this paragon in order that other Scotsmen
should emulate his disinterestedness, the poet switches
abruptly to another exemplary Scotsman. William Soutar, to
whom the poem is dedicated, was a bedfast poet who over-
came his disability to the extent of becoming one of Mac-
Diarmid's most accomplished poetic disciples. Like Tam he
lives in 'The pure world o' the spirit' (378). MacDiarmid, at
this juncture, was certainly trying to democratise his poetry,
to humanise it with portraits of particular people. Once again
he was at a critical stage in his career and exploring several
options.

Although it was shaping up impressively as a creative endeavour big enough even for MacDiarmid, *Clann Albann* was
abandoned around the time the poet moved from the mainland to the little Shetland island of Whalsay. The move was
more of a traumatic upheaval than a mere change of scenery
and MacDiarmid felt his work should change in accordance
with the direction his life was taking. In 1933, the year in
which he virtually dropped the project, MacDiarmid had
some valedictory remarks on *Clann Albann*:

As to when the first volume [*The Muckle Toon*] is likely to
be ready, I can give no idea . . . though I have practically
finished writing it. It is longer than my *Cencrastus* and
much more varied alike in matter and manner, but these
are difficult days for poetry publishing, especially on such
a magnitude in a linguistic medium debarred from most
of the English reading public and otherwise of a kind
which cannot appeal to any large body of readers. Of the
other four volumes I have also completed considerable
portions, but 'the spirit blows where it listeth,' and I
cannot set any date for the finish of the undertaking. In
these circumstances [it is possible that] the whole scheme

may never be carried out and much of it secure only posthumous publication.[10]

No one could accuse MacDiarmid of lack of ambition. He had created a one-man Scottish Renaissance in 1922, he had been a pioneer of political poetry in 1931, and now he was anxious to devise a new test for his talents.

Chapter Five
THIS STONE WORLD

I must get into this stone world now.
Ratchel, striae, relationships of tesserae,
    Innumerable shades of grey,
    Innumerable shapes,
And beneath them all a stupendous unity
    'On a Raised Beach' (426)

In 1933 MacDiarmid moved to the little Shetland island of
Whalsay where he was to remain for the next eight years. It
was a productive period but also a time of severe psychological stress under the strain of which MacDiarmid's health
broke down, though he rapidly recovered after undergoing
hospitalisation. In some respects the Zarathustrian period of
exile on the island was a traumatic test of the poet's aston-
ishingly resilient character. Though he had the companionship of his second wife, Valda, and his new baby, Michael,
the poet had to endure an intellectual isolation. As he summed
up the period in 1941, he felt it had been enervating rather
than excruciating:

Except for [some] brief visits in Scotland and England,
and the rare occasions in the summertime when I have
friends – authors, artists, and students – to stay with me
in Shetland, I see nobody who has read widely enough to
possess grounds on which to base, if not opinions, at least
reasonable speculations. I hear nothing but the inane
phrases of women. 'It's all in the Bible, you know. . . .

Moore, you know, Old Moore. He knew, and they do say
that the Queen had a dream. . . . And you remember
what Churchill said. . . ?' And the men are as ignorant
and incoherent as the women, even the young men,
sailors who have been all over the world and soldiers in
the present War and the previous War. . . . They have
read nothing, seen nothing – never open a newspaper,
even. [Ironically, although I have] a score of books to my
name, and a measure of international reputation, I am
perhaps the poorest, and certainly the most precariously
situated on this poor little island, where there is no one
else who comes within a million miles of conceiving, let
alone sharing or comprehending in any degree, any of my
major interests. (LP, xxvii–xxviii, 423)

Financially MacDiarmid was in a difficult position, though
this was nothing new; since he had left Montrose he had been
deprived of security. The disturbing element in his life was
the possibility, however remote, that he had actually failed
Scotland – had sacrificed himself and those closest to him
without fully realising the potential spirit of Scotland. To
contemplate this was to acknowledge, theoretically, the spectacle of defeat. During the war years MacDiarmid had suffered from depression but, as his letters to George Ogilvie
show, always assumed that he would triumph over adversity.
On Whalsay there were moments when he almost wholly lost
the self-assurance he had enjoyed in Montrose when he produced his masterpiece in Scots.

Difficulties, to MacDiarmid, were obstacles to overcome
with work and at no time in his creative career did he offer
alibis for inactivity. If one idea faltered on a creative level he
developed another, more artistically rewarding, notion. During the 1930s he brought the Gaelic Idea to the forefront of
his consciousness and its spiritual qualities seemed to com-
pensate for his private problems. On moving to Whalsay
MacDiarmid embarked on a new plan of action, a new poetic
programme and a new way of life. It was a challenge. He
was, as always, fiendishly busy. There was the completion of

Scottish Scene (1934), his book with Lewis Grassic Gibbon; and the work published as *Stony Limits and Other Poems* (1934). He set about securing a regular income by working for Routledge: he was (in 1934) retained by the firm at the rate of £1 per week to advise on Scottish subjects; he acted as editor (after the death of Lewis Grassic Gibbon in 1935) of the Voice of Scotland series of books (which, ironically, included Muir's *Scott and Scotland*); and he wrote, for the Voice of Scotland series, a book on *Red Scotland* which Routledge rejected, first because it was too long (100,000 words instead of the 50,000 contracted for), then (after MacDiarmid had reduced its length) because of its stylistic content and political contentions. Throughout this period there was political upheaval: in 1933 he was expelled from the National Party of Scotland and the following year, during which the poet's mother died, he joined the Communist Party of Great Britain. MacDiarmid saw CP membership as a partial antidote to isolation, but it was not enough. In 1935 he broke down under psychological pressure and, thanks to the humane intervention of Francis George Scott, was hospitalised for seven weeks in Perth. Mac-Diarmid was neither a confessional writer nor a man who paraded his private affairs in his work. Inevitably, though, the psychological crisis informs some of the lines composed on Whalsay and in the period leading up to his departure from the Scottish mainland. The poet of evolutionary idealism and individuality was in pursuit of a fundamentally revolutionary approach to poetry. At times he felt his work should have an impeccably Marxist acceptance of the importance of the masses and also display a uniquely inspirational quality. In order to achieve a new synthesis he was willing to discard, at least in principle, that belief that had permeated *A Drunk Man*:

> All sources of individual pride
> Are like straws on a whirling tide
> Or like trees which have dried up but still sway
>   In the breeze with the others (407)

So, in the interests of a collectivist ethic MacDiarmid considered, in principle, suppressing the individuality that had sustained him. He had convinced himself that poetry had to be socially responsible and sympathetic to the aspirations of the masses. As lyricism (so MacDiarmid then felt) could convey little more than a mood he attempted to express his socialist sympathies in verse carrying an equal measure of information and affirmation. 'Etika Preobrazhennova Erosa' (from which the four lines above come) portrays the poet as a political leader bringing the people up towards the promised land on a plateau on a MacDiarmidian mountain:

> Let us climb to where the people can be found
>> Ranged in their millions
> As history is climbing to world unity
> – As who, when he gains a great summit
> Finds he has no need to look below
> To know his altitude (410)

MacDiarmid concludes the poem with the supposition that 'no individual deed/Eventually matters individually' (411). As the philosophical individual moves towards universal unity, so MacDiarmid suggests, the political individual aspires to a global unity. For MacDiarmid this means the establishment of a Social Credit base and the creation of a socialist superstructure; MacDiarmid's solution involved a willingness to mix apparent opposites like Social Credit and Marxism. In his volume *Stony Limits and Other Poems* MacDiarmid exhibited the range of his new interests. This large book contains more variation than the poet usually admitted to any one collection and the poems relate in clusters concerned with the exploration of various thematic and linguistic areas. There are poems in a discursive English either accepting Social Credit or, more momentously, announcing the Gaelic Idea; there are lyrics in English and Synthetic Scots; there are pathological poems in an idiom hovering insecurely between Scottish accented English and the Aggrandised Scots developed in *Scots Unbound and Other Poems* (1932); there are poems in what MacDiarmid was to call Synthetic English.

MacDiarmid's belief in Social Credit was developed in tandem with his declared faith in Communism. There is something poignantly ironical in the predicament of a poet who, while reduced to economic poverty, nevertheless felt in a position to make confident assertions about the financial affairs of the world. MacDiarmid was angrily impatient with the economic anomalies that deprived him of even a semblance of security; consequently he was, as he insisted in 'The Belly-Grip', anxious to 'give/Every man at least ample means to live' (394). MacDiarmid's political pantheon was a characteristically eclectic affair. He could refer to 'The eternal lightning of Lenin's bones' (386) and also cite his Social Credit friends as examples of men shaped by the forces of evolutionary idealism:

> Douglas, Orage, and a few
> Others of that highbrow crew! –
> Are further already from most men
> Than average humans from monkeys got
> For many a long aeon. (397)

In his urgent desire for an abrupt economic solution there is a MacDiarmidian impatience to sweep aside practical matters that interfere with the expression of spiritual concerns. MacDiarmid's Social Credit, like his Communism, is a pragmatic means to a metaphysical end. In a Social Credit poem, 'Genethliacon for the New World Order' (dedicated to A. R. Orage's daughter Ann), MacDiarmid sums up his programme as a biblical call for 'Life and that far more abundantly'. (404).

What MacDiarmid meant by life was increasingly identified with his growing interest in Gaelic. In 'Thalamus' he expanded Hopkins's assertion that 'the mind, mind has mountains; cliffs of fall' ('No worst, there is none') into an exploration of inner space since few 'Have glimpsed the medial nuclei yet/Of their thalamus – that Everest in themsel-

ves'. (413) Having embarked on the ascent of his own cerebral
Everest MacDiarmid felt that the gaps in his consciousness
were caused by an awareness of what was lost when Gaelic
culture was systematically undermined by the English (and
Lowland Scottish) victors of Culloden. MacDiarmid had frequently dissociated himself from the Celtic Twilight and its
sentimental portrayal of the Gael. He wanted to replace such
whimsy with a powerful depiction of what Gaelic culture had
amounted to before 1746. He wanted to recover the 'Lost
world of Gaeldom', (415) he said, in a poem 'In Memoriam:
Liam Mac'Ille Iosa'. That name is the Gaelic version of
William Gillies who was associated with MacDiarmid and
Hon. R. Erskine of Marr in the Scots National League, an
extremist association strong on the subject of a Gaelic cultural
revival. In his elegy for Gillies MacDiarmid alludes to 'the
big music' (414) and describes Gaelic as an 'incomparable
instrument' (415). Spiritual progress would depend on a
language made in the image of an ideal Gaelic:

> O come, come, come, let us turn to God
> And get rid of this degrading and damnable load,
> So set we can give our spirits free play
> And rise to the height of our form. (415)

Like other passionate Scottish Nationalists, MacDiarmid
was haunted by the tragic history of Scotland and by the
catastrophic consequences of the defeat of the clans at Culloden. A culture with its own dress, speech and music was
the object of a sustained attack by successive governments.
As a result the 'great music' had gone and Gaelic had dwin-
dled to a minority language. Recalling Dostoevsky's Russian
Idea, MacDiarmid countered with his own Gaelic Idea:

> This Gaelic Idea has nothing in common with the
> activities of An Comunn Gaidhealach, no relationship
> whatever with the Celtic Twilight. It would not matter so
> far as positing it is concerned whether there had never
> been any Gaelic language or literature, not to mention

clans and tartans, at all. It is an intellectual conception designed to offset the Russian Idea: and neither it, nor my anti-English spirit, is any new thing though the call for its apt embodiment in works of genius is today crucial. (SE, 67–8)

On the one hand MacDiarmid extended this to his belief in 'a sort of Celtic Union of Socialist Soviet Republics' (LP, 26) and, on the other, he designed poems expressly in the interests of the Gaelic Idea. Among the first, and finest, of these poems is 'Lament for the Great Music', which came into *Stony Limits* as a substitute for 'Ode to All Rebels'.

This is a long meditative poem addressed to the MacCrimmons who, as hereditary pipers to MacLeod of MacLeod, ran a college of piping at Boreraig on Skye.[1] They practised their art for two centuries before the college was closed in the aftermath of Culloden. Thematically and stylistically 'Lament for the Great Music' marks a decisive development in Mac-Diarmid's poetry. In it he took a particular manifestation of the Gaelic Idea and explored it exhaustively. Moreover he was exhilarated by what he took to be a new structural principle in his own art. For some time MacDiarmid had been searching for an expansive alternative to the lyric and he was given a new lease of creative life by his conviction that he could emulate in verse the open-ended improvisatory quality of the pibroch. In 1936 he rose to the theoretical occasion in this manner:

[The pibrochs of the great period] knew no 'bar'. They were *timeless* music – hence their affiliation with plainsong, with the neuma. Barred music – accented music – finds its ultimate form in symphony. Unbarred music – quantity music – expresses itself in pattern-repetition; hence the idea that the Celt has no architectonic power, that his art is confined to niggling involutions and intricacies – yet the ultimate form here is not symphony; it is epic. [And it] is epic – and no lesser form – that equates with the classless society. (SE, 75–6)

Whether or not MacDiarmid's poetry is a verbal equivalent of the pibroch is not the point; he believed he was evolving a quintessentially Celtic epic form for the coming classless society.

The term Great Music is a translation of the Gaelic *Ceòl-Mór* which is the most advanced form of pipe-music as this informative exposition suggests:

> *Ceòl-mór* possesses its own unique musical forms and phrase-patterns; and, though distinctly clannish, the exultant spirit which it most-often expresses is also essentially heroic. It is said to have been developed mainly by the hereditary pipers maintained by some Highland chiefs throughout the period of incessant clan warfare, civil war, and rebellion which began in the late sixteenth century and finally ended with the abolition of the hereditary jurisdictions in 1748; and most of its special characteristics may be ascribed to the fact that it was composed solely for oral transmission in an exceptionally martial and aristocratic preliterate society.[2]

To MacDiarmid this infinitely unfolding form is irresistibly attractive and offers a shape capable of containing his increasing artistic urge for extended meditations. In pibroch the progression involves variations on a theme, or *urlar*. MacDiarmid's theme is the glory that was Gaeldom and he improvises three principal variations on it. First, he approaches the theme ironically in a section stretching from the first lines to the speculation 'Who can guarantee that two and two/Are not five on Jupiter?' (470) Second, he responds ecstatically to the theme and delivers himself of a mystical manifesto before invoking shadows for Hebridean 'grey rocks/Are gaining ground and the seas are black with their shadows' (475). Finally he relates the haunting music of the MacCrimmons to his own physical isolation which, paradoxically, turns out to be a precondition for acting responsibly in the poetic service of humanity.

After opening on four lines of adaptation sustaining a pastoral note[3] MacDiarmid relates the image of Christ aban-

doned on the cross to the cultural crucifixion of Gaelic music.
Both examples are aspects of betrayal. Just as Christianity
has betrayed its founder by atrophying into an organisational
routine, so Scotland has turned its back on the Gaelic glory
and degenerated into a small nation with small ambitions.
Deprived of its greatest indigenous art form Scotland staggers
forward into greater and greater banality, forever taking the
idea of 'vast progress' (464) seriously. Emphasising the irony
of it all MacDiarmid offers evidence of Scotland's appalling
decline with regard to the Great Music:

> And, besides, as *The Scotsman* says, it is likely enough
> The great music has had a real if imponderable
>   influence
> On subsequent piping after all – like Christ on the
>   Kirk!
>   – My God, can you not read history and see
>   They have never had what you are fain to save?
> (464)

and again

> We have no use for the great music.
> All we need is a few good-going tunes. (468)

The comparison between Christ and the Great Music is sustained and MacDiarmid realises that the use of this specific
symbolism might only be approximate in this case and show
'how far from the great music I am'. (466) The poet therefore
expands his referential repertoire; animated by 'Platonic intellectualism' (470) and 'the style of Plotinus' (477) he pours
withering scorn on the atrocious state that Scotland finds
itself in. He would be happier, in fact, if there was only a
Platonic Idea of Scotland – an image uncontaminated by the
hideous reality. It would have been better, he supposes, had
the catastrophe of Culloden been followed by total destruction
instead of a cultural genocide that permitted the survival of
a collective memory of the vanished glory:

Sumeria is buried in the desert sands,
Atlantis in the ocean waves – happier these
Than Scotland, for all is gone, no travesty
Of their ancient glories lives
On the lips of degenerate sons as here. (467)

This first, heavily ironical section, ends on a powerful anecdote. MacDiarmid takes the reader into his confidence by
telling him he would have loved to have witnessed the silence
observed by pipers as a protest against the imprisonment of
a MacCrimmon. The story has its own symbolism for a poet
who is forever advancing towards a metaphysical silence.

The second variation on the *urlar*, and central section of the
poem, opens on an image of a sunset as a symbol of the fading
of Gaelic culture as represented by the Great Music. Watching the light fading, however, the poet senses an inner light,
a spiritual glow that is to spread throughout the remainder
of the poem:

> With the passing of the splendour from the heights
> The middle distance and foreground were suddenly lit
>   up
> With a light (like that in which shingle lies under the
>   sea-tide's forefoot)
> Bursting from some hidden spring of the afterglow. All
>   else
> Was darker save the quickened feeling – like the sense
>   of a man
> Who returns from foreign scenes to the country of his
>   blood and birth. (471)

MacDiarmid is alone in the afterglow; he is illuminated by a
vision of the Great Music which only emphasises the tragedy
of modern Scotland. If the sun finally sets then the darkness
of modern Scotland will be seen as a disaster, an inferno of
urbanisation: 'How can I think of you/In these cities you
never saw' (472). MacDiarmid turns scornfully to Scots who
live their lives in ignorance of the Great Music, indifferent

apparently to the extirpation of their cultural heritage. As a poet MacDiarmid has to dissociate himself from contemporary Scotland: 'My native land should be to me/As a root to a tree' (472). Moreover, he claims that all Scots are to some extent responsible for the perpetuation of the tragedy: 'These denationalised Scots have killed the soul/Which is universally human' (472). However, a sunset is a symbol with its own logic and MacDiarmid believes that Scotland might be lit up again by a turning of the earth toward a new light. In expressing this faith in the rediscovery of the creative source MacDiarmid issues a mystical manifesto:

> It is the realisation of the light upon which
> Not only life but the very existence of the universe
>   depends;
> Not only animal life but earth, water, air.
> If it faded it would mean the end of 'everything.'
> It does not fade. Our spirit is of a being indestructible.
> Its activity continues from eternity to eternity.
> It is like the sun which seems to set to our earthly eyes
> But in reality shines on unceasingly.
> It is the movement which the mind invents
> For its own expression not otherwise than the stars.
>   (473)

The sunset is an illusion imagined by men; similarly the spirit of the Great Music lives on in eternity and is accessible to the creative individual. What MacDiarmid seeks is neither the appearance of reality nor the subjective illusion of reality but a spiritual unity with an evolutionary ideal which is a different order of reality because 'The supreme reality is visible to the mind alone' (475). MacDiarmid's neoplatonic intellectual vision reveals this spiritual reality:

> It is the supreme reality (not the Deity of personal
>   theism)
> Standing free of all historical events in past or future,
> Knowable – but visible to the mind alone (474)

In this state of mind it is possible to have 'a rapt and mysterious/Communion with the spiritual world' (474). Such a metaphysical assumption sustained the improvisatory genius of the Great Music and it is the ultimate end of MacDiarmid's long poetic search for the hidden source of creativity.

In the last section of the poem MacDiarmid speaks for himself; tells the great MacCrimmon pipers that he is with them and therefore cut off from his fellow men. He is a man seeking spiritual harmony more than human companionship:

> I am as lonely and unfrequented as your music is.
> I have had to get rid of all my friends,
> All those to whom I had to accommodate myself.
> If one's capital consists in a calling
> And a mission in life one cannot afford to keep friends.
> I could not stand undivided and true amongst them.
> Only in the solitude of my thought can I be myself
> Or remember you clearly. (475–6)

The poet does not feel that his isolation condemns him as an antisocial escapist. On the contrary the determination to inhabit the metaphysical sphere allows MacDiarmid to serve others as his sacrifice saves humanity by communicating the spiritual insight and solace of great art. MacDiarmid's poetry is a gift he presents to humanity:

> So those who have had to dwell
> In solitude, at the furthest remove from their fellows,
> Serve the community too. Their loneliness
> Is only because they belong to a wider community
> Than that of their immediate environment,
> Not to one country or race, but to humanity,
> Not to this age but to all time,
> As your pibrochs reached to Eternity (476–7)

Just because he is so serious about his sacrifice MacDiarmid is 'horrified by the triviality of life, by its corruption and helplessness'. (477) He condemns urbanisation as an insult

to the free spirit of man, then soars above cities by putting
them beneath him. Socialism can solve all the economic problems – 'The struggle for material existence is over. It has been
won' (478). But that is only the beginning, a means of clearing
the way for the revelation of the great spiritual end. To attain
that end humanity needs a poetic saviour who will discover
the source of creativity which 'resembles the ray of a fountain;
it rises, sparkles' (478). In earlier lines, MacDiarmid had
referred to birdsong – 'a dipper's song' (476) – and he recalls
the ornithological image. He is not a wanderer but a poet
who has adapted himself to the particular conditions in
Scotland:

> I am only that Job in feathers, a heron, myself,
> Gaunt and unsubstantial – yet immune to the
>   vicissitudes
> Other birds accept as a matter of course; impervious to
>   the effects
> Of even the wildest weather, no mean consideration in
>   a country like this;
> And my appetite is not restricted to any particular fare.
>   (479)

Aware that too much abstract speculation can create chaos,
the poet, 'no dilettante of chaos' (480), turns away from the
formless nebulosity of 'ultimate Incoherence' (480). Instead
he comes back to earth with his favourite images of renaissance and resurrection. Although his search is spiritual it is
conducted in the spirit of humanity:

> I believe in the necessary and unavoidable
>   responsibility of man
> And in the ineluctable certainty of the resurrection
> And know that the mind of man creates no ideas
> Though it is ideas alone that create.
> Mind is the organ through which the Universe reaches
> Such consciousness of itself as is possible now, and I
>   must not brood

On the intermittence of genius, the way consciousness
    varies
Or declines, as in Scotland here, till it seems
Heaven itself may be only the best that is feasible
For most people, but a sad declension from music like
    yours. (480)

Once more MacDiarmid is prepared to be reborn, about to
focus his 'cosmic consciousness' (481) on a new facet of the
terrible crystal,

      the creative instant, the moment of divine
        realisation,
    When the self is lit up by its own inner light
    Caused in the self by its intensity of thought (481)

His obligation is to the spirit of Scotland contained in the
Great Music and so he ends by addressing the MacCrimmons
and sharing 'the eternal light' (482) with them as the future
is seen as a creative spirit rising to resurrection. MacDiarmid
fuses this 'eternal light' with the earlier evocation of a sunset
and closes on a rhetorically optimistic question:

    Look! Is that only the setting sun again?
    Or a piper coming from far away? (482)

In the 'Lament for the Great Music', MacDiarmid reaches
back into the historical past in order to discover a cultural
cradle for the new Scotland. For years he had been producing
images of renaissance and rebirth; now he increasingly felt
that birth was a particularly fertile theme and contemplated
a metaphysical and symbolic nativity. The birth had to be
something new, not a repeat performance of a stage in Scotland's history. MacDiarmid, intellectually isolated on his island, was in a valedictory mood when considering 'The
Progress of Poetry':

The spirit rises, and all my friends are here,
Every myrionous human Calvary of modern life,
And I bid farewell to the melancholy, the disillusion,
The ideal heavenly virgins, the moon, the hate of our
    kind,
Vanished youth, and all juvenile enthusiasms (458)

To prepare the way for a spiritually immaculate conception
MacDiarmid has to shock the reader out of his complacent
acceptance of what is a diseased modern world. A world
disfigured by disease and death can only be saved by the
creation of a new saviour who might be a Lenin or a Mac-
Diarmid or a synthesis of the politic and the poetic. What
MacDiarmid demonstrated in two pathological poems was
the extent of decay, both physical and metaphysical, in the
modern world and the implications of the atrophy.

'Ex-Parte Statement on the Project of Cancer' is a deliberately shocking poem. It is narrated by a man dying of cancer
who attracts the reader's attention through the extremity of
his situation and his frankness

And I needna refer to the way
We cancerous ken each ither – almost as 'homo's' dae
    (445)

The poem is hesitant, hovering between colloquialism and
Aggrandised Scots, and the lack of direction is accentuated
by the to-ing and fro-ing of the discussion and the narrator's
references to earlier parts of the poem – 'Cast back your
mind's eyes/Owre the five phrases I've had to italicise'. (448)
We see, though, clearly where the logic (or pathologic) of the
poem is leading. Since cancer is 'a livin' thing' (447) it is an
apt symbol for modern life since in both cases the evidence
of cultural virulence obliterates humanity. Therefore the
phenomenon of cancer teaches man an evolutionary lesson
for he can only survive, as a species, by confronting physical
death with metaphysical life:

There's been nae advance in the human intellect for
   the past
Twa thoosand years at least, and if Nature at last
Has given up hope, found that a cul-de-sac,
The increase o' cancer may mean she's harkit back
(Changed her gait to gang – if you nab
My seely punnin' – sidelins like a crab)
To an alternative she's aye had up her sleeve. (449)

These lines would have pointed towards the thematically
terminal 'Ode to All Rebels'. However, the publisher found
the ode distasteful and obscene and deleted it.

'Ode to All Rebels' is MacDiarmid's most determined
attempt to write an expressionist poem in Scots; indeed this
somewhat bizarre composition mixes Gothic elements, supernatural touches and deliberate bits of blasphemy in a calcu-
lated assault on the expectations of the reader of 1935 who
assumed he knew his MacDiarmid. The title assumes some
knowledge of the Rebel Angels of the Apocrypha who were
(in the words of a modern novelist) 'real angels [who] betrayed the secrets of Heaven to King Solomon, and God threw
them out of Heaven [so] they gave mankind another push up
the ladder, they came to earth and taught tongues, and healing and laws of hygiene.'[4] The Ode is written in a conversationally casual dialect Scots fortified by rhyme. In fact the
Scots texture is really a matter of orthography. After the poem
was banned, MacDiarmid Anglicised parts of it for publication in *Second Hymn to Lenin and Other Poems* (1935): 'Kate's
eyes were sea-green' (488) becomes 'A Pair of Sea-Green
Eyes' (552); 'Here at the heicht o' passion' (495) becomes 'As
Lovers Do' (540); 'Are the livin' sae muckle use' (501) becomes 'At the Cenotaph' (538); 'O weel may timid and gras-
pin' folk' (502) becomes 'Thanksgiving' (546); 'Think not
that I forget a single pang' (503) becomes 'Think Not That
I Forget' (548) and there is also an Anglicised extract from
the Ode beginning 'As the heavy earth is the same below'
(543) which corresponds to the lines starting from 'But as the
lourd earth is the same alow'. (505) The difference between

the Scots and English versions is minimal, though in the
following example the poet has made a slight verbal adjust-
ment in the interests of a revised rhyme:

> *O weel may timid and graspin' folk*
> *Rejoice that aince as the Scriptures state*
> *An innocent man was tortured to Daith*
> *For their benefit: and be pleased – noo they hae't.* (502)

becomes

> O well may timid and grasping folk
> Rejoice that once according to Holy Writ
> An innocent man was tortured to death
> For their benefit; and be content – now they have it!
>   (546)

To convey the neurotically unsettled quality of a pathological vision MacDiarmid never establishes a single speaking
voice for the melodramatic monologue. Instead it is carried
by different voices that eerily issue from the same uncertain
source: there is the voice of the poet (who comments on
poetry), the voice of the fictional narrator (who speculates on
marriage and sex) and the voice of the Rebel Angel (who
indicates the challenge of the evolutionary ideal). The poem
is meant to be a disturbing psychological experience and the
texture of the verse is riddled with images of disease and
death. Indeed the poem opens with a necrophiliac confession.
Recalling the death of his first wife, Kate, the narrator describes his reaction to the lowering of her coffin:

> Even as frae lowerin' the coffin I raze
> Conscious o' my nature in a wud amaze
> And strauchtened up my muckle animal frame
> That kent what it wanted and kent nae shame
>   And stood in a burst o' sun
>   Glowerin' at the bit broken grun'. (488)

[173]

This perverse manifestation of sexual vitality in the presence of death is a way of shocking the reader into a consideration of the startling implications of the poet's evolutionary ideal which challenges physical death with metaphysical immortality.

The narrator, having introduced himself as an unpredictable character, supplies the reader with the information that he has been married twice. Kate, now dead, had sea-green eyes; Jean, now divorced from him, had sky-blue eyes. Despite these, and other, physical differences they amounted to the same thing: sexual objects arousing desire and offering comfort. To the narrator all women are to be regarded as creatures useful principally for confirming the assertive individuality of the male. With a large measure of arrogance, the narrator remembers all the women he has known sexually:

> And wi' a' their differences the life I'd ha'e led
> Wi' ony ane o' them I micht ha'e wed
>   'Ud ha'e been fell near the same
>   As wi' yon particular dame. (490)

According to such sexual opportunism individuality is synonymous with what commonsense calls selfishness. Similarly, misfortune becomes simply a matter of chance. Two men might find in their sexual partners two quite different propositions:

> *They turn to meet their natural need,*
> *One finds domestic bliss;*
> *The other a lock hospital*
> *To rot with syphilis.* (490)

The omnipresence of disease is crucial to the poem. MacDiarmid is making his narrator deliberately unsympathetic, a character clearly differentiated from the poet while holding certain views that travesty the poetic vision associated with MacDiarmid. Having regarded women as sexual comforters, the narrator gives his opinion on children. His affection for his own offspring is qualified by coarseness:

> Yet I lo'ed them as dearly as ony man
>   Can lo'e his spawn (491)

With such sentiments it is not surprising that he distrusts 'the faitherly instinct'. (492) He contends that evolution makes an instrument of the individual who is therefore directed towards 'Refinements o' sensibility'. (492)

Complacent in his cynicism, the narrator moves on to dismiss as absurd the romantic concept of love, then launches into a comical encomium for laundries – 'Thank God for laundries' (493) – as a mechanical means whereby male privacy might be preserved. So far we can recognise the narrator of the poem as a self-styled Rebel though he displays none of the traditionally heroic features of the romantic Rebel. He is a negative presence who denies romantic love and dismisses domestic responsibility. His perception of the proximity of death and life gives rise not to a celebration of the joy of living but to a macabre anecdote designed to shock and disgust the reader. In describing his period as a medical student, the narrator is reminded,

> O' hoo Kate a'e day afore we were mairried,
> And students still, aince turned her bit heid
>   (Her hair that shone in the sun
>   As sae mony weemun's has done)
> And watched me wi' quizzical een
> As I cam' on her heels up to the obscene
>   Case spread oot for the class. I returned her look
> Wi' ane strictly accordin' to the book,
> As I fingered the vagina lyin' afore me
>   – Carcinoma o' the uterus – while o'er me
>   Swept the thocht: 'Darlin' the neist may be you'
>   – I saw deep eneuch then, and saw true,
>   And yet lo'ed her, I confess,
>   Gin nane the mair certes nane the less. (495–6)

MacDiarmid has, by this time, established the iconoclastic nature of the Rebel who narrates his poem. Suddenly the tone of the poem changes, at a passage beginning 'I tae ha'e been ta'en up the mountain heich' (497), and we are aware that the Rebel has become aware of his angelic responsibilities. By a process of instant evolution the Rebel has been metamorphosed: he is an angel 'born/Deaf and blind' (497) who can, none the less, see and hear. The Rebel Angel has, in fact, a vision that sets him apart from 'maist folk' (498):

> They believe in ither things they canna see
> Then why should they no' believe in me
> But presume to pick and choose atween
> The things they themsel's ca' the unseen?
> Nonsense? But dae they get as muckle fun
> Frae my antics as frae theirs I've whiles won,
> – Tho' angels lack humour and it's no' sae easy
> To divert me noo as it used to be. (498)

MacDiarmid has sprung a surprise on the reader who took the narrator for a mere Rebel when he was, actually and imaginatively, a Rebel Angel. The objectionable Rebel has become an amoral 'Angel o' Daith' (506). He is aware of pathological aberrations – 'the woman in cancer's toils' (503), 'venereal disease' (504) – and able to rise above them. His supreme disgust is reserved for the inability of man to realise that just as God made an Angel into a Rebel so it is within the power of man to begin as a Rebel and transform himself into an Angel. The process is available to those with a knowledge of MacDiarmid's evolutionary idealism:

> O magical change. O miracle.
> I am suddenly beyond mysel'.
> > Reid, white, and square,
> Tearin' the soul to rags. (505)

The Rebel Angel is a link between the earthly paradise and

eternity. He has seen it all and his visionary knowledge categorises him as an outcast:

> I am Ishmael, the only man,
> Wha's the freend o' a' men.
> (And wha has ever been certain o' ocht
> Here recognises certainty's voice again.)
> I tell you a' else is vain.
> Eden's wide-open, unchanged; and nocht shuts us
> frae't
> But impious delusions o' oor ain. (507)

Having established an entrance to Eden, the poem moves towards a conclusion through a catalogue of avoidable misfortunes. At the end of all this evidence of man's folly the Rebel Angel has identified with his friends on earth, the Ishmaels and outsiders and misfits and inmates, and addresses his old friend:

> *Your song, O God, that none dare hear*
> *Save the insane and such as I*
> *Apostates from humanity*
> *Sings out in me with no more fear*
> *Than one who thinks he has the world's ear*
> *From his padded cell*
> *— Insane enough, with you so near,*
> *To want, like you, the world as well!* (512)

In insisting on creative equality with God in this manner we see that MacDiarmid has placed himself on the side of the most outspoken of the angels.

It is impossible, considering the deletions and substitutions involved in the making of the first edition, to consider *Stony Limits* as a general statement of thematic or linguistic principle. It is the most varied of all MacDiarmid's collections and it is only with hindsight that we can see which poems led directly to his late manner of discursive poetry. In *Stony Limits* the poet considers several options and displays a mastery of

many manners. There are sharp socialist poems such as
'Edinburgh Toun' and 'John Maclean (1879–1923)'; there
are English poems using the poet's ornithological imagery
and lyrics, like 'The Little White Rose', presenting Scottish
sentiments in an elegant English; there are disparate items
such as the satire 'On The Oxford Book of Victorian Verse'
and the universalist 'Hymn to Sophia: The Wisdom of God'.
Some of the poems seem to be leftovers from *The Muckle Toon*
volume of the *Clann Albann* project, for the dedication comprises two quatrains in praise of Langholm, there is a piece
about 'The Monument' on White Hill and a consideration of
'The Point of Honour' at the river Esk brings MacDiarmid
back to his creative source:

> *Nay, the last issue I have all but joined,*
> *But my muse still lacks – and so has missed all –*
> *The right temper, like yours, which goes to the point*
> *Of the terrible; the terrible crystal.* (390)

Restless as ever, MacDiarmid wants to choose a new way
forward. There was no question of rationalisation after the
event of a creative breakdown for, as the magnificent set of
'Shetland Lyrics' show, there is no sign of his Scots lyrical
source drying up:

> I suddenly saw I was wrang when I felt
> That the gapin' mooths and gogglin' een
> O' the fish were no' what we should expect
> Frae a sea sae infinite and serene. (438)

MacDiarmid had tired of the lyric and felt that his evolutionary idealism demanded an appropriately extensive form. His
desire to convey the notion of a miraculous nativity led him
to experiment with this theme in Aggrandised Scots. In the
sustained creative spasm that is 'Harry Semen', the language
gushes forth in a simulation of the universalism that is implicit
in the formal harmony that links sperm to stars:

Sae Joseph may ha'e pondered; sae a snawstorm
Comes whirlin' in grey sheets frae the shadowy sky
And only in a sma' circle are the separate flakes seen.
White, whiter, they cross and recross as capricious they
    fly,
Mak' patterns on the grund and weave into wreaths,
Load the bare boughs, and find lodgements in corners
    frae
The scourin' wind that sends a snawstorm up frae the
    earth
To meet that frae the sky, till which is which nae man
    can say.
They melt in the waters. They fill the valleys. They
    scale the peaks.
There's a tinkle o' icicles. The topmaist summit shines
    oot.
Sae Joseph may ha'e pondered on the coiled fire in his
    seed,
The transformation in Mary, and seen Jesus tak' root.
  (485)

Although the Scots makes a memorable fusion of concepts, it
no longer satisfied MacDiarmid who wanted to give his mysticism the benefit of a scientific terminology. The result was
what he came to call Synthetic English. (SE, 79) The intention was to save his metaphysical approach from a superfluity
of abstraction and imprecision:

With regard despite my political and linguistic
propensities to my latterly writing so much in English,
this has been due to a shift in my fundamental
intellectual interests. More and more I have been
concerned with scientific matters, and I found it
impossible to express these at any rate with the necessary
precision even in my aggrandised Scots – even English
does not have anything like an adequate scientific
vocabulary – one must use all sorts of *ad hoc* neologisms,

and that is one of the reasons why I have had to eke out
my English with all sorts of words and phrases from
other languages – of course that is the very way English
itself has been built up.[5]

The first example, in *Stony Limits*, of the Synthetic English
MacDiarmid was evolving is given in the poem 'In the Caledonian Forest' where the alliteration suggests the
dictionary-derived basis of the medium:

> The geo-selenic gimbal that moving makes
> A gerbe now of this tree now of that
> Or glomerates the whole earth in a galanty-show
>   Against the full moon caught
> Suddenly threw a fuscous halation round a druxy
>   dryad
>   Lying among the fumet in this dwale wood
> As brooding on Scotland's indecrassifiable race
>   I wandered again in a hemicranic mood. (391)

'Vestigia Nulla Retrorsum', in memory of Rilke, brings the
imagery of Synthetic English down to earth in geological
detail and the title poem of *Stony Limits* offers a patron saint
of Synthetic English. MacDiarmid's verbal monument to
Charles Doughty is apt since Doughty's work, particularly
The Dawn in Britain (1906) with its idiosyncratic English and
metaphysical longing, anticipated MacDiarmid's search for
a Celtic counterpart to English culture. MacDiarmid felt for
Doughty the same kind of empathy he had extended to John
Davidson in *Scots Unbound*:

> [Doughty's] significance today dwarfs all the other
> English poets since Elizabethan times into utter
> insignificance. . . To those of us who are concerned about
> a Scottish renaissance, Doughty's unique preoccupation
> with – and marvellous penetration into – ancient British
> (Celtic) consciousness is [totally] convincing . . .
> Doughty's idea was to make a fresh channel for English
> direct from the upper reaches, from the vernacular as it

was before the Renaissance, and so freshen and purify the corrupt main flood. (SE, 76, 85)

MacDiarmid's poem uses an abstruse vocabulary worthy of Doughty and salutes the man as a colleague, a fellow worker in the field of language. MacDiarmid is able to produce a poem that transcends the literary exercise through the pressure he brings to bear on a worthy subject who is described thus in a poetic conclusion memorable for its final flourish:

> red as Adam you stood
> In the desert, the horizon with vultures black-winged,
> And sang and died in this still greater solitude
> Where I sit by your skull whose emptiness is worth
> The sum of almost all the full heads now on Earth
> – By your roomy skull where most men might well
>   spend
> Longer than you did in Arabia, friend! (422)

To satisfy himself that Synthetic English was worth the effort of the creative lifetime that remained to him, MacDiarmid had to experiment with it over a longer stretch. The result was a meditation 'On a Raised Beach'.

Just as *A Drunk Man* is MacDiarmid's masterpiece in Synthetic Scots, so 'On a Raised Beach' is his most memorable poem in Synthetic English. It is a poetic contemplation of a Shetland storm beach as a structure shaped by the creative force at large in the universe. Though the beach has an apparently random form determined by the ferocity of the elements, it is an important part of MacDiarmid's argument that its appearance is the result of external pressure exerted by the creative principle. In the first verse-paragraph Mac-Diarmid moves from a statement of fact to an enquiry. Everything around him, at the time of writing, is apparently inhuman, born of stone. The static stones are, though, capable of creation. MacDiarmid juxtaposes the still lithogenesis with a dynamic image of Christ's resurrection as a movement indicative of some divine intervention. The force that lifted

the stone from the sepulchre is capable of endless creation
and recreation; it is the same force that activates the universe
and motivates the poet. MacDiarmid's opening verse-paragraph, with its dictionary-derived alliteration, is both majestic
and moving:

> All is lithogenesis – or lochia,
> Carpolite fruit of the forbidden tree,
> Stones blacker than any in the Caaba,
> Cream-coloured caen-stone, chatoyant pieces,
> Celadon and corbeau, bistre and beige,
> Glaucous, hoar, enfouldered, cyathiform,
> Making mere faculae of the sun and moon
> I study you glout and gloss, but have
> No cadrans to adjust you with, and turn again
> From optik to haptik and like a blind man run
> My fingers over you, arris by arris, burr by burr,
> Slickensides, truité, rugas, foveoles,
> Bringing my aesthesis in vain to bear,
> An angle-titch to all your corrugations and coigns,
> Hatched foraminous cavo-rilievo of the world,
> Deictic, fiducial stones. Chiliad by chiliad
> What bricole piled you here, stupendous cairn?
> What artist poses the Earth échorché thus,
> Pillar of creation engouled in me?
> What eburnation augments you with men's bones,
> Every energumen an Endymion yet?
> All the other stones are in this haecceity it seems,
> But where is the Christophanic rock that moved?
> What Cabirian song from this catasta comes? (422–3)

Man, represented by the poet, has moved from his original
oceanic element on to the land. He has taken for granted the
physiological fact of evolution; now he is required to will a
new stage of evolutionary idealism. The poet has come to this
stony element as a uniquely gifted individual created in the
shaping image of the creative force that men have codenamed
God. Like a God the poet has to bring forth creation; has to

make the spirit rise from the stone. As the poem gets under-
way MacDiarmid reveals that he is lying on his back. This
horizontal man has to lift himself up in a metaphysical sense.
MacDiarmid focuses his attention on the storm beach and is
touched by the movement of a bird as it soars above the
stones. The lifting movement reminds MacDiarmid of his
evolutionary idealism and he too is inclined to soar, especially
as he is aware that 'these stones have dismissed/All but all of
evolution'. (424) The poet has to bring speech from stone in
order to approach the wordless eloquence of the elements.

Surrounded by hard evidence of stony indifference Mac-
Diarmid contrasts his physical vulnerability with the persistence of the stones and advances the central proposition of the
poem:

> We must be humble. We are so easily baffled by
>   appearances
> And do not realise that these stones are one with the
>   stars.
> It makes no difference to them whether they are high
>   or low,
> Mountain peak or ocean floor, palace, or pigsty.
> There are plenty of ruined buildings in the world but
>   no ruined stones. (425)

MacDiarmid thus links the earthly with the eternal, the stony
silence with the speed of light, the squalid with the sublime.
He is aware of the metaphysical presence of the stones; in
touch with their essential meaning. They inspire awe in him.
Whereas the creations of man can be destroyed and reduced
to rubble, the creations of the universe are unbreakably eternal. A building can be ruinously reduced, but the beach that
is battered by storm and shattered by sea is only impercep-
tibly altered into another equally valid form. Nature's architecture is not arbitrary but affirmative. Urbanisation, on the
other hand, is transient. To MacDiarmid the stones are the
embodiment of a creative intensity. They are examples of the
shapes assumed by a universally creative intelligence. As his

poetry is a literary transcription of the universal spirit of creativity MacDiarmid connects the divine source with

> This more divine rhythm, wholly at one
> With the earth, riding the Heavens with it, as the
>   stones do
> And all soon must. (425)

Anticipating the impasse that would result if he surrendered entirely to the pathetic fallacy, MacDiarmid immediately tells himself 'it is wrong to indulge in these illustrations/Instead of just accepting the stones'. (425) Thinking of his own impulsive personality, he feels the need for a Wordsworthian moment of tranquillity as 'Impatience is a poor qualification for immortality.' (425)

To MacDiarmid, a poet whose best work places a cerebral conception in an emotional matrix, there is an ambivalent attitude to emotional exhibitionism; the poet suspects that 'Hot blood is of no use in dealing with eternity' (426). He wants to deal almost exclusively with eternity, so offers up to the universal creative principle the battleground of his own consciousness with its dialectical movement of mind, its ebb and flow of extremes:

> It is essential to know the chill of all the objections
> That come creeping into the mind, the battle between
>   opposing ideas
> Which gives the victory to the strongest and most
>   universal
> Over all others, and to wage it to the end
> With increasing freedom, precision, and detachment
> A detachment that shocks our instincts and ridicules
>   our desires. (426)

Everything in the universe, and therefore in MacDiarmid's world, is created; the creations that endure eternally are those that go beyond the exigencies of day-to-day life and embrace a timeless significance. Since the stones constitute the basic artistic material used by the creative force they are indispensable:

> the world cannot dispense with the stones.
> They alone are not redundant. Nothing can replace
>   them
> Except a new creation of God. (426)

Such cogitation brings MacDiarmid the evolutionary ideal-ist back to the essentials; back to the stones and the force that moves them for 'These stones go through Man, straight to God, if there is one.' (427). In a recapitulation of lithogenesis MacDiarmid pushes back the imaginative curtains to spot-light the first stage of evolution. We are given a poetic account of what it was like in the beginning when the stones emerged in the shape of things to come:

> Only in them
> If in anything, can His creation confront Him.
> They came so far out of the water and halted forever.
> That larking dallier, the sun, has only been able to
>   play
> With superficial by-products since;
> The moon moves the waters backwards and forwards,
> But the stones cannot be lured an inch farther
> Either on this side of eternity or the other.
> Who thinks God is easier to know than they are?
> Trying to reach men any more, any otherwise, than
>   they are?
> These stones will reach us long before we reach them.
> Cold, undistracted, eternal and sublime. (427)

So astonishing is this evidence of the creative force that the poet applauds it and responds to its promise of immortality. Eternally alive with the spirit of creativity he produces a moving passage concerning his conquest of the fear of death:

Death is a physical horror to me no more.
I am prepared with everything else to share
Sunshine and darkness and wind and rain
And life and death bare as these rocks though it be
In whatever order nature may decree,
But, not indifferent to the struggle yet
Nor to the ataraxia I might get
By fatalism, a deeper issue see
Than these, or suicide, here confronting me.
It is reality that is at stake. (428)

In many of his previous poems MacDiarmid had taken
solipsism seriously enough to compose poems in its honour;
he had acted out an egotism so sublime that his poems assumed a part in the creation of the universe. Now he understands how his poetic creations relate to universal creations
and appreciates the interstellar distance between literary ut-
terances and the silent 'music of the spheres'. (428) Mac-
Diarmid feels that the individual habitually makes artistic
models of a secondary world since the primary spiritual world
(the source of creativity) is beyond sight, speech and sense
and therefore linguistically indefinable and epistemologically
unknowable:

    the kindred form I am conscious of here
  Is the beginning and end of the world,
  The unsearchable masterpiece, the music of the
      spheres,
  Alpha and Omega, the Omnific Word.
  These stones have the silence of supreme creative
      power,
  The direct and undisturbed way of working
  Which alone leads to greatness. (428–9)

Such a thought allows MacDiarmid to come to a new visionary synthesis that reconciles his evolutionary idealism with
his obligations to his fellow men, and his unversalism with
his isolation. The artistically autonomous individual makes

his contribution to the universe precisely by being alone with
the elements in order to communicate to other men unique
teleological conclusions:

> It will be ever increasingly necessary to find
> In the interests of all mankind
> Men capable of rejecting all that all other men
>   Think, as a stone remains
> Essential to the world, inseparable from it,
>   And rejects all other life yet.
> Great work cannot be combined with surrender to the
>   crowd. (429)

Here MacDiarmid puts the reader under pressure, demands
that he dissociate himself from mob morality, requires a concentration so complete that it corresponds to the creative
force. The reader has to accept the poet's word on questions
of creativity:

> Listen to me – Truth is not crushed;
> It crushes, gorgonises all else into itself. (430)

From his position as a creative individual MacDiarmid
surveys civilisation and treats it critically as a collective creation of an evolving species. As this essentially rural poet sees
it, extant civilisation amounts only to urbanisation; mankind
has passed its time either building monuments to house citizens or destroying these structures. Compared to the teleological end of creativity these civilised structures are
primitive:

> All human culture is a Goliath to fall
> To the least of these pebbles withal. (431)

In his awareness of the transience of earthly artefacts Mac-
Diarmid speaks as a man who has, through intense inner
contemplation, come close to the source of creativity and seen
its glow

> Superhumanly, menacingly clear – the reflection
> Of a brightness through a burning crystal. (431)

MacDiarmid the erstwhile intellectual elitist now takes the hand of MacDiarmid the man of the people. The twin attitudes of the poet are fused in an act of lifting at once symbolic and serene, physical and metaphysical:

> These bare stones bring me straight back to reality.
>   I grasp one of them and I have in my grip
> The beginning and the end of the world,
> My own self, and as before I never saw
> The empty hand of my brother man,
> The humanity no culture has reached, the mob.
> Intelligentsia, our impossible and imperative job! (432)

The new and stupendous task of the poet is to lift the stones one by one so that the spirit of the people – the despised 'mob' – can rise to resurrection. Implicit in the image is the concept of the 'The masses' (432) having been held down by the intolerable burden of economic oppression. From the act of lifting the stones a new poetic spirit will be born. The poet of the future must participate in life fully and yet honour his obligations to the spiritual reality that ultimately shapes him and the world he inhabits:

>   It is not
>   The reality of life that is hard to know.
> It is nearest of all and easiest to grasp,
> But you must participate in it to proclaim it.
> – I lift a stone; it is the meaning of life I clasp
> Which is death, for that is the meaning of death;
> How else does any man yet participate
>   In the life of a stone,
> How else can any man yet become
> Sufficiently at one with creation, sufficiently alone,
> Till as the stone that covers him he lies dumb
> And the stone at the mouth of his grave is not
>   overthrown? (432–3)

Again, as in *A Drunk Man*, the artist is a saviour willing to make a supreme sacrifice in the name of humanity. Immortality is attained by artistic integrity and physical death absorbed into spiritual life:

So let us beware of death; the stones will have
Their revenge; we have lost all approach to them,
But soon we shall become as those we have betrayed,
And they will seal us fast in our graves
As our indifference and ignorance seals them;
    But let us not be afraid to die.
No heavier and colder and quieter then,
No more motionless, do stones lie
    In death than in life to all men.
It is not more difficult in death than here
– Though slow as the stones the powers develop
To rise from the grave – to get a life worth having;
And in death – unlike life – we lose nothing that is
    truly ours. (433)

Alive again with the notion of resurrection MacDiarmid makes a serious attempt to reach 'The humanity no culture has reached, the mob' (432) in the Other Poems in *Second Hymn to Lenin and Other Poems* (1935). Though it is MacDiarmid's most incisively political volume, rich in emphatic poems that bear comparison with the work of Brecht, it does not abandon evolutionary idealism in favour of party politics. In fact it features the concept of a mystical and metaphysical nativity and the penultimate poem offers a vision of the terrible crystal of creativity buried in the slums of Glasgow. As counterpoint to the three visionary poems ('Birth of a Genius Among Men', 'Lo! A Child is Born', 'In the Slums of Glasgow') MacDiarmid includes some didactically direct poetry demonstrating the force of his provocative couplet asserting

In short, any utterance that is not pure
Propaganda is impure propaganda for sure! (558)

With polemical skill and a good deal of political indignation MacDiarmid produces poems speaking for the masses. 'After Two Thousand Years' is an attack on Christian institutions as hypocritical organisations bestowing blessings on 'any murderer or fraud' capable of exploiting the 'working-classes' (559). 'Reflections in an Ironworks' calls for an injection of iron into the souls of the mob so they can overcome the superior irony of the master-class. 'The End of Usury' impatiently dismisses economic injustice as an evolutionary hangover from 'an obscene incredible past' (554). 'Another Epitaph on an Army of Mercenaries' takes issue with A. E. Housman's qualitative distinction between volunteers and regular professional soldiers; to MacDiarmid the 'professional murderers' (551) are simply despicable enemies of life. 'In the Children's Hospital' satirises the susceptibility of the working-classes to flattery and 'In the Slaughterhouse' uses the familiar image of the people as sheep blundering willingly towards slaughter.

As we have seen several of the propagandist poems – 'At the Cenotaph', 'One of the Principal Causes of War', 'As Lovers Do', 'From an "Ode to All Rebels" ' – are part of the 'Ode to All Rebels' rendered into English. They are, in other words, particular parts of a general vision. In this volume MacDiarmid's propaganda leads, as it invariably does, towards an affirmation of spirituality. The quest for the terrible crystal, or the supreme reality, goes on simultaneously with a concern for political justice. MacDiarmid the political activist (to whom party membership was always important) longs for the embrace of the universal, for harmony with the infinite:

> And quicken me to the gloriously and terribly
>   illuminating
> Integration of the physical and spiritual till I feel how
>   easily
> I could put my hand gently on the whole round world
> As on my sweetheart's head and draw it to me. (539)

MacDiarmid's renewed metaphysical interest in the notion of

spiritual nativity was probably prompted by the fact that, in 1932, his second wife, Valda, gave birth to his third child, Michael. The event is alluded to in 'An Unknown Quantity' and 'The Two Parents'. In response to the political climate of the 1930s MacDiarmid felt, at times, that the greatest priority of a socialist poet was to act in the interests of 'the humanity no culture has reached, the mob' (432) and some poems go through the motions of qualifying the fundamental belief in the inviolability of individuality.

In *Second Hymn to Lenin and Other Poems*, MacDiarmid returns to his earlier faith in the coming of 'A greater Christ, a greater Burns' (86). The earth is to be liberated by a saviour who has either the political skill of a Lenin or the poetic vision of a MacDiarmid; the representative of the future has to combine these talents. Two poems dwell on the circumstances of a saviour arriving on earth, delivered up like a gift for the good of humanity. 'Birth of a Genius Among Men' describes the birth as the result of a metaphysical union between a selfconsciously creative individual and the feminine personification of God (or Sophia, though MacDiarmid does not name names in this poem). The philosophical argument of the poem suggests that individuals are taken up and used by timeless creative forces anxious to express their eternal ideas in human form. Each actual birth is, as it were, a rehearsal for the ideal birth, each genius an example of the evolutionary ideal:

> To both of us it seemed as if we had never loved
>   before.
> A miracle was abroad and I knew that not merely I
> Had accomplished the act of love but the whole
>   universe through me,
> A great design was fulfilled, another genius nigh. (540)

'Lo! A Child Is Born' is an evocation, through a cascade of connected images, of the birth of a genius so precocious that he instinctively stage-manages his delivery from the womb to the waiting world. There is little doubt that Mac-

Diarmid had in mind the figure of Lenin who was his favourite symbol of a mind so decisive that it could dismiss the difficulties of the present, sum up the past and create the future in a revolutionary series of events. The Marxist critic David Craig, commenting on the Leninist nature of the poetic nativity, notes that 'Lenin's mastery ... evidently typified for MacDiarmid a kind of clarity he ... desperately wanted'. (Festschrift, 91). It is for this reason that MacDiarmid uses the phrase 'Springing into history' (548); history, in this context, is not a record of the past but a dynamic force the revolutionary directs by the exercise of his will. This is the whole point of the presentation of the 'new-born son' as a creation disowned by the past and instantly ready to face the future:

> A strategic mind already, seeking the best way
> To present himself to life, and at last, resolved,
> Springing into history quivering like a fish,
> Dropping into the world like a ripe fruit in due time –
> But where is the Past to which Time, smiling through
>   her tears
> At her new-born son, can turn crying: 'I love you'?
>   (548)

The question is rhetorical and refers back to the Scots lyric 'O Jesu Parvule'.

The isolation of the individual, a common enough theme in modern literature, derives from the apparent incompatibility of cities with individual sensitivity. Late Victorian and twentieth-century literature shows a deep distrust of urban life: the swarms of nameless people who trudge across London Bridge in Eliot's *The Waste Land* are only the most celebrated examples of anonymity in modern poetry. In his poems on 'Edinburgh' and 'Glasgow' – where we find references to 'the darkness of industrialism' (646) and 'darkness of spirit' (1049) – MacDiarmid articulates his contempt for cities. Though, theoretically, a Marxist with a belief in the means of production as a weapon in the fight to secure the future for 'the feck'

MacDiarmid always stresses the negative aspects of industrialisation. In his poetry the individual who rises above the squalor of city life is either a revolutionary giant such as Lenin (able to control the movement of masses) or a poetic nonconformist such as John Davidson (who finally found himself defeated by circumstances hence MacDiarmid's distress at his death). It is this background that makes 'In the Slums of Glasgow' such a special poem for MacDiarmid's evolutionary vision enables him to see through the depressing details of urban squalor. He looks through the shadows to the substance and finds spiritual enlightenment in a mystical awareness of the goodness of the human species: 'I too look on the world and behold it is good.' (562). The lack of concern for identifiable individuals is sometimes held to be a weakness of MacDiarmid's poetry. Here we see its strength for MacDiarmid believes that by a stupendous effort of will the visionary poet can see in 'the despised slum-crowd' (564) what they hardly apprehend in themselves. They are but dimly aware of what the poet knows as a result of his inspirational insight: that the human spirit can survive the most appalling environment. MacDiarmid's faith in 'the feck' is crystal-clear and the slum-dwellers will emerge from their darkness when guided by 'a shining light' (562): in 'In the Slums of Glasgow' MacDiarmid the poetic prophet illuminates the city; in 'Third Hymn to Lenin' the Russian revolutionary provides the light.

'In the Slums of Glasgow' is a mystical poem that considers poverty as a spiritual condition rather than an economic status. As a persistent critic of urbanisation – 'There are plenty of ruined buildings in the world but no ruined stones' (425) – MacDiarmid habitually uses the city as a symbol of destruction. In this poem he takes his urban antipathy to extremes as he considers the squalid slum conditions prevailing in Glasgow in the 1930s. In an area where life is physically distressing the spirit still rears its lovely head. MacDiarmid finds in the slums a creative quality and conveys it in an eight-line stanza rhyming *abcbdbeb*:

I have caught a glimpse of the seamless garment
And am blind to all else for evermore.
The immaculate vesture, the innermost shift,
    Of high and low, of rich and poor,
The glorious raiment of bridegroom and bride,
    Whoremonger and whore,
I have caught a glimpse of the seamless garment
And have eyes for aught else no more. (562)

The archaic ring of the 'aught' helps to place the poem in a
biblical perspective for MacDiarmid has come to the slums
to consider the meek who are, according to both Christian
and Communist mythology, about to inherit the earth. The
poet examines their spiritual credentials for communism.

MacDiarmid's fellow feeling with the 'folk of these slums'
(563) persuades him that they can be disfigured by poverty
but not entirely destroyed by it. They survive on a metaphysical level that is evidence of the central mystery of life.
Buried beneath the layers of indifference and ignorance is the
terrible crystal of creativity; it exists, even in the slums, as
'the inner radiance, the mystery of the hidden light' (564).
The glimpse of eternity in the slums transfigures the poet who
indulges the ecstasy of his Pauline moment:

I have not gained a single definite belief that can be
    put
In a scientific formula or hardened into a religious
    creed.
A conversion is not, as mostly thought, a turning
    towards a belief,
It is rather a turning round, a revolution indeed.
It has no primary reference to any external object.
It took place in me at last with lightning speed.
I suddenly walk in light, my feet are barely touching
    the ground,
I am free of a million words and forms I no longer
    need. (563)

With this attitude MacDiarmid condemns capitalism (as Pound, in his Cantos, condemned usury) as a crime against nature, a sin against the 'free impulse of life' (564). Capitalism has attempted to crush the working people into caves but they have used these hovels as Platonic caves of creation, simulating spiritual ecstasy through sexual bliss which is 'The bliss of God glorifying every squalid lair.' (564)

Seven years after 'In the Slums of Glasgow' appeared in *Second Hymn to Lenin and Other Poems*, MacDiarmid was himself living in Glasgow and 'doing hard manual labour in big Clydeside engineering shops' (LP, xxxiii). He left Whalsay in February 1942 and in Glasgow he completed his 'Third Hymn to Lenin'. It is conceived on a different, more discursive, level than the two previous hymns. Whereas they lectured Lenin on the superiority of poetry to politics, this 'Third Hymn to Lenin' calls on the spectre of Communism to haunt Glasgow. Indeed MacDiarmid felt that an alternative title might be 'Glasgow Invokes the Spirit of Lenin' (893). By using the internationally infamous Glasgow slums as a symbol of capitalism MacDiarmid depicts an industrial inferno on which Lenin is summoned to descend like an avenging angel. Recalling the metaphysical nativity of 'Lo! A Child Is Born' and the image of the 'strategic mind', (548) MacDiarmid attributes miraculous powers to Lenin:

> On days of revolutionary turning points you literally
>   flourished,
> Became clairvoyant, foresaw the movement of classes,
> And the probable zig-zags of the revolution
> As if on your palm;
> Not only an analytical mind but also
> A great constructive, synthesizing mind
> Able to build up in thought the new reality
> As it must actually come
> By force of definite laws eventually (894)

The metaphorical content of Marxism – the dialectical movement of a personified History, the advance of the anonymous masses, the revelation of hidden structures and superstructures – is irresistibly attractive to MacDiarmid who is characteristically able to soar above the squalid confines of the industrial city. He examines all the evidence around him – the slums, the genteel tea-rooms, the 'mindless mobs, the gangsters' (898) – and returns to the basic assumption that sustained him through the 1930s. This is the belief that 'thought is reality – and thought alone!' (899) MacDiarmid wants a Lenin to make the world fit for the kind of poetry he was composing towards the end of the 1930s. This poetry of the future is to be on a scale grand enough to occupy Mac-Diarmid for the remainder of his creative lifetime. In comparison to his new project, compositions such as 'Third Hymn to Lenin' were to be classed as occasional poems suitable for insertion in one scheme or another for during the 1930s Mac-Diarmid contemplated a Scottish *Faust* and the Leninist hymns, for instance, could have suited that book as well as *Clann Albann*. MacDiarmid's new endless epic was 'in the nature of a comprehensive manifesto [designed to exemplify] the aspiration to world-consciousness which has been the guiding principle in all my more recent work.' (LP, 114)

Chapter Six
ALONE WITH THE ALONE

You are at aince the road a' croods ha' gane
And alane wi' the alane.
> 'Depth and the Chthonian Image' (349)

So in the speech to which all our efforts converge
Vanish all the complications of human life
Before the exultant note of universal joy.
The Mature Art – alone with the Alone.
> *In Memoriam James Joyce* (786)

Some of the most critically acclaimed English poetry of the twentieth century shares a vision that reaches back to the dreamy promise of childhood. T. S. Eliot nostalgically recalled 'the children in the apple-tree' ('Little Gidding'), Edwin Muir harked back to a place where 'incorruptible the child plays still' ('The Transmutation'), and Dylan Thomas fondly harped on the time when he was 'young and easy under the apple boughs' ('Fern Hill'). It is an enduring image of Eden, a recollection of childhood as the point of emotional perfection with the subsequent unfolding of life as an anticlimax. Though MacDiarmid, in the Muckle Toon poems, used the landscape surrounding Langholm as an emblem of Eden it was not an obsessive quest and he virtually abandoned it as an irresistibly poetic subject when he left the Scottish mainland to settle in Whalsay in 1933. MacDiarmid had a good national reason, too, for avoiding in principle the theme of repossessing the lost Eden of childhood. He was

painfully aware of how J. M. Barrie had turned the Gaelic
myth of Tir nan Og into Neverland and wanted a poetry that
would forever rid Scotland of its infantilism:

> Peter Pan nae langer oor deity'll be
> And oor boast an endless infantilism.
> Away, wi' the auld superstitions. Let the sun up at last
> And hurl a' sic spooks into their proper abysm. (382)

These lines are from 'Envoi: On Coming Home', one of the
last poems he consciously composed to fit into *The Muckle
Toon*. They have the valedictory mood that MacDiarmid enjoyed at moments when he was about to embark on yet
another project.

What MacDiarmid hoped to achieve was an alternative
vision, an entirely adult conception of the world. He wanted
to do for the scientific age what Dante had done for the
medieval period and Milton for a sceptical era: he wished to
sustain a persuasive vision in verse. Under the pressure of a
creative idea he would lift language to new heights of expression and, simultaneously, explore a theme that would bring
humanity up to a new evolutionary level. The new poem was
to penetrate into the future, it was to look ahead – and it is
no accident that he planned to call the last part of it either
Impavidi Progrediamur or *Haud Forrit* (Lap, 11). MacDiarmid's
epic would be an intellectual odyssey towards the source of
creativity and it would be charted in language designed to
raise the spirit. In *In Memoriam James Joyce* MacDiarmid has
a reference to language as a force of nature:

> Language,
> Accomplishing what it pleases, traversing all things,
> By subtlety of nature; rising to colossal dimensions,
> Or standing on the tops of the filaments of a flower,
> Or rising to the solar sphere on a sunbeam (786)

MacDiarmid's neoplatonic proclivities gave rise to a key concept: the earthly language he employed would correspond to

an ideal language composed of the creative elements of all extant languages. MacDiarmid's new long poem would therefore be in the nature of an experimental exploration of this ideal language and he insisted that 'I'm looking for a diversity in unity, not for a unification of languages.' (Uncanny, 171) It was an immensely ambitious project though MacDiarmid's sense of humour allowed him to understate it:

> We only seek the full unobstructed light
> Of the speech of our own star – the speech of all
>   mankind. (742)

Exiled on his Shetland island, MacDiarmid was forced back on his own imaginative resources and the long poem he composed was a staggering individual effort in the interests of isolating the source of creativity. As planned in autobiographical stages *Clann Albann* was not epic enough for MacDiarmid's latest poetic programme and he was becoming increasingly convinced that length was a poetic virtue in itself, a demonstration of belief in the future. As he put it, at a later date, 'I'm all for GIANTISM in the arts. Everything that means the expansion of creative genius to a point where all the little people simply can't comprehend it and are excluded automatically.' (Company, 56) During the Whalsay years, therefore, he put *Clann Albann* aside and began work on his new sequence. He wanted to survey Scotland from the apparently inaccessible heights of what he referred to, in 'Cornish Heroic Song' (705) and *In Memoriam James Joyce* (746) as his *aonach*, a Gaelic word meaning '(1) a solitary place, a mountain top, a hill; (2) a place of union.' (705) The poem would confront appearance with the 'supreme reality' (745) and show that evolutionary idealism is attainable, that creativity can be traced to its source, and that the individual can gain access to a universal unity. In a deliberately misleading comment on the epic MacDiarmid said

> Any theology is quite inacceptable to me, however, since like Joyce and Pound I hold no supernatural faith, but I

believe that this unification [of human knowledge] will be achieved ultimately 'in a society in which the participant aspect of action attains its maximum expresion' – a society which I naturally visualise as Marxist. (Joyce, 17)

MacDiarmid certainly did not subscribe to any institutional theology or superstitious dogma but the whole poem is animated by a supernatural faith in the spiritual future of humanity in general and the Celtic people in particular.

MacDiarmid had long wanted to write a national epic with international cultural connotations. It was to be a poetic solution to the problem of Scotland's cultural fragmentation. As Sergeant Grieve in Salonika during the First World War he had greatly admired Maurice Hewlett's *The Song of the Plow* (1916), a celebration of the indigenous English peasantry as personified in the hero Hodge who champions the cause of the Angles. The older English poets MacDiarmid admired most – Milton, Blake, Doughty – had also written patriotic epics. Whitman and Pound, MacDiarmid's favourite American poets, had given their country a rich cultural consciousness. Yet Scotland or, more specifically, Gaeldom still lacked an appropriate modern epic. MacDiarmid wanted a poem big enough to contain his nationalism as well as his philosophy so it was to have the patriotic push of, say, *The Song of the Plow* plus the verbal fluidity and thematic sweep of, say, *Leaves of Grass*. It was not to rely on a dogmatically supernatural system but was to explore and express the MacDiarmidian metaphysic.

The new sequence as a whole was to be called *Mature Art* or perhaps *Cornish Heroic Song* or perhaps (as the subtitle of *In Memorian James Joyce* has it) *A Vision of World Language*. MacDiarmid changed his mind about the most suitable title for the complete work as publishing difficulties made the sequence a work perpetually in progress. In 1947 he placed a section from *The Kind of Poetry I Want* in a larger context by identifying it as 'an extract from one of the long poems in Mr MacDiarmid's 20,000 line poem, 'Mature Art', which was to have been published by the Obelisk Press, Paris – a project squashed by the war and the Fall of France.' (Kist, 31) In 1962 the complete epic was still very much in his mind as he explained his use of the title *Impavidi Progrediamur* as 'One of the four volumes of the huge poem of which 'In Memoriam James Joyce' (1955) was the first.' (Collected, 41) In the Prefatory Note to *A Lap of Honour* (1967) he said:

> I am now seventy-five, and cannot therefore promise that there will be any substantial further addition to the corpus of my poetry, except for my very long, · unpublished, and still uncompleted 'Impavidi Progrediamur', to which, however, I will, instead of that Latin title, give the Scots one of 'Haud Forrit'. (Lap, 11)

And in the Author's Note to *Complete Poems* he wrote, two years before his death,

> [*Impavidi Progrediamur*] is still unpublished: I have simply abandoned the whole project. . . Other large-scale projects, such as 'Clann Albann' (with its parts 'The Muckle Toon' and 'Fier comme un Ecossais') and the complete 'Cornish Heroic Song for Valda Trevlyn', were either abandoned or subsumed in other works, and are not recorded here. (vi)

In 1938 MacDiarmid submitted *Mature Art*, as it then stood, to Faber and T. S. Eliot replied (on 8 June 1938) giving his opinion that 'it seems to me an extremely interesting, individual, and indeed very remarkable piece of work. There can be no doubt that it is something that ought to be published, but the question is how, and by whom.' Eliot considered the poem to be courageous but commercially unviable whereupon MacDiarmid submitted it to Jack Kahane who agreed to publish it with his Obelisk Press in Paris. Accordingly, Mac-Diarmid prepared a prospectus headed *Mature Art: An Exercise in Schlabone, Bordatini, and Scordattura* and invited subscribers to reserve (at two guineas per volume) a copy of the 20,000 line poem dealing with

the interrelated themes of the evolution of world literature and world consciousness, the problems of linguistics, the place and potentialities of the Gaelic genius, from its origin in Georgia to its modern expressions in Scotland, Ireland, Wales, Cornwall, Galicia and the Pays Basque, the synthesis of East and West, and the future of civilisation.

It is a very learned poem involving a stupendous range of reference, especially to Gaelic, Russian, Italian and Indian literatures, German literature and philosophy, and modern physics and the physiology of the brain, and while mainly in English, utilises elements of over a score of languages, Oriental and Occidental.

When Jack Kahane died in the autumn of 1939 this ambitious publishing project died too and MacDiarmid had to shelve the poem and content himself, subsequently, with retouching the text from time to time.

What the reader has, then, is an unfinished epic, an open-ended discussion of a poem, a colossal edifice in which MacDiarmid's mind is processed through books and ideas. It is a poem about the poetic search for the source of creativity since MacDiarmid realises that 'in ages like our own all the ostensible themes and subjects of the poet will tend to be in the first place simply allegories for the creative process itself.' (LP, 337) It is also an epic with a hero for an idealised MacDiarmid is presented as the poetic saviour, 'The Man for whom Gaeldom is waiting':

> He was the wind, the sea, the tempest, the hurricane.
> He was the marvellous embodiment
> Of the complete identification
> Of the Celtic mind with all nature and all life
> That before his emergence had been long
> Totally beyond the comprehension
> Of the vast majority of modern Gaels,
> Who had been in full retreat for over a century,
> Fearing reality, passion, tragedy, communal assertion,
> Fearing even the imputation of sadness

And blind and deaf to the things of the mind
And the intricate high arts of their ancestors (1375)

Mature Art was, as these lines suggest, conceived as a Celtic
contribution to the art of the twentieth century; a concept
first adumbrated in 'Lament for the Great Music'. MacDiarmid wanted to give the Gael the benefit of a twentieth-century
consciousness so that the great music would be combined
with the imaginative resources of the scientific age. Mac-
Diarmid was quite clear on the Celtic nature of *Mature Art*:

> I want all this highly complicated poetry – and regard
> myself in this way as in others (although not in language)
> as a purely Celtic poet, carrying on (newly applied in
> vastly changed circumstances) the ancient bardic
> traditions of a very intricate and scholarly poetry, and
> with all the bardic powers of savage satire and invective
> as well as the bardic concern for the Celtic countries –
> Scotland, Ireland, Wales, and Cornwall – and for Celtic
> history and the continuity of Celtic civilization. (LP, 166)

In the poem Scotland is represented by the author, Ireland
by the likes of Joyce and Yeats, Wales by Dylan Thomas and
Cornwall by the poet's wife Valda. Above all that there is the
assumption that the quintessentially spiritual quality of Celtic
art will result in an intellectual unity and universal harmony.
Mature Art is designed as 'A poetry full of erudition, expertise,
and ecstasy' (1019); it follows the linguistic example of Joyce,
who fashioned his own philological instrument in *Finnegans
Wake* (1939) and is influenced by Pound whose Cantos convinced MacDiarmid that the mode of poetry suitable for his
evolutionary idealism and intellectual universalism should be
multilingual, allusive, ostentatiously cerebral and highly subjective. It is possible to see MacDiarmid's idea in action by
looking at the extant parts of *Mature Art* (assuming that, and
not *Cornish Heroic Song*, might have been the overall title)
which shapes up as the projected *Cornish Heroic Song for Valda
Trevlyn* (including the three 'Dìreadh' poems and *Poems of the
East-West Synthesis*); *The Kind of Poetry I Want*; *In Memoriam*

James Joyce and *Impavidi Progrediamur*. The fact that the first and last parts of the poem were never completed does not detract from its interest and MacDiarmid could (and no doubt would) have argued that his work was perpetually in progress, to cite his definition of 'Bagpipe Music' (which he intended to include in *Impavidi Progrediamur*):

> Let me play to you tunes without measure or end,
> Tunes that are born to die without a herald,
> As a flight of storks rises from a marsh, circles,
> And alights on the spot from which it rose. (665)

The Celtic connexion provided the structural principle of the epic which was to be read as a pibroch-like improvisation on a theme (or *urlar*) consisting of a consideration of 'the creative processes themselves' (LP, 337). When the poem was first shaped for publication MacDiarmid intended to preface it with an explanatory note on the structure:

> With regard to the formal character of my poems – or the informal character; the formless or chaotic character, or lack of architectonic power as it may appear to many readers – I am also not only quite impenitent, but venture to suggest that it bears out one of my main themes by its resemblance in this respect to what most Occidentals perhaps find most disconcerting and unlikeable in Oriental art and music – as in Scottish pipe music. (LP, 335)

MacDiarmid's desire for a Gaelic cultural revival began as a theoretical affair. As a child he had, on holidays near Dingwall, been able to 'learn a little Gaelic from the Ross-shire woman who was my uncle's second wife' (LP, 5) and in 1934 he came into contact with a man widely regarded as the greatest of all Gaelic poets – Sorley Maclean. On a visit to Edinburgh, MacDiarmid met Maclean and in 1935 Maclean spent a week with MacDiarmid on Whalsay. Maclean was able to assist and encourage MacDiarmid in his attempts to reclaim the remnants of Gaelic culture and to form, from the

fragmentation, a visionary account of what Gaelic might have
been had it avoided the persecution that followed Culloden.
As a first step in the realisation of his Gaelic Idea MacDiarmid wrote 'Lament for the Great Music' and then translated,
'from the Scots Gaelic of Alasdair MacMhaighstir Alasdair'
(513), 'The Birlinn of Clanranald'. In *To Circumjack Cencrastus*,
MacDiarmid had addressed Alasdair MacMhaighstir Alasdair in these terms: 'Your genius copes wi' a' that is/In
endless ecstasies'. (211) In translating this poetic hero Mac-
Diarmid produced an impressive sea-narrative with much
alliteration – 'brangled first with the brine' (515) – and some
adroit rhymes:

> Though the hoary heaving ocean
> Swell with even more commotion,
> Toppling waves with drowning notion
>   Roar and frown (520)

MacDiarmid later translated 'The Praise of Ben Dorain' from
the Gaelic of Duncan Ben MacIntyre, who was also the subject of a poem 'Further Talk with Donnchadh Bàn Mac an
t-Saoir'. Thus MacDiarmid felt entitled to claim some credit
as the man who 'provided what are generally acknowledged
by competent authorities to be the best translations of the
two greatest Scottish Gaelic poems' (LP, 175).

Mature Art was to do justice to the fact that MacDiarmid
was 'born a Scottish Gael/Of earth's subtlest speech, born
with a clever tongue' (1009). *Theoretically*, Gaelic was Mac-
Diarmid's native language since it was the language the
English had taken from the Scottish people as part of the
spoils of their military victory over the clans. It did not matter
if MacDiarmid's knowledge of Gaelic was minimal just as it
'would not matter so far as positing [the Gaelic Idea] is
concerned whether there had never been any Gaelic language
or literature. . . It is an intellectual conception' (SE, 68).
Typically, MacDiarmid was enormously impressed by two
controversial books that claimed to rescue the lost Gaelic
glory from propagandist hostility. L. A. Waddell's *The British*

Edda (1930) and L. A. Albert's *Six Thousand Years of Gaelic Grandeur Unearthed* (1936) provided MacDiarmid with a platform from which to launch an intellectually challenging Gaelic revival. According to MacDiarmid, Roger O'Connor (*Cier-Rige*) was to be accepted as a reliable transmitter of the ancient Celtic chronicles which were to be read in conjunction with the work of Doughty:

> These books – Doughty's poems, Waddell's *British Edda*, and the *Chronicles* – preserved and transmitted through *Cier-Rige*, afford a basis for . . . changing the whole course of our literary history, and torpedoing the culture associated with the English Ascendancy policy. And that is the aim of the Scottish Renaissance Movement. (LP, 296)

Apparently the books by Waddell and Albert also offered MacDiarmid 'proof that the original impetus to civilisation was an Ur-Gaelic initiative, *nota bene* in the very region, Georgia, the original home of the Scots, which has given Stalin to the world!' (LP, 369–70). Though the notion has obvious eccentricity MacDiarmid used it as a poetic impulse. In 'The Fingers of Baal Contract in the Communist Salute' (written in the late 1930s as the opening stanza about events in Spain confirms) we have

> 'Stalin the Georgian,' I have said. We are Georgians all.
> We Gaels. (679)

In 'Dìreadh III' he says the Scottish Gael

> initiated the idea of civilization
> That to-day needs renewal at its native source
> Where, indeed, it is finding it, since Georgia,
> Stalin's native country, was also the first home of the Scots. (1191)

And in 'Lamh Dearg Aboo', dedicated to Stalin, he addresses the Soviet dictator as follows:

Ah, Stalin, we Scots who had our first home
In Caucasian Georgia like yourself see how
The processes of history in their working out
Bring East and West together in general human
    triumph now. (1323–4)

These lines do not represent MacDiarmid at his best but they
do indicate how open he was to whatever ideas could serve
him in a poetic capacity. *Mature Art*, in fact, is full of ideas
that could be construed as outrageous.

A more important notion than the Georgian genesis of the
Scots is the project MacDiarmid called the East-West
Synthesis:

I have in recent years been greatly preoccupied with
what I call the East-West synthesis, the bridging of the
gulf between the East and the West, believing that the
clue to the process lies in the Gaelic genius – that this
indeed must be the world mission of the Gaelic
refluence. . . The ideas of the East-West synthesis and the
Caledonian antisyzygy merge into one and lie at the root
of any understanding of, for example, that greatest
Scottish musical achievement, the *piobaireachd* or great
pipe music, and it is impossible to communicate any idea
of pibroch to people who are not effectively seized of this
joint-idea. (LP, 14, 375)

MacDiarmid's *Cornish Heroic Song to Valda Trevlyn*, planned as
the first part of *Mature Art*, comprised – inter alia – *Poems of
the East-West Synthesis* (1946), with its reference to the Georgian
genesis of the Scots; the section of 'Cornish Heroic Song' that
appeared in the *Criterion* in 1939 and *A Kist of Whistles* (1947);
and the three 'Dìreadh' poems, since the first of these was
advertised as 'One of the shorter separable lyrics interspersed
in an immensely-long as-yet-unpublished poem, *Cornish Heroic
Song for Valda Trevlyn*' (Festschrift, 216). At one time it seems
that MacDiarmid intended to use the title *Cornish Heroic Song*
for the complete epic since he refers to *The Kind of Poetry I
Want*, as it appeared in *Lucky Poet*, as 'a sequence which runs,

appearing and reappearing at intervals, through the entire immense bulk of my *Cornish Heroic Song*' (LP, 165). The three *Poems of the East-West Synthesis* sound like a prelude to the Heroic Song proper; they envisage 'the Gaelic refluence, and the re-emergence/Of the Gaelic spirit at the Future's strongest and deepest root', (680) speak of 'the need/To refresh the Gaelic genius at its oldest sources' (681) and celebrate Cornwall as the land associated with 'Tristan and Iseult' (683).

'Cornish Heroic Song for Valda Trevlyn', as printed in the *Criterion,* was described as 'a long portion of the introductory section' and carried the superscription 'Carbonek, St Tib's Eve, 1936'.[1] It is a toast to his wife as both woman and feminine personification of the Celtic spirit of Cornwall. Mac-Diarmid had once joked about the cultural significance of his two marriages:

> I could never, by any possibility, have had anything to do with an English girl, but married first of all a Scots girl of old Highland descent, and as my second wife a Cornish girl, symbolizing the further development of my pro-Celtic ideas. (LP, 7)

As the spirit of Cornwall, Valda is both alluring and enchanting as she offers the possibility of a union between Celtic Cornwall and Celtic Scotland:

> Witch, you foreknew my mood to-night. I see you wear
> The golden lunula I had copied for you
> From the finest of the four found in Cornwall yet,
> Linking the Early Bronze Age and the Twentieth
>   Century,
> This crescentic collar or gorget of thin gold,
> Linking Scotland and Cornwall too,
> For was not the lunula a Scots creation? (705)

MacDiarmid celebrates Cornwall as 'Chip of Atlantis', 'This granite-bound corner', 'epic *intime*', 'little world apart' (706). In his marital merger with Valda he sees a symbolic fusion of Celtic elements. As he considers the power of this combination he recalls the symbol of Melville's Moby-Dick which had already surfaced in *A Drunk Man Looks at the Thistle*:

> The Celtic genius – Cornwall, Scotland, Ireland, Wales –
> Is to the English Ascendancy, the hideous khaki
>   Empire,
> As the white whale is to the killer whale,
> The white whale displaying in its buccal cavity
> The heavy oily blood-rich tongue which is the killer's
>   especial delight. (708–9)

The poem moves into a colourful description of Valda's hair which changes with the inspirational moment and the poet feels he must define his relationship with one woman as a partner representing a human and eternally creative principle:

> His attitude towards woman is the basic point
> A man must have thought out to know
> Where he honestly stands. (711)

MacDiarmid therefore broods on his beloved in whom he realises both the image of Cornwall and an emotional affirmation:

> To see the sun through its branches
> When the tree is in full bloom
> Is a thing that can never be forgotten.
> Nor the sight of your eyes now, Valda,
> Through the toppling wave of love.
> Love's scarlet banner is over us.
> We conquer Chaos, a new Creation. (712)

In his Scots lyrics MacDiarmid frequently employed the God's eye view of the earth which was anthropomorphised as a result. In his three 'Dìreadh' poems, designed as lyrical sections of the *Cornish Heroic Song for Valda Trevlyn*, he comes

closer to the contours of the earth by looking at Scotland from
an inspirational height so arranged as to reveal the actual
details of the Scottish landscape. In his first book the poet
had referred admiringly to 'a bird's-eye view, as Milton's
Satan first saw Paradise', (Annals, 99) and he later wrote the
three 'Dìreadh' poems to 'give birds'-eye views – or, rather,
eagles'-eye views – of the whole of Scotland, each from a
different vantage point' (LP, 255). These poems, whose collective title of 'Dìreadh' is the Gaelic word meaning the 'act
of surmounting' (1163), amount to a vision produced by a
Celtic consciousness. 'Dìreadh I' begins by parading Gaelic
words whose meanings are either given in parentheses or in
footnotes. The poet describes himself as 'Looking, *cromadh*, at
all Scotland below us' (1164). Because of the infusion of
Gaelic words the opening of the poem reads like a primer in
Gaelic, or pages from a phrasebook. However MacDiarmid
surmounts this philological obstacle and considers the nature
of his own work. He then produces a description of the ideal
of his poetry (though the irony of the first line of the following
extract should be noted):

> Without the least self-consciousness
> I achieve the ideal of so many poets,
> The union of poetry and science,
> My theme being nature *in solido*,
> That mysterious presence of surrounding things
> Which imposes itself on any separate element
> That we set up as an individual for its own sake.
>   (1167)

Nature, so far as the 'Dìreadh' sequence is concerned,
means Scottish nature (in both topographical and psychological senses). MacDiarmid tests his own Scottish nature as
a product of the Scottish earth-mother:

> I am the primitive man, Antaeus-like,
> Deriving my strength from the warm, brown, kindly
>   earth,
> My mother. (1167)

However, MacDiarmid is not about to succumb entirely to the sensuous charm of nature poetry which is too passive a medium to satisfy him. He desires to be a participant in any environment that appeals to him, claims to use his vision of a Scotocentric universe in the interests of poetry,

> To raise his theme to a higher level
> And transform it into a philosophic ideal
> In successive poems, realistic, idealistic, historical,
> And, finally, triumphantly, all three combined,
> Like the clear, sharp, changing looks of the Shetland
>   Islands
> That gain by not being a separate fact. (1168–9)

This higher level of consciousness is attainable both physically and metaphysically as the poet demonstrates by placing himself on summits. Regarding 'all Scotland/In my vision now' (1170) he sees in the physical diversity of the landscape the source of the Caledonian Antisyzygy. As a man on a mountain MacDiarmid sees the quintessential Scot as 'a world in himself . . . full of darkness like a mountain' (1170). Anticipating objections that his nationalistic vision and Scotocentric universe might be finite MacDiarmid redefines Scotland in a timeless dimension. He asks and answers a crucial rhetorical question in an evocation of landscape that goes back to an Edenic recollection of Langholm:

> Scotland small? Our multiform, our infinite Scotland
>   *small?*
> Only as a patch of hillside may be a cliché corner
> To a fool who cries 'Nothing but heather!' where in
>   September another
> Sitting there and resting and gazing round
> Sees not only the heather but blaeberries
> With bright green leaves and leaves already turned
>   scarlet
> Hiding ripe blue berries; and amongst the sage-green
>   leaves

Of the bog-myrtle the golden flowers of the tormentil
  shining;
And on the small bare places, where the little Blackface
  sheep
Found grazing, milkworts blue as summer skies;
And down in neglected peat-hags, not worked
Within living memory, sphagnum moss in pastel
  shades
Of yellow, green, and pink; sundew and butterwort
Waiting with wide-open sticky leaves for their tiny
  winged prey;
And nodding harebells vying in their colour
With the blue butterflies that poise themselves
  delicately upon them;
And stunted rowans with harsh dry leaves of glorious
  colour.
'Nothing but heather!' – How marvellously descriptive!
  And incomplete! (1170–1)

Scotland then is both microcosm and world-in-itself; both
symbol and source. In the same way the poet is both example
and exception:

Remember, I speak
Never of the representative individual man as man,
But always of the artist as the great exception
To the whole human order of things (1172)

After a plea for the extension of human consciousness Mac-
Diarmid goes back to his mountain and soars:

So, we scale the summit and leap into the abyss,
And lo! we have wings. (1174)

'Dìreadh II' surveys Scotland 'from the view-point of Berwickshire' (LP, 256) and its wealth of agricultural details
recalls the work the poet did as a young man for the Fabian
Research Committee on *The Rural Problem* (1913). Indeed the

essentially rural nature of MacDiarmid's background is seen
in an ecstatic passage near the beginning of the poem where
the poet recalls an experience that came to him at the top of
a glen when, in the presence of scores of stags, he saw 'golden
eagles, safe/In their empyrean liberty' and knew that 'squad-
rons of bomber planes' could never take their place:

> Here is the real Scotland,
> The Scotland of the leaping salmon,
> The soaring eagle, the unstalked stag,
> And the leaping mountain hare.
> Here, above the tree-line, where the track
> Is the bed of an amethystine burn
> In a bare world of shining quartz and purple heather,
> Is the Scotland that is one of the sights of the earth
> And once seen can never be forgotten. (1175)

In comparison to that spectacle cities, including Edinburgh
and Glasgow, are 'rubbish' (1175). And so MacDiarmid remembers his days in Berwickshire which is presented as an
agricultural paradise to be compared to Wales and then contrasted with England in the period 1760 to 1830. MacDiarmid's rural expertise is used to build up a precise picture of
Berwickshire as a land, like Eden, 'Brimming with prosperity
and no waste anywhere' (1179). Unlike obsessively Edenic
poets, though, he does not wish to go back to it, preferring a
new way of life that will retain this landscape as an important
example for future reference. He is always the figure in the
landscape, present as person (in various anecdotes) or as a
natural metaphor:

> Chafing always upon a rocky bed
> The river gathers round it
> All that fine tangle of foliage
> You see only upon impetuous streams. (1180)

MacDiarmid has said that these four lines are 'applicable to
and give a picture of my own life' (LP, 261). His search for

the source of creativity runs into river-imagery since his boy-hood was dominated by three rivers.

'Dìreadh III' begins with a glorious description of the poet standing on the summit of Sgurr Alasdair looking at the Cuillin peaks. Here is MacDiarmid's natural element for he is in a 'simple place of clear rock and crystal water' (1186), alone with nature which is seen as a spiritual manifestation, a mystical configuration, a work of natural art at once actual and ideal:

> I lie here like the cool and gracious greenery
> Of the water-crowfoot leafage, streaming
> In the roping crystalline currents,
> And set all about on its upper surface
> With flecks of snow blossom that, on closer looking,
> Show a dust of gold. (1187)

As a man 'possessed by this purity' MacDiarmid is visited by 'the Gaelic genius' (1187) that sustains him and his poetic work. He is pushed back into experiences that matter to him; he thinks of the first rock-pigeon he ever saw, remembers his early lyrics in Scots, and goes forward from the past into a new level of evolutionary idealism where he can 'covet the mystery of our Gaelic speech' (1191). MacDiarmid signals to the reader his ascension to a new spiritual and poetic level. He is a man inspired by the Celtic genius, is 'with Alba – with Deirdre' (1193). As the poem moves towards a climax the poet avails himself of a liquid euphony and finally reaches the summit where he sees the legendary deer whose reap-pearance signals the resurrection of Scotland:

> Let what can be shaken, be shaken,
> And the unshakeable remain.
> The Inaccessible Pinnacle is not inaccessible.
> So does Alba surpass the warriors
> As a graceful ash surpasses a thorn,
> Or the deer who moves sprinkled with the dewfall
> Is far above all other beasts
> – Its horns glittering to Heaven itself. (1193)

From his description of it as a 'small part' of his 'immensely long poem' (LP, 114) MacDiarmid surely planned to follow the complete *Cornish Heroic Song for Valda Trevyln* with *The Kind of Poetry I Want* although, such is MacDiarmid's bibliographical complexity, it did not get the benefit of an authorised order until after the appearance in book-form of *In Memoriam James Joyce*. In *Lucky Poet* MacDiarmid's references to 'my enormous poem' and 'my vast poem' (LP, 135) presumably relate to *Mature Art* as a whole; *The Kind of Poetry I Want* would fit into the scheme of things as a manifesto which would come immediately after the euphoric opening of the poem. Having written a kind of poetry MacDiarmid wants to distinguish it as *The Kind of Poetry I Want*. As it exists the manifesto-poem is an extended exercise in free-association; the poet takes as the source of his speculation the idea of poetic evolution then subjects it to a series of illustrative examples. Poetry is the target of MacDiarmid's attention and he approaches it from every angle he can conceive of in an effort to demonstrate exhaustively the truth of his central contention that the poetry of the future must be 'A learned poetry, rich in . . . historical and linguistic knowledge.' (1030) In common with the whole of the *Mature Art* epic, this section was to be made in the structural image of the pibroch, specifically

> the fourth and greatest movement of the *pìob mhòr,*
> The most fantastic music in all the range of the pipes,
> The *crunluath a-mach* – where miracles of improvisation
> Form themselves of their own volition under the
>   fingers;
> The expert ear may trace the original melody
> Of the *ùrlar* weaving its faint way
> Through the maze of gracenotes
> But the very gracenotes are going mad
> And making melodies of their own
> As the player conceives new and ever louder diversions.
>   (1007–8)

MacDiarmid's aim, in this sequence, is to replace inspiration with information and to substitute science for sentiment. He assumes that the poetry of the future will be a supremely didactic medium and so seeks to enthrall the reader by instructing him. His illustrative examples include references to Gestapo Guards (607), firearms (609), bridge(609), billiards (611), the thought of Martin Buber (616), the philosophy of 'Chestov, my master' (622), the position of the foetus in the womb (1003), the bread-knife that cuts three slices at once (1005), the terpsichorean virtuosity of Fred Astaire (1006), the delights of angling (1008), the character of Indian culture (1013), Coleridge's esemplasy and coadunation (1016), the vastness of the mineral world (1018), Marya Sklodowska at her laboratory table (1019), hedge-laying (1025), the 'conception of evolution' (1027), the interpenetration of languages (1031); in short

> A poetry in which the images
> Work up on each other's shoulders like Zouave
>   acrobats,
> Or strange and fascinating as the Javanese dancer,
> Retna Mohini, or profound and complicated
> Like all the work of Ram Gopal and his company.
>   (1024)

There is an exhilaration in this piling up of examples and in the way in which MacDiarmid enjoys the counterpoint between scientific jargon, as in 'group-reagents for every known poison'; and colloquial phrases such as 'A poetry that can put all its chips on the table' (625).

Although there are occasional quatrains and couplets throughout *Mature Art*, the form is free and the line-endings are determined by the poet's instinct for what is improvisationally apt. MacDiarmid's phenomenal memory and omnivorous reading demanded an open-ended idiom and the repetitive technique of *The Kind of Poetry I Want* is an indication of MacDiarmid's ability to pursue a subject until he feels he has explored every aspect of it. Before the sequence closes rather cunningly on two lines containing an internal rhyme and pararhyme –

> The sound of a rock falling perpendicularly into a lake,
> . . . . Or loch! (1035)

– the reader is in a position to appreciate the poet's views on the subject specified in the title. MacDiarmid has the courage of his aesthetic convictions as he pushes his argumentative line to the limit, using epic similes and catalogues of conventionally unpoetic items. When he feels there is a need for some human interest then he admits his own provocative personality into the sequence:

> – I am forty-six; of tenacious, long-lived country folk.
> Fools regret my poetic change – from my 'enchanting
> early lyrics' –
> But I have found in Marxism all that I need –
> (I on my mother's side of long-lived Scottish peasant
> stock
> And on my father's of hardy keen-brained Border mill-
> workers).
> It only remains to perfect myself in this new mode.
> This is the poetry I want – all
> I can regard now as poetry at all,
> As poetry of to-day, not of the past,
> A Communist poetry that bases itself
> On the Resolution of the C.C. of the R.C.P.
> In Spring 1925: 'The Party must vigorously oppose
> Thoughtless and contemptuous treatment
> Of the old cultural heritage
> As well as of the literary specialists. . . .
> It must likewise combat the tendency
> Towards a purely hothouse proletarian literature.'
> (615)

The only resolution MacDiarmid's epic is based on is his own poetic will.

Although there are vicarious elements in the poem much of it is, literally, a matter of opinion and MacDiarmid's poetic authority is stamped on the majority of the verse-paragraphs that make up the poem. It is, therefore, understandable that he should cite the sequence as one of the works miraculously delivered to him. MacDiarmid's feeling is that he has not so much written poetry as acted as an instrument on which the universe has played poetry:

> A poetry full of the crazy feeling
> That everything that has ever gone into my life
> Has pointed to each successive word
> And I couldn't have failed to write it if I'd tried,
> Since a man cannot duck away from the pattern
> That life lays out for him. (625)

However there is an element in *The Kind of Poetry I Want* that was to get rather out of proportion in *In Memoriam James Joyce*: the practice of absorbing, without acknowledgment, the work of other authors. Eliot's *The Waste Land* used quotations to define a cultural context; Joyce's *Ulysses* raised the art of parody to a new level of creativity; and Pound's *Cantos* were widely allusive in a multilingual fashion. MacDiarmid was impressed by the rich literary texture of this mode of modernism and as early as *A Drunk Man* had adapted it to his own ends. In *The Kind of Poetry I Want* he went a stage further. This is a section from *The Kind of Poetry I Want*:

> The poetry of one who practises his art
> Not like a man who works that he may live
> But as one who is bent on doing nothing but work,
> Confident that he who lives does not work,
> That one must die to life in order to be
> Utterly a creator (1021)

And this is a passage from Thomas Mann's story 'Tonio Kröger' in the translation H. T. Lowe-Porter published in 1928:

He worked, not like a man who works that he may live;
but as one who is bent on doing nothing but work;
having no regard for himself as a human being but only
as a creator [knowing] that he who lives does not work;
that one must die to life in order to be utterly a creator.[2]

MacDiarmid's theoretical justification for this wholesale
appropriation of the words and cadences of other writers is
to cite Gorky's *One Day of the World* as an example of 'collective
creative work' (LP, 135). Since MacDiarmid, in Shetland,
was not in a position to collaborate with other writers (apart
from Lewis Grassic Gibbon with whom he wrote a book) he
simply adapted extant writing as a means to his end. In *The
Kind of Poetry I Want* he described himself as a man who, in
principle, lived by books alone:

This is the testament of a man who has had
The supreme good luck ever since he was a lad
To find in himself and foster a vast will
To devote himself to Arts and Letters, and still
(Constantly in 'devout prayer to that eternal Spirit
Who can enrich with all utterance and knowledge')
Is happily in middle age insatiable yet,
An omnivorous reader and passionate lover
Of every creative effort the whole world over (1030)

MacDiarmid's prose, like his poetry, depended on a mass of
quotations and he discussed the derivative technique in a
defensive manner:

I may add here, since the way in which I bespatter all
my writings with innumerable quotations from the most
heterogeneous writers of all times and countries is one of
the most frequent points of complaint against me, that
this habit springs from the omnivorous reading in which
I have indulged ever since I learned to read, and that
though I understand the prudential consideration which
counsels against quoting other writers too much, since the
effect of this on the minds of most readers is that the

writer himself tends to be lost in the multitude of writers
he is drawing upon, I have never been of those who are
afraid of being 'too literary' (deeming that to be as
literary as possible is precisely the writer's job, just as it
is a professional strong man's job to be as physically
powerful as possible). . . (LP, 27)

The problems began when MacDiarmid failed to identify his
quotations and simply incorporated them into his work. He
came in for a lot of criticism in 1965 when, in a letter to the
TLS, Glyn Jones revealed that the poem 'Perfect' was a ty-
pographical arrangement of his fictional prose. Subsequent
correspondents pointed out that two passages from *In Memoriam James Joyce* were not actually written by MacDiarmid:
the passage on a Chinese calligrapher (765) was from a review
by Hugh Gordon Porteus and the long discussion of Karl
Kraus (767–75) was from a review of a book on Karl Kraus
in the *TLS* of 8 May 1953.[3] In an essay on MacDiarmid, the
composer Ronald Stevenson pointed out that the opening of
the final section of *In Memoriam James Joyce* (871–2) consisted
of 'a huge quotation from an essay which Busoni wrote in
America in 1910'. (Festschrift, 146) Examples could be multi-
plied considerably. There are two verse-paragraphs in the
'England Is Our Enemy' section of *In Memoriam James Joyce*
which reproduce, verbatim, this Ford Madox Hueffer quotation which is also reproduced in *Lucky Poet*:

> The best writers of to-day can find only a handful of
> readers apiece in the United States; and only one handful
> for all the lot of them in the British Empire – say 14,000.
> The populations of the British Empire and the United
> States are, say, three hundred millions; thus,
> mathematically put, the fraction of readers for the best
> work *of* to-day *in the English-speaking world* is 14,000/
> 300,000,000. It means that in each 100,000 souls, five are
> reasonably civilized. (LP, 103)

Only the words italicised above are omitted from the quotation as it appears, without any acknowledgment, in the text

of *In Memoriam James Joyce* (862). One further example of MacDiarmid's method occurs at the end of the first section of the poem, the 'In Memoriam' proper, when MacDiarmid refers to

> such new discoveries
> As the Goad, the female Shriek,
> The Garble with an Utter in its claws (804–5)

without citing the origin of these animals in James Thurber's *The Beast In Me* (1948). However, the Thurber references could be construed as a clever use of allusion whereas the other examples indicate a methodological flaw in MacDiarmid's all-embracing epic.

It is important to approach *In Memoriam James Joyce* as a literary experiment; indeed the title proclaims the name of the most egregious experimentalist of the twentieth century, though the poem is not so much an elegy as an example of what MacDiarmid feels is poetry written in the revolutionary tradition of Joyce. It has been the assumption of this book that MacDiarmid's greatest poetry depends on placing a cerebral conception in an emotional matrix. In *In Memoriam James Joyce* there is a conspicuous absence of emotion and often only the theory remains. The finished product is, therefore, generally arid except for isolated passages when MacDiarmid brings emotional pressure to bear on the poem. *In Memoriam James Joyce* is a theoretical poem based on a questionable proposition. It puts forward propositions and premises that can be refuted and so eschews the persuasive power of poetry in favour of the spurious advantages of argumentation. For example, the assertion that man will only evolve into something higher by accepting evolutionary idealism, 'Otherwise we shall go the way of the dodo and kiwi' (842), is a powerful notion in MacDiarmid's poetry when he is enthused by the possibility of spiritual change in himself. Reduced to an analytical abstraction the idea is less impressive. Again MacDiarmid's claim that 'England Is Our Enemy' (858) is little more than a slogan when it only introduces a section of the poem apparently lifted from prosaic sources. Essentially Mac-Diarmid is demonstrating the technical appearance of the kind of poetry he wants in the belief that it is a development of his earlier work which of course it is on a purely theoretical level:

> It's not true to say my more recent poetry has marked a retreat from my earlier standpoint. *In Memoriam James Joyce*, over which the battle seems to have been joined, was to my mind a natural development. It is more obviously a natural development from my first work before I began writing in Lallans, or *synthetic* Scots – but the argument behind it, for a world language which isn't an esperanto but an interpenetration of all languages, accommodates as far as I am concerned the Lallans movement and similar movements in various European countries. I'm looking for a diversity in unity, not for a unification of languages. (Uncanny, 171)

In Memoriam James Joyce was first put together in the Shetland Islands in 1941, shortly before MacDiarmid left for Glasgow in February 1942. At least he claims that this is the case in his Author's Note to the 1955 edition of the poem (Joyce, 11). However, as the sequence includes a long passage taken from the *TLS* in 1953 and alludes to a Thurber item collected in 1948, the version of 1941 must have been considerably shorter than the text eventually approved by MacDiarmid. In 1973 the poet recalled that the Joyce poem was written between 1940 and 1945.[4] It thus represents a sustained literary war effort and there is, indeed, a combative quality about the poem. It calls for a universal harmony and a global linguistic unity yet seeks to exclude England since 'England is Our Enemy'. The use of the royal plural is a signal that MacDiarmid is speaking on behalf of all mankind, save the English, and that the pan-Celtism of his Gaelic Idea has been fused with the mystical aspects of the East-West Synthesis. Interested in extracting from the East the essence of contemplative wisdom, MacDiarmid informs the reader that 'a greater interest in Indian thoughts and ideas/Exists nowhere

in the world than in my mind' (856). His visionary synthesis
of the most creative elements of all languages is not to be
thought of as favouring one strong language over less developed languages. The poet who resuscitated Scots and adapted
English to his own ends is open to all languages:

> – All dreams of 'imperialism' must be exorcised,
> Including linguistic imperialism, which sums up all the
>   rest. (790)

In fact MacDiarmid's philological paradise is a dynamic and
eternally evolving ideal:

> Metaphysical and empirical language communities,
> With a continuous interweaving of threads between
>   them,
> Between inner, mobile, emphatic, and therefore
> Untranslatable language forms, crossed by countless
> Isophones, isolexes, isorhemes, and outer, rigid,
> Metaphorical forms – all external language
>   communities,
> All the systems and structures of language usage,
> Existing and resting on the bosom of linguistic thought,
> Which envelops, carries, and fructifies them
> Like the ocean the Earth! (785)

In addressing Joyce, who died in 1941, on the subject of
world language MacDiarmid is speaking to a dead man who
was once gloriously alive to all the creative possibilities of
language and who attempted to create his own linguistic
universe in *Finnegans Wake*. Just as *A Drunk Man Looks at the
Thistle* was inspired by *Ulysses*, so *In Memoriam James Joyce* is
inspired by Joyce's later and more extreme experimental
work. MacDiarmid never met Joyce, a fact he regretted, but
regarded his fellow Celt as a creative colleague and the supreme linguistic innovator of the century. Nevertheless Mac-
Diarmid is confident enough in his own work to approach

Joyce as an artistic equal so his first words are a mixture of banter and booklore:

> I remember how you laughed like Hell
> When I read you from Pape's 'Politics of the Aryan
>   Road':
> 'English is destined to become the Universal
>   Language! . . .' (738)

This ambivalent tone is sustained throughout the poem; it is by turns colloquial and arcane. MacDiarmid feels that the ubiquitous presence of English means that the English mentality has conquered large areas of the world and has obliterated indigenous cultures. The removal of the hegemony of English will be a revolutionary act and allow a new cultural interdependence and range of self-expression. India, in the 1940s, is used as a symbol of a nation that has had English imposed on it; thus MacDiarmid's poem seeks to liberate Indian philosophy from English political domination and represent it to the Western reader. Similarly Chinese culture is to be revered and in one of the parenthetical units that occur in the poem MacDiarmid takes Joyce aside and gives him some advice:

> (For unlike you, Joyce, I am more concerned
> With the East than the West and the poetry I seek
> Must be the work of one who has always known
> That the Tarim valley is of more importance
> Than Jordan or the Rhine in world history). (801)

World language is the central theme of the poem and Mac-Diarmid frequently finds it a big enough subject to contain many of the concerns from his thematic repertoire. There are moments when the poet breaks into lyricism, occasions when he broods on his childhood in Langholm, there are angling anecdotes and paradoxical assertions such as 'The universal *is* the particular.' (845) Inevitably, since it is the foundation of his faith in the future, there is an incidental exposition of

evolutionary idealism and there is the familiar MacDiarmidian notion of the poetic saviour. Joyce is clearly singled
out as a man who has achieved greatness at the cost of self-
sacrifice:

> I praise you then, Joyce, because you too
> Were – like all Gongorists – one of those altruists
> (However their conscious motives may be mixed)
> Risking contemporary misunderstanding, personal
>   obloquy even,
> For the sake of enriching the inheritance
> Each administers in his generation. (826)

There are also tributes to Celtic culture-heroes such as Yeats
(756–8) and Dylan Thomas (828–30) and references to old
friends such as Patrick Geddes 'Revealing more on one sheet
of paper/Than whole volumes of science or philosophy' (802),
Cunninghame Graham with his 'magnificent presence' (869)
and 'my friend Ruaraidh Erskine of Marr' (869). To complete
the MacDiarmidian picture there are obligatory references to
figures from the pantheon such as 'my great master, Chestov'
(745) and Plotinus (745).

   In orchestrating the poem MacDiarmid abandons the exigencies of poetic rhythm, except for lyrical interludes, and
exercises an arbitrary control over line-endings. He also uses
two technical devices which allow him to indulge, theoretically anyway, in pibroch-like variations on the *urlar* of world
language. MacDiarmid relies heavily on the epic simile and
the catalogue. In an early and important passage of the poem
MacDiarmid combines the two techniques by dissolving from
a catalogue of poets into an epic simile in parenthesis:

> Davidson, too, with his angry cry
> 'Our language is too worn, too much abused,
> Jaded and overspurred, wind-broken, lame, –
> The hackneyed roadster every bagman mounts';
> Patmore with 'shaw,' 'photosphere,' 'prepense-
>   occulted,' 'draff,'

Thompson calling that the time had come
To raise a banner (but not raising it himself)
– 'I who can scarcely speak my fellows' speech' –
Against the Praetorian cohorts of poetry, whose
   prescriptive aid
Every aspirant to the poetical purple invokes!
And on to Doughty and Hopkins – then the younger
   men
(Name after name after name comes to me now
As a climber night-bound on a high wind-swept pass
Sees the world recreated peak by peak at dawn
And instinctively rises to his feet in homage
As, *parvis componere magna*, those who sit and wait
Rise at their Sovereign's coming)
Who go back to Langland's homely Anglo-Saxon verse.
   (740)

Once the reader has accepted the structural mechanism of
the poem and the matter-of-factual rhythms then the book
makes more demands on the reader's stamina than his intelligence. It is a long poem with a stunning range of references
derived from MacDiarmid's vast reading. It is not, concep-
tually, a difficult poem. In fact MacDiarmid has aimed at
clarity of expression that comes through even the most
scholarly-sounding passages. There is humour too in the way
the poet contrasts dense passages of word-lists or book-titles
with colloquial references to himself – as 'one of the "funny
ones" ' (741) or 'the salt of the earth' (741) – and generally
mixes his linguistic and referential modes. For example, the
following passage moves from a reference to *The Kind of Poetry
I Want* (which is, after all, part of the same *Mature Art* sequence), throws in a foreign word, introduces an illustrative
anecdote, moves to a quatrain in dialect Scots, then conjures
up an *ad hoc* conclusion:

For this is the kind of poetry I want,
Wandering from subject to subject
And roaming back and forth in time

[226]

Yet always as essentially controlled
As a *saeta* or a flamenco song.
As a poet I'm interested in religious ideas –
Even Scottish ones, Wee Free ones even – as a matter
    of fact
Just as an alcoholic can take snake venom
With no worse effects than a warming of the digestive
    tract.

To fules the spirit seems to be active
When the senses alane are really spry
Even as the mune appears to move
When it's nocht but the clouds ga'en by.

Once one's attuned to the elemental
One's banished by the superficial for ever. (797–8)

The poem is therefore well defined as

This rag-bag, this Loch Ness monster, this impact
Of the whole range of *Weltliteratur* on one man's brain.
    (755)

The closest thing to MacDiarmid's poem is the prose of
Lucky Poet which contrives ingenious links between favourite
passages from the poet's reading. So when the poem is prosaic, as it is for long stretches, then at least the texture of the
prose is MacDiarmidian. This recognisably polemical style is
well suited to the personal element in the poem. MacDiarmid's own speech-rhythm is present in an apparently incongruous expression such as 'adze, cusp, ogee, and the like'
(739) and MacDiarmid is capable of moving from Plotinus to

my own kinsmen, Lindley Murray, the father of
    English Grammar,
And Alexander Murray, who studied the languages
Of Western Asia and North-East Africa and Lappish
And wrote the 'History of European Languages,'
And others of my contemporaries living still (745)

Similarly his elaborate parentheses can contain anecdotal illustrations of his intellectual expansionism:

> (Moreover as I have often told
> My angling friend Norman MacCaig
> If I went fishing I could not be content
> With salmon or brown trout. . .
> I'd remember with Herman Melville
> That behind Leviathan
> There's still the kraken,
> And no end to our 'ontological heroics.'
> And MacCaig has laughed and said
> 'Let me see you catch anything yet
> Big enough not to throw in again.') (851)

The title-sequence of *In Memoriam James Joyce* is an exposition of the theme of language; extant languages are treated as instruments capable of contributing grace notes to a universal harmony. Lacking the multi-lingualism of Pound, Eliot and Joyce, MacDiarmid is content to cite books on the subject and to give an exotic texture to his own idiom by importing specialist terms and scientific jargon. He launches into 'Countless references, all close as a Cumnock Hinge' (745), states the obvious by saying 'I am dealing particularly/With literature here' (749) and announces his intention of healing 'the breach/Between genius and scholarship, literature and learning' (752). Having established a working duality between genius and scholarship, MacDiarmid proceeds on the assumption that his previous work has demonstrated his genius so the present work will display his scholarship. Intent on reassembling the 'broken unity of the human spirit' (753), he tends upwards for 'it is in literature as it is in mountaineering' (752). Evolutionary idealism comes naturally to a poet who knows

> The painful and ecstatic awareness
> Of language as the central mystery
> Of the intellectual life, the great obsession
> With language and the point of consciousness. (763)

Although he claims to know Shelta, Hesperic Latin, Béar-
lagair na Sāer, the Cretan Mantinades (762) and to be *au
fait* with quantum mechanics, Heisenberg, the matrix calcu-
lus, and wave mechanics (782), MacDiarmid qualifies his
apparent omniscience with the confession that he 'can speak
no Greek' (797), although he spent the First World War years
in Greece. MacDiarmid's knowledge is on a theoretical level
just as the language he is discussing is an ideal one. He is
aware of this difficulty and seeks a fusion in the future:

> For there are two kinds of knowledge,
> Knowing about things and knowing things,
> Scientific data and aesthetic realisation,
> And I seek their perfect fusion in my work. (782)

He does indeed. It seems, however, that MacDiarmid is
aware of the apparent inconsistency of the position he has so
confidently taken up in the poem. He has proposed the necessity of a world language and has dismissed 'the adoption of
English as the supra-national language' (789) on anti-imper-
ialist grounds. His poem, however, is written in English,
albeit Synthetic English. MacDiarmid does not seek to resolve
this crucial contradiction on an argumentative level. Instead
he breaks into poetry, producing an In Memoriam within an
In Memoriam. Though the whole poem is specifically directed
to the living memory of Joyce, MacDiarmid remembers another Irish writer. Yeats, who died in 1939, was on friendly
terms with MacDiarmid who thus feels justified in confessing
his contrariness to a poet whose variety is a cause for celebration in his native Ireland. In addressing Yeats, Mac-
Diarmid produces a selfconsciously ornate passage complete
with Victorian diction – 'dight', 'ruddily bright' (756) – and
inversion – 'in pleasing harmony bound' (756) – determined
by the exigencies of rhyme. In the context of the catalogues
of *In Memoriam James Joyce* the section written in memory of
Yeats stands out clearly on account of its imagery and
euphony:

Let the only consistency
In the course of my poetry
Be like that of the hawthorn tree
Which in early Spring breaks
Fresh emerald, then by nature's law
Darkens and deepens and takes
Tints of purple-maroon, rose-madder and straw. (756)

Throughout his career MacDiarmid has been fascinated by
the Keatsian notion of poetry coming to the poet as leaves
come to the tree. It is the basis of the symbolism of 'A
Moment in Eternity' (3–10) and in his poem to Goethe, 'The
Oon Olympian', MacDiarmid recalls 'Keats'/Poetry that comes like leafs to a tree' (358). In 'A Moment of Eternity'
MacDiarmid was transformed into 'a crystal trunk' and this
tree through which creativity courses had 'Meteors for roots'
(5) and crystal-like stars shining on its branches. Affected by
the death of Yeats, MacDiarmid returns to this tree. He
wonders exactly what survives the physical death of the poem.
His creative conjecture is an affirmation of poetic immortality
for the leaves (poems) may have scattered and the trunk
(body) may die but the creative light still dances around the
tree. In thinking thus of Yeats, MacDiarmid contemplates
his own physical death and poetic survival and is content:

And when the leaves have passed
Or only in a few tatters remain
The tree to the winter condemned
                    Stands forth at last
          Not bare and drab and pitiful,
But a candelabrum of oxidised silver gemmed
By innumerable points of ruby
Which dominate the whole and are visible
Even at considerable distance
As flame-points of living fire.
That so it may be
With my poems too at last glance
Is my only desire. (756)

The roots that tap the power of the terrible crystal are, so MacDiarmid supposes, too deep for death.

'The World of Words' recasts the argumentative matter of the first section in more personal terms. MacDiarmid refers to angling, his 'favourite sport' (811), gives a long catalogue of impressive friends he has known (817), pays eloquent tribute to Dylan Thomas through an epic simile of archery (828–30), varies the pace of the poem by inserting at inappropriate moments such irreverent asides as

> One thing sticks out. You must agree
> Poetry apart, as life you scan,
> The whole thing's due, in human terms,
> To woman taking a rise out of man. (818)

In this section MacDiarmid seeks to go, like Nietzsche, beyond good and evil towards an evolutionary idealism that language supports at its most creative moments. Here MacDiarmid the mystic takes priority over MacDiarmid the materialist:

> I know that in the final artistic
> – The highest human – vision
> There is neither good nor evil,
> Better nor worse,
> But only the harmony
> Of that which is,
> The pure phenomenon
> Abiding in the eternal radiance. (835)

The 'eternal radiance' issues from the terrible crystal of creativity. MacDiarmid apparently feels close to the completion of his long quest and declares his faith in a revised mystical manifesto:

> In this realistic mood I recognise
> With a grim animal acceptance
> That it is indeed likely enough that the 'soul'

Perishes everlastingly with the death of the body,
But what this realistic mood, into which
My mind falls like a plummet
Through the neutral zone of its balanced doubt,
Never for one single beat of time can shake or disturb
Is my certain knowledge,
Derived from the complex vision of everything in me,
That the whole astronomical universe, however
    illimitable,
Is only one part and parcel of the mystery of Life;
Of this I am as certain as I am certain that I am I.
The astronomical universe is *not* all there is. (822)

In rising to a creative harmony with the universe and a
glimpse of eternity MacDiarmid has achieved some certainty
of immortality. Like Joyce, MacDiarmid knows there is a
creative life after death

    For beyond the four dimensions of space-time
    There is the fifth dimension, individuality (836)

which survives in the work an artist leaves behind. In this
timeless dimension the poet is an explorer, a man as imaginatively adventurous as the most advanced scientists who make
predictions about the nature of space-time.

MacDiarmid's mysticism is drawn from the philosophical
wisdom of the whole world. In 'The Snares of Varuna' and
'The Meeting of the East and the West' he pays tribute to
the East. This empathy with Eastern thought has strong
political repercussions. MacDiarmid does not accept the
West's claim to be the most enlightened area of the world,
the home of intellectual distinction and physical freedom. In
a powerful catalogue of human misery he draws attention to
the reality of the European situation:

    The concentration camps, the cat o' nine tails,
    The law more lawless than any criminal,
    The beatings-up by the police,
    The countless thuggeries of Jacks-in-office,

The vile society women, infernal parasites,
The endless sadism, Gorilla-rule,
The live men hanging in the plaza
With butcher's hooks through their jaws (841)

With such repulsive manifestations of Western culture there
is clearly an urgent need for an earthly alternative. Mac-
Diarmid turns to the Indian God, Varuna, whose magical
powers maintain universal order: 'he wields the universe/As
gamesters handle dice'. (840) Seeking a coalescence of all
philosophical wisdom, a combination of 'Plato and the East',
(845) MacDiarmid insists on the necessity of a human will
towards evolutionary idealism:

It is unlikely that man will develop into anything
    higher
Unless he desires to and is prepared to pay the cost.
    (842)

There is to be no vague escapist abstraction in the East–West
Synthesis but a precise articulation of existence as MacDiarmid demonstrates by, once more, breaking into poetry and
recalling the landscape he loves:

Look! Here and there a pinguicula eloquent of the Alps
Still keeps a purple-blue flower
On the top of its straight and slender stem.
Bog-asphodel, deep-gold, and comely in form,
The queer, almost diabolical, sundew,
And when you leave the bog for the stag moors and the
    rocks
The parsley fern – a lovelier plant
Than even the proud Osmunda Regalis –
Flourishes in abundance
Showing off oddly contrasted fronds
From the cracks of the lichened stones.
It is pleasant to find the books
Describing it as 'very local.'

Here is a change indeed!
The universal *is* the particular. (845)

Like Goethe (852), MacDiarmid seeks a meeting of heaven
and earth, a visionary unity, a 'spiritual sympathy and affinity' (856); in the name of this unity-in-diversity he cites
Buddhism (855–6) and refers to, for example, 'the soul of
Chinese music' (857). In the penultimate section of the poem,
'England Is Our Enemy' (which reads like a rearrangement
of critical prose), MacDiarmid excludes England from his
vision of world language and instead evokes an alternative to
academically approved English literature:

The glorious names of all the imaginative writers
From Homer to the Brothers Grimm,
From Flaubert back to Apuleius,
From Catullus to Turgenev,
All these form the glories of Europe,
Their works going together to make one whole,
And each work being one stone
In a gigantic and imperishable fabric. (870)

This catalogue leads into the final section opening on the
words of Busoni to convey an image of the wordless eloquence
of 'the realm of music' (871). 'Plaited Like the Generations
of Men', as the closing section is called, refers to Aodhagán
Ó Rathaille's aisling 'Gile na Gile' which had already fea-
tured as part of the referential ritual of *To Circumjack Cencrastus*
(224). Poignantly MacDiarmid alludes to this as a vision of
eternity in a Scottish glen:

Oh, Aodhagán Ó Rathaille meets again
The Brightness of Brightness in a lonely glen
And sees the hair that's plaited
Like the generations of men! (872)

MacDiarmid has come, at this valedictory point in the poem,
to a consideration of his own life's work. He is aware of the

direction he has taken and recalls how he has tended ever upwards towards an eternally feminine principle in order to combine his individuality with the vastness of the universe. It is a mystical synthesis which might elude the majority and he asks:

> Have I failed in my braid-binding
> At this great crisis
> When the impending task of mankind
> Is to help to bring to a close the 'conflict' stage
> Of the present process of the discontinuous
> And to usher in the 'harmony' stage
> By means of an abandonment
> Of the interlocking and proselytizing technique
> Of 'Warfare' and 'persuasion'?
> At this moment when braid-binding as never before,
> The creation of the seamless garment,
> Is the poet's task? (876)

That rhetorical question brings MacDiarmid to a statement of his poetic position, an acknowledgment that his poetry of philosophical complexity and evolutionary idealism has rejected simplistic positivism and schematic materialism:

> Being in short as where literary art
> Overpowers philosophical precision
> And finding no intellectual solution
> For this notorious conflict
> Between the 'intellectual love' of the universe as it is
> And the moral will that it should be other,
> Concluding that perhaps the only solution
> Lies in the faith, or the mystical perception,
> That the welter of frustration in the parts
> Is instrumental to some loftier perfection
> In the universe as a whole?

> Ah! no, no! Intolerable end
> To one who set out to be independent of faith
> And of mystical perception.
> It does not after all seem certain
> That the peace I have found is entirely
> Free from mystical elements. (881)

On that reference to peace the poem turns to resolve itself on a characteristic counterpoint. MacDiarmid describes, in detail, the dawning of world consciousness on the foetus and then turns to the hush of Joyce's death chamber (887–8). Nothing, it seems, is destroyed. The survival of the source of creativity after physical death is also a promise of immortality.

In Memoriam James Joyce was the last sustained poetic effort produced by MacDiarmid and the remainder of his creative life produced isolated poems (as fine as 'The Glass of Pure Water', with its celebration of creativity and denunciation of capitalism as a negation of life) and poems that were intended to form part of the unfinished *Impavidi Progrediamur* which was always intended to be the last lap of *Mature Art*. Several of the contributions planned for *Impavidi* present an idealised version of MacDiarmid. In one of these he is 'The Kind of Scot I Want':

> He was especially full
> Of this love of movement
> And zeal of observation.
> He manifested anew
> All the leading characteristics
> (The high spirits conspicuous as the valour)
> Of the Scots before the Union
> – Breaking anew
> 'An enchanting and amazing crystal fountain
> From the dark rocky caverns below'. (629)

So we come back to the terrible crystal of creativity. MacDiarmid's consistent search for the source of creativity was a

long one. Having realised, as early as 'A Moment in Eternity',
that his poetic gift transformed him into a symbol where

> I was a crystal trunk,
> Columnar in the glades of Paradise (5)

he continued in pursuit of 'the terrible crystal, the ineffable
glow' (352). This creative source was a power the poet could
reach by rooting himself in the right landscape or reaching
out, imaginatively, to the stars shining like crystals in the
night sky. Watching the river Esk he could see 'the terrible;
the terrible crystal' (390) and in 'The Terrible Crystal' looked
at its underground aspect:

> This is the hidden and lambent core I seek.
> Like crystal it is hidden deep
> And only to be found by those
> Who will dig deep.
> Like crystal it is formed by cataclysm and central fires;
> Like crystal it gathers into an icy unity
> And a gem-like transparence
> All the colour and fire of life;
> Like crystal it concentrates and irradiates light;
> Like crystal it endures. (1094)

In his later work, in Synthetic English, he felt he had found
the 'single creative ray' (823), 'the eternal radiance' (835)
though he had once claimed:

> Just as a glass can be shattered by striking a certain note
> on the fiddle or – if an alleged American case is authentic
> – a suspension bridge can be broken down in the same
> way . . . so it is only in the Scots language I can achieve
> or maintain if not, in certain senses, integrity of
> expression, at least 'the terrible crystal'; its sounds . . .
> bring me fully alive. (LP, 35)

The terrible crystal was either buried in the earth of Scotland, deep under the surface; or it was shining in the universal

sky. Its form was constantly changing, so it could assume the shape of 'living fire' (756) or a human seed, a 'lurid emission, whirlin' lint-white and green' (484). To avail himself of its power MacDiarmid had to nurture a cerebral conception in an emotional matrix fully aware that the resulting nativity would be metaphysical. When he looked into the crystal he saw a vision. At his greatest moments the image of the terrible crystal holds and he shapes its form with many facets. The man who could, at his best, concentrate into an individual vision of universal unity insights derived from a mass of speculative material and a heavenly host of images could say, with some justification, 'I may have paid in pain for my insights into the universe, but the pain has gone – the insights remain.' (LP, 44–5) He found the terrible crystal of creativity in himself, held it up to the universal radiance and cast new light on Scotland as he saw, in all its facets, fragments that would ultimately cohere in an ideal form of the future:

> Diallage of the world's debate, end of the long auxesis,
> Although no ébrillade of Pegasus can here avail,
> I prefer your enchorial characters – the futhorc of the
>   future –
> To the hieroglyphics of all the other forms of Nature.
> Song, your apprentice encrinite, seems to sweep
> The Heavens with a last entrochal movement;
> And, with the same word that began it, closes
> Earth's vast epanadiplosis. (433)

NOTES

CHAPTER ONE   THE MIND ALONE

1 Bertrand Russell, *History of Western Philosophy*, London, Allen & Unwin, 1946, 2nd edn 1961, p. 289.
2 In a letter of 15 February 1982 J. K. Annand mentions MacDiarmid's 'claim to have been educated at Edinburgh University, which is quite untrue, as C.M.G. once admitted to me when I challenged him about it.'
3 Naomi Mitchison, *You May Well Ask*, London, Gollancz, 1979, p. 122.
4 Robert Louis Stevenson, *Dr Jekyll and Mr Hyde. Weir of Hermiston*, London, Thomas Nelson, 1956, p. 75.
5 Francis Steegmuller (ed.), *The Letters of Gustave Flaubert 1830–1857*, London, Faber, 1982, p. 79.
6 *TLS 4: Essays and Reviews from The Times Literary Supplement 1965*, Oxford, Oxford University Press, 1966, p. 183.
7 Ibid., p. 194.
8 Maurice Lindsay (ed.), *John Davidson: A Selection of the Poems*, London, Hutchinson, 1961, p. 16.
9 Maurice Lindsay, *Francis George Scott and The Scottish Renaissance*, Edinburgh, Paul Harris, 1980, p. 24.
10 William Soutar, *Diaries of a Dying Man*, Edinburgh, Chambers, 1954, p. 60.
11 G. Gregory Smith, *Scottish Literature*, London, Macmillan, 1919, pp. 4–5.
12 Edwin Muir, *Scott and Scotland*, London, Routledge, 1936, p. 178.
13 Ibid., p. 21.

CHAPTER TWO   NAMES FOR NAMELESS THINGS

1 Ezra Pound, *Literary Essays*, London, Faber, 1954, p. 5.
2 Grieve took the title of his first book from G. Gregory Smith:

'It may not appear unreasonable to lay this emphasis on the contrariety in northern literary mood, especially as certain conditions, or accidents, in the later national development . . . too readily obscure the second element and leave the Muse the narrower reputation of being painfully concerned with the Annals of the Five Senses.' (*Scottish Literature*, London, Macmillan, 1919, p. 33)

3 Duncan Glen, *Hugh MacDiarmid and the Scottish Renaissance*, Edinburgh, Chambers, 1964, p. 73.

4 Ibid., p. 65.

5 G. Gregory Smith, *Scottish Literature*, London, Macmillan, 1919, pp. 138–9.

6 *The Scottish Chapbook*, vol. 1, no. 3, October 1922, pp. 62–3.

7 In *The Scottish Chapbook*, vol. 1, no. 7, February 1923, p. 182. MacDiarmid wrote of 'the possibility of a great Scottish Literary Renaissance deriving its strength from the resources that lie latent and almost unsuspected in the Vernacular.' Denis Saurat's article on 'Le groupe de "la Renaissance Écossaise"' ' appeared in *Revue Anglo Américaine*, Première Année, no. 4, April 1924.

8 Lavinia Derwent, *A Border Bairn*, London, Hutchinson, 1979, pp. 13–14.

9 Ibid., p. 126.

10 Arthur Koestler, *Kaleidoscope*, London, Hutchinson, 1981, p. 109.

11 *The Scottish Chapbook*, vol. 1, no. 3, October 1922, p. 63.

12 *The Scottish Chapbook*, vol. 1, no. 8, March 1923, p. 210.

13 In preface to Hugh MacDiarmid, *Sangschaw*, Edinburgh, Blackwood, 1925, p. x.

14 Ann Edwards Boutelle, *Thistle and Rose*, Edinburgh, MacDonald, 1980, p. 79.

15 *The Scottish Chapbook*, vol. II, no. 3, November–December 1923, p. 70.

CHAPTER THREE   TO PROVE MY SAUL IS SCOTS

1 *The Scottish Chapbook*, vol. 1, no. 3, October 1922, p. 72.

2 Ibid., vol. 1, no. 7, February 1923, p. 183.

3 J. K. Annand (ed.), *Early Lyrics by Hugh MacDiarmid*, Preston, Akros, 1968, p. 16.

4 G. Gregory Smith, *Scottish Literature*, London, Macmillan, 1919, pp. 19–23.

5 Maurice Lindsay, *Francis George Scott and the Scottish Renaissance*, Edinburgh, Paul Harris, 1980, p. 55.

6 Ibid.

7 William Johnstone, *Points in Time*, London, Barrie & Jenkins, 1980, p. 73.

8 J. K. Annand (ed.), op. cit., p. 15.

9 Duncan Glen, *Hugh MacDiarmid and the Scottish Renaissance*, Edinburgh, Chambers, 1964, p. 91, quoting MacDiarmid's address to the Edinburgh University Nationalist Club, April 1958.

10 Kenneth Buthlay, in *Hugh MacDiarmid*, Edinburgh, Oliver & Boyd, 1964, discloses that the MacDiarmid translations in *Sangschaw*, *Penny Wheep* and *A Drunk Man* are in fact adaptations from books of translations by Babette Deutsch and Avrahm Yarmolinsky, and by Jethro Bithell: 'There can be no doubt that [MacDiarmid] has a remarkable facility in picking up a working knowledge of diverse languages, but there is no convincing evidence to show that he is in full command of any foreign tongue.' (p. 75)

11 *The Scottish Chapbook*, vol. 1, no. 3, October 1922, p. 70.

12 Gordon Wright, *MacDiarmid: An Illustrated Biography*, Edinburgh, Gordon Wright, 1977, p. 21.

13 Hugh MacDiarmid, *A Drunk Man Looks at the Thistle*, edited by John C. Weston, Amherst, University of Massachusetts Press, 1971, p. 70.

14 Herman Melville, *Moby-Dick*, edited Harold Beaver, Harmondsworth, Penguin, 1972, p. 24.

CHAPTER FOUR   FRAE BATTLES, MAIR THAN
BALLADS

1 Maurice Lindsay, *Francis George Scott and the Scottish Renaissance*, Edinburgh, Paul Harris, 1980, p. 56.

2 Patrick Geddes (ed.), *To Marjory Kennedy-Fraser*, Edinburgh, Patrick Geddes, 1931.

3 Hugh MacDiarmid, *Francis George Scott: An Essay*, Edinburgh, MacDonald, 1955, p. 42.

4 Duncan Glen, *Hugh MacDiarmid and the Scottish Renaissance*, Edinburgh, Chambers, 1964, pp. 215–16.

5 Ibid., p. 216.

6 W. R. Aitken, 'Hugh MacDiarmid's "Unpublished" Books', in Frank McAdams (ed.), *Of One Accord*, Glasgow, Scottish Library Association, 1977, pp. 65–6. Aitken also notes that 'Only one poem has been found that is specifically attributed to [Parts IV and V] of *Clann Albann*. . . A moving short poem, "By a Lifting of the Head," was published in the *Modern Scot* for July 1933 as "From the fifth volume of *Clann Albann*," but when it was reprinted in 1935 in *Second Hymn to Lenin and Other Poems* it was called "With a Lifting of the Head," which was to have been the title of Part 5 of *Clann Albann*. This poem was later seen to be part of

the "Ode to All Rebels," one of the five poems deleted from the 1934 edition of *Stony Limits.*' (p. 63) That comment by Aitken indicates the problematic nature of any reconstruction of MacDiarmid's various projected books.

7 In a letter to the present writer, written on 4 October 1972, MacDiarmid described his Aggrandised Scots as a way of adapting a neglected language to an entirely new subject-matter.

8 Gordon Wright, *Hugh MacDiarmid: An Illustrated Biography*, Edinburgh, Gordon Wright, 1977, p. 56.

9 Eric Linklater, *Magnus Merriman*, London, Cape, 1934, pp. 71–2.

10 W. R. Aitken, op. cit., p. 65.

CHAPTER FIVE   THE STONE WORLD

1 In an article in the *Scotsman*, 9 October 1981, p. 11, G. A. Dixon of the Scottish Records Office confirms the documentary authenticity of an indenture of 1743 'confirming the existence of the MacCrimmon school or college of piping – the classic centre of Scotland's greatest national music.'

2 R. L. C. Lorimer in David Daiches (ed.), *A Companion to Scottish Culture*, London, Edward Arnold, 1981, p. 289.

3 In an essay on 'The Seamless Garment and the Muse', in *Agenda*, vol. 5, no. 4 and vol. 6, no. 1, Autumn–Winter 1967–8 (Double Issue on Hugh MacDiarmid and Scottish Poetry), the Irish poet John Montague suggests that MacDiarmid's opening lines

Fold of value in the world west from Greece
Over whom it has been our duty to keep guard
Have we slept on our watch; have death and dishonour
Reached you through our neglect and left you in lasting sleep?
(462–3)

are derived from Eoin MacNeill's translation of Grainne's lullaby over Diarmid in the *Duanaire Finn*:

O fold of valor of the world west from Greece,
over whom I stay watching,
my heart will well-nigh burst
if I see thee not at any time.

Montague adds: 'MacDiarmid transposes [the four lines] so that they become a lament, not over a boy, but the civilisation to which he belonged, the original tradition, may it be said, of these islands. And the whole movement of the lines is changed to match the theme so that an almost naive cry of tenderness is keyed to a Whitmanian skirl.' (*Agenda*, p. 28)

4 Robertson Davies, *The Rebel Angels*, London, Allen Lane, 1982, p. 257.
5 Letter to Alan Bold, 4 October 1972.

CHAPTER SIX   ALONE WITH THE ALONE

1 W. R. Aitken, 'Hugh MacDiarmid's "Unpublished" Books', in Frank McAdams (ed.), *Of One Accord*, Glasgow, Scottish Library Association, 1977, p. 67.
2 Thomas Mann, *Death in Venice. Tristan. Tonio Kröger*, translated by H. T. Lowe-Porter, Harmondsworth, Penguin, 1955, pp. 148–9.
3 *TLS 4: Essays and Reviews from the Times Library Supplement 1965*, London, Oxford University Press 1966, pp. 176–95. In the preface to the fourth edition of *The Disinherited Mind*, London, Bowes & Bowes, 1975, Erich Heller clarifies the Karl Kraus passage as follows: 'Part of my essay on Karl Kraus was originally written for *The Times Literary Supplement*. It appeared anonymously (as used to be the custom of the journal) on the front page of no. 2, 675, dated May 8, 1953. I was surprised as well as flattered to discover much later that with this article I had contributed not only to the *T.L.S.* but also to the poetry of Hugh MacDiarmid (Dr C. M. Grieve), the renowned Scots poet. His poem "And above all, Karl Kraus", from his cycle *In Memoriam James Joyce*, consists of 157 lines of which 149 are taken from my essay – with their essential identity preserved – even though they suffered a little breakage in the process of being lifted up into the poetic mode. My slight anxiety that this transference might be detected by some readers and ascribed to me as plagiarism is caused by the (may I say deserved) notoriety of Hugh MacDiarmid's poem. It was selected, without acknowledgment of my *T.L.S.* essay for the Penguin Book *The Mid-Century English Poetry 1940–1960*, which enjoys wide circulation. I have sometimes wondered whether this episode should not serve as footnote to my essay "Rilke and Nietzsche", and with its discourse on the relationship between poetry and other forms of linguistic expression.'
4 Hugh MacDiarmid, letter to Alan Bold, 9 January 1973.

GLOSSARY

abaw, abash
abies, except
abuneheid, overhead
adreigh, distant
agley, wrong
aiblins, perhaps
airt, direction
antrin, rare
arselins, backwards
aucht-fit, eight-foot
ava', at all

baggit, enceinte
bairnie, baby
bauchles, old shoes
bawaw, contemptuous look
beek, show
begood, began
bellwaverin', uncertain
benmaist, inmost
bensils o' a bleeze, big fire
beshacht, crooked
binna, except
birssy, bristly
blate, bashful
blether, bladder
blinterin', gleaming
bobby, policeman
bool, bowl
borne-heid, headlong

boss (of body), front
boutgate, roundabout way
breenge, burst
brent, wrinkled
brent-on, straightforward
broukit, neglected
bubblyjock, turkey
byspale, precocious child

ca' o' whales, school of whales
camsteerie, disorderly
canny, gentle
cantles, summits
canty, jaunty
clanjamfrie, collection
cleiks, hints
corneigh, enough
cree legs wi' (no' to), not safe to
   meddle with
crine, shrink
crockats up, on one's dignity
cull, testicle
cullage, genitals
cundy, drain
curjute, overwhelm

datchie, secret
deed, died
devaul, cease
ding, bang down

[244]

dirlin', throbbing
doonsin', dazzling
dree, endure
dry-gair-flow, place where two hills
  meet and form a bosom
dumfoonderin', astonishing
dwine, decline

eel-ark, breeding ground for eels
eelied, vanished
eemis, insecure
een, eyes
emerauds, emeralds
emmle-deugs, tatters fluttering
  from a dress

fash, trouble
feck, majority
fegs, faith
fell, clever (*adj.*)
fell, very (*adj.*)
ferlie, wonder
fidge, move
fidged, worried
flauchter, flutter
flauchter-spaed, two handed spade
  for cutting peat
fleg, frighten
flegsome, frightening
fog-theekit, moss-thatched
forenenst, in front of
forenicht, early evening
fu', full
fug, moss

gangtrees, planks for putting barrel
  on
gar, make
geg, trick
get, bastard
geylies, very much
gleids, sparks
glit, slime

gundy, violent

haingles, state of ennui
hair kaimed to the lift, on the go
hauf, half
hazelraw, lichen
heels-owre-gowdy, head-over-heels
heich, high
heich-skeich, crazy
hines, rasps
howe, bottom

ilka, every
ingangs, intestines

jaup, splash

kaa, drive
kail, cabbage
kaim, comb
keeks, looks slyly
keltie, bumper
ken, know
kite, belly
kittle, tickle
knedneuch, sour

laich, low
laverock, lark
lift, sky
loup, jump
lourd, heavy
lowe, flame
lowse, loosen

muckle, big
Muckle Toon, Langholm
mutchkin, half bottle of liquor

nesh, nervous

ocht, anything
on-ding, downpour

Glossary

oorie, weird
ootby, outside
or, before

peerie-weerie, diminished to a
  mere thread of sound

radgie, excitable
raff o' rain, drizzle
ratch, scratch
reek, smoke (There was nae reek i'
  the laverock's hoose, it was a
  dark and stormy night)
reistit, dried
rive, tear
rouch, rough

samyn, deck of ship
scansin', glinting
scaut-heid, disfigured
scouth, scope
seil o' your face, fortune favour
  you
seilfu', blissful
shot, freed
skimmerin', glimmering
skirl-i'-the-pan, fried oatmeal
skrymmorie, frightful
snod, neat
spilth, overflow

splairgin', spluttering
stound, throb
swither, hesitate
syne, afterwards

tapsalteerie, topsy turvy
thrapple, throat
thring, shrug
tine, lose
tint, lost
toom, empty
tousled, untidy

ullage, deficiency in contents of
  barrel
unco, strange (*adj.*)
unco, very (*adv.*)
unkennable, unknowable

waesome, woeful
watergaw, indistinct rainbow
wecht, weight
weet, wet
whiles, sometimes
whummle, overturn

youk, itch
yow-trummle, ewe-tremble (cold
  spell at end of July after sheep-
  shearing)

Index of Poems

After Two Thousand Years, 190
Allelauder, 31
Amiel, 35–6
Another Epitaph on an Army of Mercenaries, 190
Another Turn of the Screw, 144
Antenora, 153
Apprentice Angel, An, 32, 153
As Lovers Do, 172, 190
At My Father's Grave, 143
At the Cenotaph, 172, 190
Au Clairè de la Lune, 66–7

Back o' Beyond, The, 153–4
Bagpipe Music, 204
Ballad of the Five Senses, 43, 69–71
Ballad of the General Strike, 91, 115
Battle Continues, The, 7
Belle Terre sans Merci, La, 47–8
Beyond Exile, 47–8
Birlinn of Clanranald, The, 205
Birth of a Genius Among Men, 189, 191
Blind Man's Luck, 74
Bombinations of a Chimaera, 75–7
Bonnie Broukit Bairn, The, 60, 66
Bonnie Lowe, The, 72
Bracken Hills in Autumn, 136
Braid Scots, 79
Bubblyjock, The, 74
Burning Passion, The, 140
By Wauchopeside, 136

Charisma and My Relatives, 140–1
Cheville, 153
Church of My Fathers, The, 143
Cloudburst and Soaring Moon, 71
Consummation, 54
Cornish Heroic Song for Valda Trevlyn, 35, 199, 203, 207, 208–9
Country Folk, 143
Country Life, 66
Crowdieknowe, 67
Currant Bush, The, 71

Dead Liebknecht, The, 71
Deep-Sea Fishing, 42
Depth and the Chthonian Image, 1–4, 148, 151–2
Diamond Body, 15

Dìreadh I, 207, 209, 210–212
Dìreadh II, 207, 209, 212–14
Dìreadh III, 37, 39, 206, 209, 214
Diseased Salmon, The, 42
Dog Pool, The, 21–2
Drunk Man Looks at the Thistle, A, 33, 38, 39, 42, 43, 84–121
Dystiscus, 153

Edinburgh, 192
Edinburgh Toun, 178
Eemis Stane, The, 67
Empty Vessel, 72, 73
End of Usury, The, 190
England is Our Enemy, 220, 222, 234
Envoi: On Coming Home, 136, 198
Etika Preobrazhennova Erosa, 160
Ex-Parte Statement on the Project of Cancer, 171–2

Farmer's Death, 66
Fatherless in Boyhood, 29
Feery-o'-the-Feet, 71, 72
Fingers of Baal Contract in the Communist Salute, The, 206
First Hymn to Lenin, 27, 136–40
Focherty, 71
Following Day, The, 53
Fool, The, 53
Fourmilière, La, 71
Frightened Bride, The, 65–6
From an 'Ode to All Rebels', 190
From 'Work in Progress', 133
Further Talk with Donnchadh Bàn Mac an t'Saoir, 205

Gairmscoile, 19, 38, 75, 78–80
Genethliacon for the New World Order, 161
Gildermorie, 37
Glasgow, 192
Glass of Pure Water, The, 19, 40–1, 236
God Takes a Rest, 77
Golden Wine in the Gaidhealtachd, A, 23

Harry Semen, 42, 43, 178–9
Hole in the Wall, The, 40, 143
Hungry Waters, 74
Hymn to Sophia: The Wisdom of God, 28, 178

Index of Poems

I Heard Christ Sing, 43, 68
In Memoriam James Joyce, 19–20, 22, 26, 198, 203–4, 220–36
In Memoriam: Liam Mac'Ille Iosa, 162
In Mysie's Bed, 72
In the Caledonian Forest, 180
In the Children's Hospital, 190
In the Slaughterhouse, 190
In the Slums of Glasgow, 41, 189, 193–5
Innumerable Christ, The, 68
Island Funeral, 15

Jimsy: an Idiot, 74
John Maclean (1879–1923), 178

Kind of Poetry I Want, The, 200, 203, 215–9, 226
Kind of Scot I Want, The, 36, 236
Kinsfolk, 29, 43, 61, 133–5

Lament for the Great Music, 163–70, 203, 205
Lamh Dearg Aboo, 206–7
Last Song, A, 54
Last Trump, The, 71
Little White Rose, The, 178
Lo! A Child is Born, 42, 189, 191–2, 195
Lourd on my hert, 125
Love-sick Lass, The, 71
Lynch-Pin, 153

Man for whom Gaeldom is Waiting, The, 12, 202
Meeting of the East and the West, The, 232
Milk-Wort and Bog-Cotton, 43, 148–9, 150
Moment in Eternity, A, 43, 50–3, 69, 125, 230, 237
Monument, The, 178
Museum Piece, 143

Nature of a Bird's World, The, 42

O Jesu Parvule, 67–8, 192
O Wha's the Bride, 103–4
Ode to All Rebels, 19, 42–3, 163, 172–7
Of John Davidson, 20
On a Raised Beach, 42, 181–9
On The Oxford Book of Victorian Verse, 178
On the Threshold, 71
One of the Principal Causes of War, 190
Oon Olympian, The, 153, 230

Pair of Sea-Green Eyes, A, 172
Parrot Cry, The, 125
Pedigree, 143
Perfect, 13, 45
Plaited Like the Generations of Men, 234
Point of Honour, The, 178
Praise of Ben Dorain, 205
Prayer for a Second Flood, 140
Progress of Poetry, The, 170–1
Prostitute, The, 143

Quest, The, 72, 73–4

Reflections in a Slum, 18
Reflections in an Ironworks, 190
Reid E'en, 66
Religion and Love, 143
Requiem: To Paula Modersohn-Becker, 125
Robber, The, 71

Sabine, 71
Salmon Leap, The, 42
Scotland, 154
Scots Unbound, 148, 151–2
Scott Centenary, The, 153
Sea-Serpent, 75, 77–8
Seamless Garment, The, 33, 144–5
Second Hymn to Lenin, 145–8, 153
Servant Girl's Bed, 72
She Whom I Love, 46
Shetland Lyrics, 178
Snares of Varuna, The, 232
Song of the New Economics, 19
Spanish Girl, 53–4
Stars Like Thistle's Floo'er, The, 89

Tam o' the Wilds and the Many-Faced Mystery, 29, 42, 154–5
Tarras, 150–1
Terrible Crystal, The, 237
Thalamus, 161
Thanksgiving, 172
There's Owre Mony Killywimples in Your Singin', 128
Think Not That I Forget, 172
Third Hymn to Lenin, 195–6
Three Fishes, The, 71
To Alasdair MacMhaighstir Alasdair, 128, 205
To Circumjack Cencrastus, 122–135, 234
To Margaret, 46
To One Who Urges More Ambitious Flights, 74
Trompe l'oeil, 74
Tryst in the Forest, 46
Two Parents, The, 191

'U Samago Moria', 71
Under the Greenwood Tree, 71
Unknown Quantity, An, 191

Valedictory, 38
Vestigia Nulla Retrorsum, 180

Water Music, 26, 149–50
Water of Life, 140–1
Watergaw, The, 29, 34, 42, 57, 60–3, 65
Wheesht, Wheesht, 71
Whuchulls, 136
Widower, The, 72
Wild Roses, 71
Wind-Bags, The, 49
World of Words, The, 231–2

Yet hae I Silence left, 89
'You Know Not Who I Am', 71
Your Immortal Memory, Burns!, 82–3

General Index

Adoratsky, 27
Aggrandised Scots, 14, 148, 151, 160, 178
Akhmatova, Anna, 71
Alasdair MacMhaighstir Alasdair, 128, 205
Albert, L. A., 206
Amiel, Henri-Frédéric, 35
Annand, J. K., 90–1
Apuleius, 234
Aristotle, 17
Astaire, Fred, 216
Auden Generation, The (Hynes), 8
Auden, W. H., 8

Barrie, J. M., 198
Baudelaire, Charles, 54
Beast in Me, The (Thurber), 221
Bell, J. J., 125
Bergson, Henri, 5
Black, Margaret, 152
Black, Robin, 152
Blake, William, 35, 53, 200
Blawearie (Cairncross), 22
Blok, Alexander, 35, 54, 96
Boethius, 41
Braid Scots, 55–6
Brecht, Bertolt, 189
British Edda, The (Waddell), 205–6
Broughton Magazine, xii, 48
Brooke, Rupert, 35, 46
Brown, George Douglas, 55
Bruce, George, 73
Buber, Martin, 216
Buchan, John, 48, 64
Burns, Robert, 29, 34, 35, 45, 87, 96, 106, 107, 112,
    120, 125, 138
Burt, Billy, 74
Burt, William, xii, 65, 74
Busoni, Ferruccio, 220, 234
Byron, Lord, 29

Cairncross, Rev. Thomas Scott, xii, 22–3
Caledonian Antisyzygy, 29–31, 211
Carlyle, Thomas, 96
Catullus, 234
Celtic Twilight, 128
Chesterton, G. K., 96
Chestov, Leo, 27, 108, 225
Churchill, Winston, 158

Cicero, 56
Cier-Rige (*see* O'Connor, Roger)
Clann Albann project, 133–56, 178, 196, 199
Clarel (Melville), 109
Clydebank and Renfrew Press, xiii
Coleridge, Samuel Taylor, 216
Colet, Louise, 13
Communist Party of Great Britain, xvi, xix, 159
Craig, David, 136, 192
Criterion, The, 207, 208

Dante, 198
Darwin, Charles, 81, 135
Davidson, John, 20–1, 27, 153, 180, 193, 225
Davidson, Thomas, xiii
Davie, G. E., 29
Dawn in Britain, The (Doughty), 180
Dostoevsky, Feodor, 28–9, 35, 79, 96, 106–12, 128,
    162
Doughty, Charles, 18, 27, 29, 35, 180–1, 200, 206,
    226
Douglas, C. H., 26, 29, 138, 161, 226
Douglas, James, 9th earl of 6–7
Douglas, Gavin, 35
Douglas-Home, Sir Alec, xix
Dunbar, William, 35, 87, 96, 151
Dunfermline Press, 56

East-West Synthesis, 207, 222
Einstein, Albert, 96
Eliot, T. S., 8, 9, 14, 36, 85, 96, 107, 145, 192, 197,
    201, 218
Ellis, Henry Havelock, 25
Engels, Friedrich, 27
Erskine, Hon. R., of Marr, 162, 225
Euclid, 96
Examiner, The, 55

Fabian Research Committee, 212
Fabian Society, xii
Finnegans Wake (Joyce), 203, 223
Flaubert, Gustave, 13, 234
Forfar Review, The, xiii
Flying Dutchman, The (Wagner), 97
Ford, Ford Madox, 220
Free Man, The, 152
Freud, Sigmund, 96, 99
Fyffe, Will, 125

Gaelic Idea, The, 129–32, 160, 162–3, 205, 222
Garden, Mary, 96
Geddes, Sir Patrick, 29, 225
Georg, Stefan, 27, 71
Georgian Poetry, 34
Gibbon, Lewis Grassic (*see* Mitchell, James Leslie)
Gillies, William, 162
Goethe, Johann Wolfgang von, 17, 153, 230, 234
Gopal, Ram, 216
Gorky, Maxim, 219
Graham, R. B. Cunninghame, 225
Grant, Duncan, 96
Graves, Robert, 138
Grieve, Andrew, xi
Grieve, Christine, xv, 74, 133–4
Grieve, Christopher Murray, works by:
Albyn, xv *Annals of the Five Senses*, xiv, 11–12, 25, 26, 50–4 *Battle Continues, The*, 7 *Collected Poems*, xix *Company I've Kept, The*, xix *Complete Poems 1920–1976*, xix, 7, 16, 201 *Contemporary Scottish Studies*, xv *Drunk Man Looks at the Thistle, A*, xv, 25, 26, 28, 31, 33, 35, 38, 39, 42, 43, 75, 76, 78, 79, 82, 83–121, 123, 124, 127, 129, 133, 134, 136, 159, 181, 189, 209, 223 *First Hymn to Lenin and Other Poems*, xvi, 3, 7, 136–45 *In Memoriam James Joyce*, xix, 9, 12, 19, 26, 198–200, 203–4, 215, 218–36 *Kind of Poetry I Want, The*, xix, 34, 36, 200, 207, 215–219, 226 *Kist of Whistles, A*, 207 *Lap of Honour, A*, 136, 201 *Lucky Bag The*, xv *Lucky Poet*, xviii, 207, 215, 227 *Penny Wheep*, xv, 65, 71–83, 92 *Poems of the East-West Synthesis*, 203 *Present Position of Scottish Music, The*, xv *Sangschaw*, xv, 39, 60, 64, 65–71, 92 *Scots Unbound and Other Poems*, xvi, 1, 8, 136, 148–153 *Scottish Scene*, 136, 154, 159 *Second Hymn to Lenin*, 3, 8, 136 *Second Hymn to Lenin and Other Poems*, xvii, 8, 189–195 *Selected Poems* 136 *Stony Limits and Other Poems* xvii, 8, 159–189 *To Circumjack Cencrastus*, xv, 5, 28, 32, 34, 50, 122–33, 134, 136, 205
Grieve, Elizabeth, xvii, 159
Grieve, James, xii, 29, 61
Grieve, Michael, xvi, 157, 191
Grieve, Mrs Peggy (née Skinner), xiv, xv, 89, 122, 133
Grieve, Mrs Valda (née Trevlyn), xvi, 29, 136, 191, 208
Grieve, Walter, xv, 133–4
Grimm Brothers, 234
Gunn, Neil M., 32
Grünewald, 68
Gurdjieff, G. I., xvii

Hamilton, duke of, xviii
Hardy, Thomas, xvi, 137
Haud Forrit project, 198
Hawthorne, Nathaniel, 96
Hegel, Georg Wilhelm Friedrich, 5
Heifetz, Jascha, 96
Heisenberg, Werner Carl, 229
Henrysoun, Robert, 35, 151
Hewlett, Maurice, 200
Hippius, Zinaida, 35, 96, 110
Homer, 17, 86–7, 234
Hopkins, Gerard Manley, 35, 226
Houseman, A. E., 190
House With the Green Shutters, The (Brown), 55
How to Read (Pound), 26
Hueffer, Ford Madox (*see* Ford, Ford Madox)

Hugh Selwyn Mauberley (Pound), 26
Hulme, T. E., 25
Husserl, Edmund, 5
Hynes, Samuel, 8

Ibsen, Henrik, 11
Impavidi Progrediamur project, 12, 42, 198, 201, 204, 236
Independent Labour Party, 25

James I, 7
Jamieson's Dictionary, 56–8, 64, 86, 128, 149
Järnefelt, Armas, 31
Johnstone, William, 89
Jones, Glyn, 13, 45, 220
Joyce, James, 8, 9, 15, 26, 29, 36, 56, 85–7, 149, 199, 203, 218, 223–4, 229, 236

Kahane, Jack, 201–2
Kahn, Gustave, 71
Kailyard School, 8, 55, 84
Keats, John, 35
Kennedy-Fraser, Marjory, 31, 128–9
Kerr, Henry, 126
Knox, John, 96, 125
Koestler, Arthur, 62
Kraus, Karl, 220

Laing, R. D., 29
Lallans, 55, 222
Lamarck, Jean Baptiste, 135
Landsmaal movement, 80
Langland, William, 226
Lasker-Schüller, Else, 96
Lauder, Sir Harry, 31, 57, 82, 96, 125
Lawrence, D. H., 63
Leaves of Grass (Whitman), 200
Lectures on Conditioned Reflexes (Pavlov), 27
Lenin, V. I., 3, 18, 27, 29, 137–9, 171, 191
Leonhardt, Rudolf, 71
Leontiev, Constantine, xvii
Lewis, C. Day, 7, 8
Lewis, Percy Wyndham, 15
Lindsay, Maurice, 89
Linklater, Eric, 151
Literature and Revolution (Trotsky), 17
Lowe-Porter, H. T., 218
Lowland Scots, 55, 222

MacCaig, Norman, 138, 149, 228
Mac Colla, Fionn (*see* MacDonald, Tom)
MacCrimmon family, 163–70
MacDiarmid, Hugh (*see* Grieve, Christopher Murray)
MacDonald, Erskine, 48
MacDonald, Ramsay, 32
MacDonald, Tom, 32
Mackenzie, Sir Compton, xv, 122, 123
Maclean, John, xiii, 59
Maclean, Sorley, 204
Macleod, Mary, 128
Macleod of Macleod, 163
Magnus Merriman (Linklater), 151
Making of a Minister, The (Cairncross), 22
Mallarmé, Stéphane, 16, 96
Mann, Thomas, 218
Mary Queen of Scots, 96

General Index

Marx, Karl, 17, 27, 30, 96
Masoch, Leopold von, 96
Mature Art project, 14, 44, 200–36
Mayakovsky, Vladimir, 136
Melville, Hermann, 96, 109–10, 209, 228
Merzhkovsky, Dmitry, 71
Middle Scots, 55
Milton, John, 34, 139, 200, 210
Mirsky, Prince D. S., 27, 137
Mitchell, James Leslie, 8, 219
Moby-Dick (Melville), 97, 109
Modern Scot, The, 133
Mohini, Retna, 216
Monmouthshire Labour News, xii
Montalk, Count Cedric de, xvi
Montalk, Count Geoffrey Potocki de, xvi
Montgomerie, John, 55
Montrose Review, The, xiv, 84, 126, 127
Moore, T. Sturge, 34
Muir, Edwin, 32, 78, 133, 197
Munro, Neil, 125
Murray, Alexander, 227
Murray, Charles, 55
Murray, Lindley, 227

National Party of Scotland, xv, xvi, 55, 159
Neill, A. S., xiii
New Age, The, xiv, 25–6
Nietzsche, Friedrich Wilhelm, 5, 35–6, 53, 96, 135, 231
Northern Numbers, xiv, 23, 34, 50
Northern Review, The, xv

O'Connor, Roger, 206
Ogilvie, George, 25, 46, 48, 87, 90, 101, 158
One Day of the World (Gorky), 219
Orage, Ann, 161
Orage, A. R., xiv, xv, 25, 161
Ó Rathaille, Aodhagán, 128, 234
Ouspensky, P.D., xiv
Owen, Wilfred, 46

Palmgren, Selim, 31
Patmore, Coventry, 225
Pavlov, Ivan Petrovich, 27
Plato, 5, 17, 96, 97, 233
Plotinus, 3, 20, 27, 165, 225, 227
Poetry of the Thirties (Skelton), 8
Poetry of the Thirties, The (Tolley), 8
Porteus, Hugh Gordon, 220
Pound, Ezra, 8, 14, 15, 25, 26, 29, 46, 136, 195, 199
Proust, Marcel, 63

Ramaekers, George, 96
Red Scotland project, 159
Reid, John Macnair, 2
Return of the Master, The (Cairncross), 22
Right Review, The, xvi
Rilke, Rainer Maria, 27, 54, 125, 144, 180
Robertson, Stanley, 152
Rocher, Edmond, 96
Rosebery, Lord, 125
Rural Problem, The (Fabian Research Council), 212

Sade, Marquis de, 96
Saltire Society, The, xviii
Sassoon, Siegfried, 46

Saurat, Denis, 29, 57, 71
Schönberg, Arnold, 96
Scots Observer, 125
Scotsman, The, 165
Scott, Francis George, 16, 24, 29, 32, 65, 89, 91, 123, 159
Scott, Sir Walter, 153
Scott and Scotland (Muir), 32, 159
Scottish Chapbook, The, xiv, 56–7, 65, 86
Scottish Literature (Smith), 30, 56, 87–8
Scottish Nation, The, xiv
Scottish National League, 162
Scottish National Movement, 55
Scottish National Party, xvii
Scottish Renaissance Movement, 3, 7, 57–9, 80, 206
Selkirk, earl of, xviii
Six Thousand Years of Gaelic Grandeur Unearthed (Albert), 206
Shakespeare, William, 17
Shaw, George Bernard, 25
Shelley, Percy Bysshe, 34
Sibelius, Jean, 31
Simpson, J. Y., 68
Skelton, Robin, 8
Skinner, Peggy (*see* Grieve, Mrs Peggy)
Sklodowska, Marya, 216
Smith, G. Gregory, 29–30, 56, 87
Socrates, 97
Solovyov, Vladimir Sergeyevich, 5, 27–9, 68, 78, 97, 101, 108
Song of the Plow (Hewlett), 200
Songs of Experience (Blake), 53
Sonnets of the Highland Hills project, 48–9
Sorabji, Kaikhosru Shapurji, 29
Soutar, William, 24, 75, 155
Spence, Lewis, 55–6
Spencer, Herbert, 135
Spengler, Oswald, 96
Stalin, Joseph, 27, 206
Stevens, Wallace, 12
Stevenson, R. L., 29, 54
Stevenson, Ronald, 220
Synthetic English, 179–81, 229, 237
Synthetic Scots, 8, 57–61, 81, 84, 85, 86, 128, 133, 160

Taylor, John, 51
Telford, Thomas, xi
Thomas, Dylan, 197, 203, 225, 231
Thompson, James, 226
Thurber, James, 221, 222
Times Literary Supplement, The, 13, 45, 220
Tolstoy, Leo, 96
Trevlyn, Valda (*see* Grieve, Mrs Valda)
Tolley, A. T., 8
Trotsky, Leon, 17
Turgenev, Ivan, 234

Ulysses (Joyce), 9, 26, 36, 65, 86–7, 218, 223
Underwoods (Stevenson), 54
Urquhart, Sir Thomas, 30

Valéry, Paul, 27, 34, 35
Vernacular Circle of the London Burns Club, 55, 56
Voice from Salonika project, 48
Voice of Scotland, The, xvii, xviii, xix
Vox, xv, 122, 123–4

Waddell, L. A., 205
Wallace, Sir William, 96, 151
Waste Land, The (Eliot), 9, 36, 85, 192, 218
Watt, Lachlan Maclean, 31–2, 125, 153
Wells, H. G., 25
Wergeland, Henrick, 80–1
Westwater, R. H., 127

What Is To Be Done? (Lenin), 139
Whistle-Binkie movement, 55
Whitman, Walt, 11, 17, 35
Wittgenstein, Ludwig von, 22, 40
Wordsworth, William, 107

Yeats, W. B., 138, 203, 225, 229